THE ESSENCE OF HUMAN LIFE

To Paddy
for Serious Reading
John Banks

THE ESSENCE OF HUMAN LIFE

Personal Living in the Culture of Man

John Amos Banks

HIGHLIGHT BOOKS

Crawfordville, Florida

Published by
Highlight Books
P.O. Box 1076
Crawfordville, FL 32327

Library of Congress Catalog Number: 86-80835

ISBN 0-9616715-0-5

Printed in the United States of America
Typography: Mediatype, Tallahassee, FL
Printing and binding: Rose Printing Co., Tallahassee, FL

Preface

Mankind exists in two distinct forms, namely, that of an individual and that of a social group, a society. They are each to the other as trees and a forest for it is individual trees that make-up a forest and there can be no forest without a group of trees. It is even so with humanity. There can be no society without individual persons and individuals cannot exist outside of a group society. But there is a major difference in these two forms of mankind for one is a biological being and the other a social association. Each have their realm of life but they are bound together with an umbilical cord that cannot be severed for to do so would mean the demise of both.

The purpose of this book is to examine these two parts of humanity in their separate manner of life and in their method of living. To this end, therefore, the volume is divided into these two parts, that of human society as a whole and that of the individual person.

As the book is a manual of human living it is addressed to all of the people of the world around without distinction of race, creed, or philosophy of thought, except as subjects of study. The core of man is that of a human being and there is no more to be said except to define the parts. Politics, religion and economic seeking are cloaks that the individual wraps around the common base of his human being. They guide the manner by which we humans pursue the needs of life but they are alien to the source of those needs which spring eternal within and without the human person.

It will aid our study of human life and living if we dispose of those intriguing words the 'mystery of life' and the 'secret of living,' for they are naught but the sayings of the poet and the preaching of the soothsayer.

Life and living is as common as day and night and as free of secrets as the breathing of air. Every human being that has ever lived on earth has engaged in the process of living, has experienced the drama of life. Not occasionally or infrequently but every day, over a period of many years.

The course of history also refutes this 'hidden mystery' to life for it is like saying that mankind has not found a proper way to conduct the course of life and living. But this can hardly be true when the written record of 6,000 years proves the contrary plus the monuments and institutions of the great civilizations to show further proof.

Now it is true that our own particular life is not an open book in which we can turn the pages to see and fore-know particular events. But it is also true that we can fore-see and shape those events because we are intelligent beings and know with clear certainty the exact manner that our living will take, namely, a seeking for well-being and in particular for food, clothing, shelter, health, an enjoyment of life. There is no mystery in this for such has been the course of human living since the beginning of human time.

Whatever mystery there is to life exists only at the beginning when we are young and have not lived much in time, in experience, in the process of living. But by the time that full maturity is reached the totality of living is well known: The care of the body, sexual fulfillment, the career of life is in force and social association is well known. These events of life are then re-lived over and over in a never-ending series of action. There will be additional learning, new and unusual events of life but in substance it will be the same process, many times repeated, with new raw material.

We each have our own Book of Life but the pages are not of paper, each is a page of life. Each morning we open a new page wherein there will be written our actions, our learning, our experience, our living. Then when evening comes and we close the page, there is a residue of knowing left in the self and when a new page is opened the following morning, the experience of yesterday is included and enlarged upon, so that the new day will in large measure be a repetition of yesterday but enriched with yesterday's living. There is no mystery in these things.

THE BOOK DIVISIONS

As stated above the book is separated into two great parts called Book I and Book II. The first is titled Human Society and reviews the origin of man, the history of man and the culture of man. The second is titled The Human Individual and reviews the reality of life for the individual, followed by personal living. These terms are quite common and need no further explanation. The Table of Contents exhibits the several chapters under each title.

Special attention is called to Book II, Part II, for this is the essence and vital substance of this manual. It contains the twelve crucial parts that make up the total life and living of every individual human. They are the twelve Tasks of Life that constantly confront each person throughout his or her entire life. They are the demands of life that each of us must solve even for a minimal condition of well-being, and beyond that for an enrichment of our life. It is through their agency that we find the meaning of life and the enjoyment of living. Indeed, Book I is largely a preparation for this section of the manual, that is, a review of the great civilizations as background and then the culture areas in which the Personal Living of the individual takes place.

This book is intended as an over-guide and could be no other for the subject matter extends across the whole of history, of society and of the individual. The detail of these subjects fill the libraries where one may turn for particular information. But this volume will serve to define the organization and structure of society as a whole and then the character of personal living.

Any book that purports to be a guide to human behavior can do no more than point the way. The individual must go forth into the world and do the living. Like a compass a book can guide and direct but the person must make the journey. Unlike the compass, however, which only shows the course, the compass-book can also inspire to follow the true course. Such is the hope expressed toward all who read this book.

Contents

BOOK I
HUMAN SOCIETY

Prologue I. Common Man 3

PART I. THE ORIGIN OF MAN

1. The Earth — Our Home 7
2. Life on Earth 12
3. Man on Earth 17

PART II. PROGRESS OF MAN

4. Man in History 22
5. The Primitive Era 28
6. The Middle Era 31
7. The Modern Era 46

PART III. CULTURE OF MAN

8. The Culture of Man 56
9. The Beliefs of Man 61
10. Man in Association 70

(TEN LIFE INSTITUTIONS)

11. The Family 75
12. Language 79
13. Education 83
14. Religion 87
15. Government 97
16. Economics 102
17. Science 107
18. Technology 113
19. Art 121
20. War 126

Epilogue I. One Earth and One People 130

BOOK II
THE HUMAN INDIVIDUAL

Prologue II. The Mission in Life 135

PART I. PERSONAL REALITY

1. The Personal World 138
2. The Experience of Life 141
3. Experience in the Body 143
4. Experience in the Mind 146
5. Experience in Events 150
6. Experience as a Process 156
7. Personality 160

PART II. PERSONAL LIVING

8. Personal Well-Being 168
9. The Goals of Life 170

(THE TWELVE GOALS OF LIFE)

10. Physical Health 176
11. Mental Health 181
12. Physical Ability 187
13. Mental Ability 190
14. Lifework Ability 200
15. Leisure Ability 204
16. Religion 209
17. Personal Safety 214
18. Economic Security 223
19. Married Association 227
20. Family Association 231
21. Small Group Association 238

PART III. ENRICHMENT OF LIFE

22. Values in Life 246
23. Ideal Values 254

Epilogue II. The Human Spirit 260

Salutation to the Dawn

Look to this day
For it is life,
The very life of life.
In its brief course
Lie all of the varities and realities
of your existence:
  The bliss of growth
  The glory of action
  The splendor of beauty
For yesterday is but a dream
and tomorrow is only a vision,
But today well lived
makes every yesterday a dream of happiness,
and every tomorrow a vision of hope.
Look well, therefore, to this day.
Such is the salutation to the dawn.

. . . *From the Sanskrit*

BOOK I

HUMAN SOCIETY

Man is the measure of all things:
  Of things that are, that they are;
  Of things that are not, that they are not.
                    ..... *Protagoras*

Prologue I

COMMON MAN

There is a commonality that marks the whole of mankind, each and all alike, where the waters of life do indeed seek and find their level, where the boundaries of race, creed and religion are naught and where political divisions are vaporous lines. It is that set of conditions that make each man and woman a human being and not a prince, a pauper, or a philosopher; it is the common path of life that each must tread whether master or slave, wise or foolish; it is the common destiny that awaits us all without distinction of class or culture. Although life is the great elevator of man it is first and foremost the mighty leveler, for there is a tolerance that we may not exceed in height or depth of living. And the median is our commonality.

We are common in the things we share alike with all of our fellowmen on earth, in our human needs, in our bodily structure, in our natural abilities to perform in the pursuit of goals. Though some are tall and some short yet the bodily make-up is no different. Again, one runs fast and another slowly, still both have the ability for motor action. One dwells in a hut and another in a house, still the need for shelter is met. Some are genius and some are average yet all perform the same mental process, all seek a life of well-being, not ill-being.

We see this common character of man quite clearly if we briefly list the parts of life that make it so, noting first the two criteria for judging. First, the traits are universal and do not belong to any one society, civilization or culture but rather to all of mankind across the face of the earth. Secondly, the traits are enduring for they were the mark of primitive man, ancient man and continue so in the modern world of today.

THE COMMONALITY OF MAN

1. Common in person. These are the characteristics that identify mankind as human.

- A physical body made-up of organs that require nutrition and senses that perceive the outer world.
- A mind with which we are able to think and reason, to experience emotions and feelings.
- The ability to perform the motor actions of walking, dancing, driving a motor vehicle, manipulate tools.

2. Common ideas and beliefs. The beliefs that mankind holds are as divergent as day and night in form, but in kind and substance they are alike. For example, in religion there are many gods and many rituals but it is still the worship of a supreme being; the methods of government vary widely but all serve the same objectives of governing people; economic policies go to opposite extremes but the goal is the same, namely, to produce the needs of livelihood and the supplies of want for the people. Ideas concerning the family, recreation and social association are identical the world around and their content is common to all.
3. Common in pattern of life. All men and women tread a similar path through life in their birth, early care and training, education and preparation for a life employment, marriage, raising children and the whole intersperced with some leisure and then finally death.
4. Common in values. Values are the good and worthy things that all persons seek and strive for. Despite the ugly marks on the record of mankind such as war, dishonesty, fraud and subjection of helpless peoples, still men everywhere hold common value judgments about right and wrong, good and bad, what is worthy and what is not. We see the great elevating effort in such works as the moral teachings of Confucius, the book of Ethics by Aristotle, the Ten Commandments of the Hebrews, Christian Golden Rule. Even from the Romans, known for their cruelty, came the beautiful Meditations, written by one of their emperors, Marcus Aurelius.

Men ever strive to elevate, not degrade, in every land. The love of freedom, justice and equality has never been the private property of a few, even though the material results do sometimes seem that it is so. The bottom line on the balance sheet shows more good than bad in the efforts of mankind.

DIFFERENCE IN MAN

Where humans differ is not in kind but in degree. We are not uncommon in the character and qualities that are the substance of a human being but the difference is rather in the degree of attainment. Some have more goods, more learning, more skills and even more health than others but still all humans have these things in some degree, in some measure.

The reasons for human difference in degree of attainment are manifold but three causes seem to dominate.

Lack of Desire to Achieve. This is characteristic of both individuals and societies. Many persons live below the level of normal or average simply because they are satisfied and contented with the condition while nearby the norm is a state of affluency. The American Indians in an earlier day and the Polynesian in the present day desire little or no change in their life style but were and are contented even though the world standard is greatly different.

Lack of Ability to Achieve. All men and women that are born with normal capacities are able to receive learning and develop needed abilities to pursue the goals of life but all do not develop these abilities to the full extent. It may be a neglect in effort to develop, perhaps an inherent lack of talent, a personal illness, or simply a downright lack of desire to upgrade one's station in life.

Lack of Opportunity to Achieve. To acquire an education, to acquire wealth, to eradicate disease — all of these achievements pre-suppose an opportunity to do so, and this opportunity is not distributed equally to the world's people. Some cannot attain higher education because there are no schools in which to do so; many people live in squalor with malnutrition and disease because the land itself will not produce sufficiently or else there is a lack of medical facilities, or both; some nations lack the natural resources necessary for a well-being of the people or else have not the means to develop those that are present.

Where the above conditions exist, man is not wholly equal on a one-to-one basis of attainment. It is a difference that divides the world into part fortunate, part distressed.

PROGRESS AND COMMONALITY

We must examine briefly the idea of progress as it affects the common man for the idea of change pervades the whole of man's thinking today. The theory of progress or the doctrine of change holds that change is of the essence of things: Matter is always in motion, planets fly through space, plants change by mutation, animals change from lower to higher forms. The idea of change derives largely from the Darwin-Wallace theory of evolution.

Now all men agree that there is such a thing as evolution or change for the mastadons are gone, men and women seldom walk but rather ride a mechanical vehicle on earth and in the sky, the housewife cooks with electric instead of a brush fire, the general level of intelligence is higher. Surely the world today, over-all, is far from that of our forefathers and if this is progress then no fault can be found in the theory. But many in high places have taken the idea of progress and declared it to be the law of all things, promising a new heaven and a new earth, if not today then surely tomorrow. It may happen but only superficially. The automobile has replaced the horse but it only moves the human body from here to there more rapidly; the radio and television only carry the message of joy or sorrow more quickly than the personal messenger; the food may be gourmet but it only nourishes the body; the efficient house is merely a shelter with more trimmings; and while the doctor truly performs a miracle in the medical arts of cure it is still the same old human body that does the healing.

If we look at humans as human beings we can discern little change in the past ten thousand years. We each of us still have, as of old, only one head, one body system, eat food for nourishment, work, play, and rest. The negatives of hate, anger and fear as well as the positives of love, good-will, and sacrifice of self still reside in every human being. The great institution of family is still just that: A father, mother and children. Government by democracy and by decree is now as it was in ancient Greece. Goods are still possessed as to the poor and as to the rich. And even the need for man to relate to God is still unchanged from primitive times. All of these aspects of mankind are still common to all men, everywhere.

Such, then, is the strata of constancy that does not change in man. We designate this unchanging level in men and women as their 'human nature,' meaning that which is anchored deep and strong. The products of science and technology have adorned this basic nature with a raiment of goods that tend to blot out the unchanging part, but it is still there and is common to all persons the world around. It is this commonality in man that is the central theme of this book.

PART I

THE ORIGIN OF MAN

Chapter I
The Earth – Our Home

The earth is the homeland of mankind. It is a round globe in space, a planet enclosed with an envelope of air. The surface of the earth is three-tenths land and seven-tenths water. Mankind lives on and makes his home on the three-tenths portion but he uses the entire earth environment, land, water and air, to extract the means of his livelihood. All of the nourishment needed for life comes from the earth with one exception and that is the rays from the sun. These rays shine down upon the earth and stimulate all of the life that exists on the earth – man, plants and animals.

The earth is one of nine planets that circle the sun. The earth spins in a circle once each day of twenty-four hours, causing day and night, and it circles the sun once each year of 365 days causing the seasons of summer and winter. The nine planets together are called the solar system, the sun system.

Our earth and our solar system are mere specks of dust, tiny lumps of matter, in the universe, and occupy a spot far out on the edge of a galaxy called the Milky Way. Now a galaxy consists of millions of stars similar to our own sun which is itself a star and it is these millions of stars that form our Milky Way galaxy. But our galaxy is still only one of millions of galaxies. The human mind cannot grasp this immensity of the universe and when we are told by scientists that the galaxies seem to be flying away from one another at fantastic speeds then the mind collapses at the idea.

ORIGIN OF THE EARTH

There are two sources for an explanation of how the earth came into existence, one is legend and the other scientific, and we shall briefly review each.

Legends and Myths of Origin. The Norsemen and the ancient Greeks devised a similar mythology to account for the creation. These legends told of gods that made the earth from a vast hole or abyss and from misty vapors. These beliefs also allow the gods to meddle directly in the affairs of mankind after they had created the earth.

Another account that existed in Sumeria and Assyria a thousand years before Christ has Marduk as the hero. There was no sky above and no firm ground below when suddenly two deities sprung into existence, named Marduk and the dragon goddess Tiamat. Marduk, seeing the dragon goddess, takes his mace and cleaves Tiamat's body in two. He then takes the upper half and forms the sky and sets in the stars, while the lower half then forms itself into firm ground.

The story of creation as told in the Judeo-Christian Bible is probably the widest known of all accounts and is accepted by the believers as fact. Here the creation includes the earth, man and all of nature.

1st day - Earth was without form and in darkness, and God divided light from darkness, calling them respectively Day and Night.

2nd day - God made the firmament by diving the waters, calling the firmament Heaven.

3rd day - The waters under the heaven were divided to form Earth and Seas.

4th day - God created the Sun, Moon and Stars.

5th day - Fish and fowls are created.

6th day - Cattle, beasts and man, both male and female, are created.

7th day - God ends His work and rests.

Scientific Theories. Plato taught that the earth, sun and stars were not creations of gods but simply things of nature made up of the elements water, air and earth, and obeying the laws of nature.

First Immanuel Kant and then Pierre de LaPlace, in 1796, stated the nebular theory of origin. In this theory there is a great ball of gas rotating in space. As it spins it cools, shrinks and hardens into separate pieces which form the solar system of sun and planets.

A modern idea known as the "big bang" theory, postulated by George Gamow, speculates that a gigantic explosion of matter took place in the dim past and scattered matter throughout space, forming the earth, sun and other heavenly bodies.

The scientific theories are mental concepts but do have some evidence to support the view, expecially the explosion theory, for the universe appears to be expanding outward into space. The ancient legends appear to be just that, having no basis in fact and no evidence to support them whatsoever.

THE PARTS OF THE EARTH

Three major divisions are assigned to planet earth, as follows.

The Air, or Atmosphere. Although not attached to the earth with a solid bond, nor can it be seen with the naked eye, still the air is very much a part of the earth. This atmosphere is a gaseous substance that encloses the entire earth-globe and extends outward from the surface of the earth a distance of 120 miles. This is the invisible 'stuff' that mankind breathes each day that is so necessary to life. But the atmosphere also serves a second most important function for it also protects humans from the harmful rays that pepper the earth from the sun.

Water, the Hydrosphere. Water covers almost three-fourths of the earth's surface in the form of oceans, seas, lakes and rivers. And the clouds above also contain water. Much of the food that man consumes is taken from the earth's waters, notably fish. In addition, the oceans and rivers are also the highways of man for travel and trade.

Land, or Lithosphere. This is the part of the earth where man dwells and it consists of mountains, plains and deserts. It is from this part of the earth that man extracts his major livelihood, cultivating crops and cattle, raising his cities in which to dwell and extracting the minerals for his use.

MOTHER EARTH

This globe that spins through space is well characterized as "mother earth" for mankind as a whole and each individual is cared for, cultured and nourished by the yield of the earth. And man is a child of Mother Earth in another very real sense in that he cannot live away from earth except for very short periods of time. When man does leave the environment of this planet for outer space, he must take with him the special means to live away from earth, such as food, clothing, air, shelter from sun rays.

Mother Earth provides the care for her earth children in four major areas, as follows.

A dwelling place. Earth is the dwelling place of man not only in a space sense but also in the domestic sense, for it is on the plains and in the mountains and along the river valleys that man builds his cities, his factories and the shelter for his family home.

A storehouse. It is out of the great storehouse of the earth that mankind extracts the food, the clothing, the shelter, the medicine and the fuel to nourish and sustain his life.

A workshop. After the raw materials are taken from the earth they are processed by hand and machine into the finished products that fill and satisfy the needs for living and the wants for pleasure.

A playground. The great outdoors of woods and rivers, mountains and seas provide the environment for mankind to relax, find leisure, enjoy the pleasure of nature and engage in a multitude of sports and games.

In addition to these four concrete areas, some religions and ethical groups hold that the earth is also a testing ground for an after-life in a heavenly paradise.

THE SHRINKING EARTH

At the beginning of the twentieth century the people of earth began to see a new aspect of their homeland that did not exist before this date, namely a depletion of the earth's abundance and capacities and consequently posing a threat to the very existence of man on earth. We may summarize the cause of this 'shrinking' under five heads, as follows:

In time. This is not a threat to existence but rather a noting of the remarkable speed of travel by modern man. Here are three approximations of travel between Europe and the United States: In the 1700's, two months; in the 1800's, two weeks; in the 1900's, two hours.

Unlike the four categories that follow, which have a negative value, this rapidity of travel has brought to the fore a greater sense of one-ness to all of the people of the earth. The separation by nationality, by east and west, by race segregation — all of these have lost their old meanings and a new understanding of these concepts is emerging.

Population growth. The world's population has grown at an enormous rate and to an enormous number, so much so that there is serious concern that if some effective controls are not begun then the number of people may exceed the capacity of the earth to support and sustain the population.

Depletion of materials. Down through the ages man has viewed the earth as a gigantic stockpile with unlimited supplies of materials, space, air and water. The great outburst of technology in the 1900's has dissipated this comfortable view. Authorities now see a limit to much of the earth's materials and resources, such as fossil fuels and minerals, materials that once consumed will be gone forever.

By pollution. Pollution of the air, the land and the water of earth means less usable air, land and water and therefore a lesser quantity for man's benefit. Pollution of the environment has been a problem for mankind since the first gatherings into large groups such as cities and towns, but the great population of earth today plus the wastes of industry have escalated the problem to a threat-to-life level. All poisoning of the earth is a shrinking of the earth-space that is wholesome and fit for man to occupy and use.

By nuclear war. The single most dreadful threat to earth and it's people is the possible use of nuclear explosives in time of war. Pollution by waste materials can be controlled with proper effort but the explosion of a nuclear weapon devastates and kills all living things, then leaves a lingering poison of radiation in the earth that may take centuries to remove. Here there is no control once the weapon has been exploded, for the pollution is complete and final.

MOTHER TO ALL LIFE

In the conceited mind of man he sees the earth as his alone, forgetting that the earth is mother to all of nature. This is best expressed in Joyce Kilmer's poem to a tree, in the verse that tells of 'a tree whose hungry mouth is pressed, against the earth's sweet flowing breast." It is against this sweet and ever-flowing breast of abundance that all of mankind and all of nature is pressed, to receive nourishment of life, of living and the enjoyment of living.

Chapter 2

Life on Earth

In ancient Greek religion there were three goddesses who controlled the course of life. First was Clotho the spinner, who starts life and then spins out the thread; Lachesis the disposer, who determines the length of life; and Atropos the inflexible, who cuts off the thread of life. Although this is the process and fate of all living things the story ignores the basic question: What is the nature of life? This is the topic we shall consider in this chapter.

Life is the most abundant thing in the world but man still has not found a precise definition for it, neither philosopher, poet, nor scientist. We can see no evidence of life with the naked eye, only an exhibition of life in things that move, grow, breathe and reproduce. When we peer into a microscope there is only a tiny bug that wiggles, not "life" itself. When we stare into space we can only wonder at it's vastness, seeing no sign of life.

The nearest that man has come to defining life is by listing the chemicals that make-up a living thing such as an ant, and then describe the changes those chemicals undergo to keep the ant alive, that is keep 'life' in the ant. This may be summed up as: Life is a system of chemical activities. Now this does trim away the myth and legend but does not lay bare that primal spark called life.

The way we know about life and living things is by their biological structure and the actions they perform, by their behavior. This is true for each of the three forms of life, plants, animals and man, whose life-activity occurs only under certain favorable conditions. If there is any failure in the action or in the conditions, then life will cease in that living thing. Before reviewing these necessities for life to exist we shall inquire into it's beginning.

ORIGIN OF LIFE

Just how life begun on earth is shrouded in the same shadows as the beginning of physical matter but here the mystery is deeper because living things change while rocks and water do not. The man and the dog we see today are much different than men and dogs who lived on earth many thousands of years ago. In those times people resembled the courseness of the ape and did not have the fine features of men and women today. Dogs were like vicious wolves. In fact, in the far, far distant past there was no such creature as man. How then did life appear on earth and man become man? Here again, as in the origin of the earth, there is only legend and theory, of which we shall briefly note three versions, religion, folklore and science.

The well known religious version in the first chapter of Genesis, in the Judeo-Christian Bible, was cited earlier. This tells us that the first acts of God were to create heaven, earth and water. Next came plants, animals and man. There is no mention of the parts of living things as we know them today, such as cells and organs and life systems. Everything came into being as a whole, as a completed product, beginning the functions of life immediately, that is, growing and reproducing.

In folklore it was asserted that life came into being by spontaneous generation. The Greek Thales taught his students that life was formed from slime when the heat of the sun shone upon it. Aristotle taught that spontaneous generation was normal in nature, claiming that insects sprang from morning dew, mice came out of moist soil fully grown, crabs and frogs came when rain fell down on slime. Even down to recent times it was believed that worms came to life in wood and cheese. The work of Louis Pasteur corrected these mis-beliefs as being facts but the folklore lingers on with many people who still believe that life can spring from inanimate things.

Statements about the origin of life are more cautious in science than in religion and folklore although the theories are similarly divergent. Perhaps the most widely held idea is that life originated in water where certain molecules were changed into a life form by energy from the sun, a process taking place over millions of years. Some think that early life may have been isolated cells or a virus that was activated by heat and then developed upwards from simple form into higher forms. Another theory speculates that a bug from outer space landed on earth, bringing the first form of life. This, of course, presupposes that there is life somewhere out in space, on other bodies in space.

Still the mystery remains: How did life originate on earth? If there is ever to be an answer it will come from the work of science. With his instruments of magic and wizardry with chemicals, the scientist is beginning to peer down into the very essence of life, is beginning to see the ingredients that are very life itself: Cells and viruses, acids and bacteria. He sees how these parts are assembled into a pattern, what their needs are to sustain life, and the conditions under which they can live, can be a living thing. From these inquiries models have been constructed to show in concrete form that which is meant by the term 'living matter.' These inquiries are not vague hope or idle dream but rather an orderly search for an answer.

LIFE PARTS

These are the most apparent parts of life, of living things.

The cell. The cell in called the unit of life for two reasons. All living things — plants, animals and man — are cellular in form. In man, for example, the muscles, the nerves, the blood, the skin, are basically a combination of millions of cells. Thus, in the human body there are about 60,000 billion cells. These cells live and die and are replaced just like all forms of life, to the tune of about 500 million every day, in the human. Although we do not notice it our bodies are enclosed with a new suit of skin every year. The tooth that aches is really a group of cells out of harmony.

The second reason that the cell is called the unit of life is because it is the smallest "thing" that performs all of the functions of a whole living thing. There are smaller forms of life such as the virus but they do not perform all of the operations of a life unit, namely, breathe, take in foodstuff and transform it into energy and excrete waste. The cell performs all of these functions.

Organs. When a group of cells are organized into a functioning whole, such as the heart, skin, glands or liver, such wholes are called an organ.

A body. When a group of organs are organized into a functioning whole, such as a child, a plant, a fish, these wholes are called a body.

Water. The most abundant substance in all forms of life such as cells and organs is water, which makes up 70 to 95 percent of the bulk of most living things. We humans like to think that we are super-structures of bone and muscle but the truth is that we are about 70 percent water.

ESSENTIAL NEEDS FOR LIFE

These needs for life are not given in any priority order because the removal of any one could result in death. There are other needs for life, of course, such as the absence of disease and the absence of disaster but these are contingent conditions while the following three needs are absolute.

Nutrition. Every living thing — a blade of grass, an elephant, a rose, a fish, a mosquito, a human being — must have food, water and air in order to perpetuate life. When these substances are assimilated into the living thing, they nourish that thing by replacing the worn parts and causing a re-growth of life, of cells.

Temperature. There is a minimum/maximum limit of temperature beyond which life cannot exist and that range is 60 degrees below to 180 degrees above F. For human beings the body range is very narrow, being only 6 degrees up or down from 98 degrees F. Beyond this limit the body cannot sustain life.

Protection from radiation. Ultraviolet and gamma rays are harmful to man and he must protect himself from their danger. The earth's atmosphere is the shield that protects from these rays that eminate from the sun. Where these rays are created by nuclear radiation then man must erect a man-made protection.

ACTION OF LIFE

In this chapter we are concerned simply with the fact of life, of living, and not human behavior, not action as a result of thinking.

A primal urge. All living things have a basic urge to act, an inner surge to move, to have motion. The smallest cell, bacteria and virus constantly wiggle, and move and shift position. Constant action is so characteristic of all living things that some scholars speculate that this urge is the vital force of life itself. This urge to act never ceases. In sleep the human continues to breath and the heart pumps blood through the veins the same as when awake, and the bear who hibernates all winter has the same bodily processes as when awake although greatly showed down.

This basic action has two rhythms. The first is an undulation, an ebb and flow at intervals. We see it in the onset of hunger at intervals, in the desire for sex that rises then falls, and the nightly sleep to relieve fatigue. We call these urges a human want or need and so they are but their nature is that of an urge that comes, is satisfied and returns again.

The second action is one of constant repetition. This is clearly seen in the beat and pulse of the heart, in breathing, in bird migration. These activities are most frequently referred to as a cycle of action.

This basic, primal urge has no satisfactory explanation except that it is the 'nature of things.' Man can define the action, even control it to some degree, but has not defined the "why," has not explained the "pusher" in this urge to do. Some physical scientists think that man may have reached the outer limits in search for physical forces. Perhaps this urge to act is the outer biological force.

Methodic growth. Nature may not have a reasoned purpose but it does have direction and aim, that of growth. To grow, to increase, to extend is the distinctive quality of all living things and nature accomplishes this in four ways, as follows.

Growth by addition. To grow by enlargement, by increase, is apparent to all: The child grows to adulthood, the mighty oak grows from an acorn and even the giant whale was once a nursing baby.

Growth by division. This is the method of cell growth, by splitting.

Growth by renewal. Like growth by addition, this is the result of nourishment. As the body parts wear out, as they constantly do, they must be replaced. In the human the organs re-grow from the food and water that is taken in while plants are renewed by sunlight and foods taken in from the soil.

Growth by reproduction. This is increase or reproduction by germinal seed. In the human and animals it is accomplished by a sexual union, in plants by a seed.

Pace and duration. The pace of life in both humans and animals is similar. In the early years life is vigorous with rapid growth and high activity. In the middle years, which is the longest period of life, the action is robust but settled into a routine and fixed habits. In the latter years all activities decline as the strength to endure strong and sustained action declines.

THE HIGHEST LIFE

The highest form of life, as all persons know, is man and this is so because of man's ability to think, to reason. With this ability man can and does control all other living things. But this observation is tinged with much conceit when we speak of a 'life' thing as a biological creature. Thinking is a mental operation while life as such is a biological condition. In this regard then, man is not necessarily the highest type of life for his biologic qualities are the same as those of other animals. As a life organism, man grades out on a par with such creatures as the ape and the horse, just another form of life on earth.

Chapter 3

Man on Earth

Man, or man-like creatures, has lived on earth for about 500,000 years and during most of that time he was distributed about the earth in small clusters of people. Beginning about 1500 A.D. with the exploration of the Americas, Africa and Australia, plus an increase in world population, it required a mere 500 years for mankind to spread out and occupy the entire surface of the globe, in density. Although the earth is far from being full of people, there is a density limit and man appears to be approaching the mark, caused largely from a lack of resources to support rather than lack of space.

ORIGIN OF MAN

Where did man come from, how did he get here on earth? That is a question still unanswered with certainty.

Like the beginning of the earth and life itself, there is no exact knowledge of the time and place of man's origin. As in the case of life, again there is only religion, legend and early scientific inquiry to explain the beginning. In these explanations there is great diversity with one exception, namely, both the Bible and scientific inquiry agree that man was a late comer in the order of things. In the Bible, God created man last of all things; in science, cats have been traced back about 40 million years while man, as man, is believed to have been here only one-half million years.

Let us briefly cite one example from each of the three sources that explain the origin of man. In mythology we have already noted the story of Marduk, in the previous chapter. After Marduk finished making the heavens and earth, we are told that he put together a man from the blood of a god.

In the Biblical version of man's beginning, it took place in the Garden of Eden. Using dust of the ground, God formed a man and then breathed into his nostrils the breath of life and thus man became a living soul.

This man was Adam and the first woman, Eve, was then made from one of Adam's ribs.

It is worthy of note that in both of the above cased man was created for a specific purpose. Marduk intended man to serve the gods while the Lord God, Jehovah, intended man to till the ground and He put Adam in the Garden of Eden to dress it and keep it.

In science, the most widely accepted version of man's beginning is the theory of evolution published by Charles Darwin in the Origin of Species in 1859. Both Darwin and Russel Wallace conceived the idea at about the same time and both after a long investigation in the field. An example of this evolution is the ape, an animal similar to man in form and actions and a mid-step between the lower animals and man, the higher animal.

Man is believed to have begun developing from the ape proper to his present form and function anywhere between five and twenty million years ago. Anthropologists disagree widely in time because there are very few fossils and little evidence remaining of the gradual change, such as shedding of hair, shedding the course appearance and gaining the fine features of modern man, shedding the stooped position and gaining the upright stance.

The theory of evolution is greatly strengthened by the finding of human-like bones that show a gradual change. Beginning with the Java man, 500,000 years ago, who was very ape-like in appearance, the bones show a modification through Peking Man (200,000 B.C.), Neanderthal Man (40,000 B.C.), Cro-Magnon Man (20,000 B.C.) and down to the current day man and his fine features. Animals also show this change of evolution, lending additional support to the descent theory.

In recent years the theory of evolution has been modified but not abandoned. The new thought is that whereas Darwin emphasized change through biological channels (nature), anthropologists now believe that social behavior or culture was also strongly influential in the process of evolution. Man did not change solely because nature selected the best and fittest, man has also changed himself by the inborn efforts to learn, to improve, to advance.

THE MARKS OF MAN

Except for the ability to think, there is no clear-cut dividing line between man as animal and man as human being, only a gray area where he is part one and part the other. The following qualities exist to some degree in animals although in man they are fully developed.

Two odd fingers. Man has five fingers on each hand, one of which is called a thumb. Unlike other animals, man's thumb works opposite to his other four fingers, enabling him to grasp, handle and maneuver tools and instruments. He can hold a pencil to write intricate signs and symbols, the surgeon can poise a knife for a delicate operation, the carpeter can grasp a hammer and saw to build a house. This backward working finger, this thumb, is an asset of humans alone.

Erect posture. Apes come close to this ability but can endure for short periods only. Standing erect enables man to move about using only two limbs instead of four, as animals do. This has freed the upper limbs, the two arms, to perform a thousand movements and operations denied other creatures such as the building of skyscrapers, constructing ships, cultivating the soil, making and handling delicate tools.

Stereoscopic vision. This is the ability to see and perceive objects with high accuracy, at a distance, and determine the size of the object.

Ability to speak. Man is not born with this ability, only with the capacity to learn to speak. Articulate speech is possible only with man, not animals.

Most animals make sounds that have meaning to them such as moaning or whining when in pain, mating calls to birds, warnings of danger by squirrels at the presence of a cat. But only man can make sounds with reasoned meaning, that have an enduring value beyond a simple, single utterance. Only man can manipulate his tongue, throat and mouth to make articulate speech. He must learn how to do these things but all humans do learn within the first several months of life.

Ability to think and reason. Again, this skill belongs to humans alone and like speech it must be learned for it is not present at birth. Animals have a basic "think," have memory, but cannot reason, plan or foresee.

Thinking consists of learning, observing, planning and problem solving. It also includes memory, the storing of facts and life experiences in the brain and then recalling this information for use in living, such as distinguishing good from bad, selecting the best way, choosing the safe method.

Above these ordinary forms of thought, man also has the ability to think in symbols and concepts. Thus, two times two equals four is symbol thinking. The two's and four's might mean apples, airplanes or fish for they are merely a symbol of the number of things, of anything. An example of concept thinking is the word 'love,' which stands for many things: Charity to the unfortunate, the heroic act to save another's life, the sharing of life together by a husband and wife, the parental feeling for children. Only humans can think and visualize in symbols and concepts.

Live in cultural relations. Animals live together to propagate and to protect, just as man does, but the human has the ability to co-operate, to work together, to construct together. It is a cultural action unknown to animals although the bee and the ant have such an instinctive inclination.

Accumulate and pass on. This is the ability to build on the past and then pass on to succeeding generations the accumulated knowledge and material wealth. In the realm of books the written record has been accumulating for 6,000 years and includes the ideas, beliefs, facts and events of man and history and of nature. The accumulated wealth in property consists in money, buildings, monuments, industrial plants, durable goods, objects of art and jewelry. Each new child that is born begins his life with this rich heritage of the generations that have passed away.

The above, then, are the marks of man, the identifying characteristics that is meant by the term man-kind, for this is the kind of creature that man is.

PERSONAL MAN

If any creature in outer space should scrutinize the earth, the great distinction that he (or it) would see in man creatures is that, sometimes they move about and act as a single being and then they bunch together and act and move about in a cluster, in a group. This is the manner in which man lives and behaves on earth, singly and in groups. For the individual person this means a dual-type of existence, with himself or herself alone, and then in association with other persons. We shall review these two elements now.

The Individual Person. All aside from our being a social animal, we are also a single, stand-apart individual, characterized by three distinct parts, as follows:

The biological part. This is the mantle of nature that all humans wear, consisting in two parts.

1. The sense organs. These are well known: Eyes with which we see, ears to hear, nose to smell, taste buds to detect and skin with which we feel. All five organs perform a similar job, that of observing the outside world and then sending a message to the brain about that which was seen, heard and felt.
2. The body systems, of which there are seven: Muscular-Bone systems, for locomotion; Nervous system, the message system to guide and direct the body; Digestive system, for absorbing food and converting it to energy; Urinary system, to carry of body wastes; Respiratory system, for breathing; Circulatory system, for circulation of the blood; Reproductive system, for reproduction of the race.

The mental part. This is the action of the mind, both thinking and feeling, that directs the personal behavior, that guides the performance of the individual.

The behavior part. Here the body and the mind join together into the whole individual to conduct the tasks of life. The simple tasks are obtaining food, clothing and shelter; walking, running and playing; protecting the body from harm, acting in association with other persons. The continuing tasks consist in the life processes: Sexual union, living a life span of seventy years during which disease and disaster are avoided while well-being and enjoyment of living is sought.

The Social Person. This is the social mantle that all persons wear in addition to their biological/mental aspect. When the individual steps forth to mix and mingle with his or her fellowmen, then a social association is taking place. This relationship occurs in three particular areas, as follows.

1. Close group. This is the association that is had within the family, with intimate friends, perhaps a work group.
2. Community relationship. Here the individual participants in the social activities that take place in or near his place of residence, such as civic projects, complying with government regulations, engaging in school, club, and church activities. The term 'neighborhood' conveys this community meaning.
3. Institutional relationship. Here there is no association of persons but rather an association with rules and regulations. The individual must obey the governing laws and must conform to group customs and so it is a case of having an association at a distance: with the government, the school, and the economic system.

These, then, are the great traits of man in his biological, thinking and social parts. Although the origin of man is obscure, his structure, method of function and behavior is well catalogued for all to see. This we shall consider in the pages to follow.

PART II
PROGRESS OF MAN

Chapter 4
Man in History

History is the record of man's achievements and his failures as an earth dweller. This record stretches back into a dim and shadowy past of a half million years where the first beginning is a total blackness. As time passed and man achieved and failed, the record began to brighten because a generation would die, leaving its artifacts and experience of living as a record. And then, six thousand years ago, at about 4,000 B.C., the record brightened to a high brilliance when man invented writing. From this point on the history of man became a recorded fact. Prior to this time the only source of history was by word of mouth and some left-over evidence such as building structures, wall paintings and artifacts at living sites. After 4,000 B.C. the record was put down in writing.

This written record of the past 6,000 years is an enormous catalog of events and happenings compiled by such men as Heroditus, Edward Gibbon, Oswald Spengler and Arnold Toynbee. It is a chronology too immense for the mind to grasp and so it must be resolved into some sort of a meaningful essence in order to visualize the whole. This we shall do with a synoptic eye, with an over-view, of the two great elements that constitute the whole of humanity, namely, the Civilizations of Man and the Cultural Institutions of Man. Before considering these in detail in the chapters that follow, we shall first establish a meaning to these two main parts of mankind as it applies to history.

CIVILIZATIONS – Man separate but similar.

After the crude beginnings of man in the early Stone Ages, man began to settle in clusters of tribes and clans, then in towns and villages and from these early beginnings arose large cities. As population increased and the manner of living became fixed, with behavior regulated by leaders and laws, these town-city people then acquired a social affinity and identity that did not exist in the wandering tribe. A tribe has a feeling of kinship, of family, but the city-town has a sense of "we people" extending beyond the immediate clan. It is an identity of social agreement or contract, not immediate clan. We know these large clusters of town-city people as Chinese, Indians, Phoenicians, Romans. And we call this social living and affinity a civilization.

The important fact to note is that mankind did not begin at one place and then spread out across the earth as one whole population but rather originated at separate sites on earth and there settled as an isolated group, developing their own way of life. Of course there were wandering peoples such as the Vikings and the Huns but these people did not found a civilization until they settled at a permanent site.

There are many and sufficient reasons for this isolated group settling which we may not examine here, merely note that it was so, and that, for whatever reason, mankind did begin and continue his course through history in clusters of people called Greeks, Sumerians, Chinese and eventually French, Japanese and Russian.

We have different names to describe these clusters of persons such as a people, a civilization or a culture, usually prefixed by their common names such as Indian Civilization, Babylonian culture and Roman people. The meaning here is that each of these groups of people, working and living in isolation from each other, built a way of life peculiar to and suitable to themselves and never banded together into a unified whole of mankind. In essence this absence of uniting marks man as a specie, as a man-kind, not a man-one.

There is no agreement by historians as to the number of civilizations that mankind has founded but it is generally agreed that the first four were as follows: Egyptian, established 3500 B.C.; Sumerian, founded 3500 B.C.; Indian, beginning 2700 B.C.; Chinese, the Yang Shao culture was flourishing at 2000 B.C. The Chinese is the oldest continuous civilization.

This separation of man into separate groups has energized much of the activities of mankind across the centuries in a long running account of wars and battles, power and control by kings and emperors, rulers and exploiters, conquerors and despoilers, triumphs and disasters. Again, without citing the many reasons for these actions, we wish merely to note that it was so, that it did occur, that it is a stark fact of history. The record of history subsequent to the Stone Ages is largely concerned with this type of intercourse between peoples, or, as we say today, nations.

CULTURAL FORMS – Man similar but separate.

The dramatic part of history such as battles, rulers and great events has tended to obscure the likeness and single identity of man which is found in his institutions, in his cultural part. These institutions, of which there are ten major ones, make up the essence of living in each of these civilizations. So that, while man may differ in his civilization-ways, he is very much alike and similar in his basic way of living, in the manner in which he lives and has lived at all times, past and present.

We know these institutions by such names as family, government and religion and each shall be reviewed in a chapter to follow. The important point to note is that these institutions are not peculiar to any one civilization but all were developed separately in each civilization at widely scattered locations around the world. If there is such a thing as unity in man it exists in his institutions.

The content of these institutions has not been the same for all cultures nor for all time within a culture, but the form has not changed. The Egyptian family of today does not live as the Egyptian family of ancient times, although the family form remains the same. The republican government of ancient Rome is far from the republican government of Italy today but the form is still republican. The content of Buddhism is different than that of Lutheranism, still both are religious institutions.

We see then, that while man may differ in his civilization mode, still he is very similar in his form of life and very must so in his manner of living. This is no new doctrine of course for as all mankind is alike biologically and mentally it seems only natural that similar forms of living would arise independently at widely scattered places. But in the recitations of history, these similar institutions of man have had a lesser viewing while the "march of civilization" has had the greater.

There is another distinction to be noted between a civilization and a culture and that is that the former die and pass away but the latter do not, and this value is passed on to succeeding generations. For example, the Phoenecians have contributed the alphabet, the ancient Arabs the arabic numerals, the Greeks much art and literature, the Romans government and laws. We use these cultural forms and content still today and view them as the common stock of mankind. But though common today, they were wrested from the maelstrom of life by our forebears at a high price, in trial and error tactics, in time and torture, as they erected and developed their civilizations.

Any effort to compare the value of civilizations to that of culture is nonsense. They are to each other as man and wife, are essential mates of humanity. But a brief contrast as to their meaning in history may be drawn. First as to civilizations, here the content is filled with a lesser meaning than that of culture. The portrayal here is one of great events, important persons and dominant actions that march across the stage of history in luminous array. But in terms of human values, of constructive effort, these actions are transient in the long story of history even though the march is made under such humanitaran slogans of "make the world safe" and "more benefit to mankind."

Secondly as to culture, it is the institutional forms that have the greater meaning for it is concerned with the meritorious acts of man and the worthy achievements in the long upward struggle from a low form of being to that of cultivated, intelligent persons and then on to a social being. These attainments are of superior worth for, as noted above, they are passed on to succeeding generations thus allowing for further advancement upward. Institutions are the outward exhibit of man's right to the title "Homo sapien, the wise one."

THEORY OF HISTORY

Many great men such as Vico, Kant, Hegel, Comte, Buckle, Marx, Collingwood, Croce and others have constructed philosophies that try to explain history in meaningful terms. Each of these is a powerful insight into the events of mankind and the progress of humanity, but none have developed a plan that explains the ultimate forces that move man-in-a-mass. Of course there are wants and needs and inspirations but there is no declaration such as is found in the physical sciences in the laws of Newton or the theories of Einstein which explain the forces of nature in exactitude. It is true that man is an organism, not a lump of matter, but this fact has been considered in offering theories, assigning basic causes to economic forces, to be god-driven, to instinctive drives and even the final cause of ultimate pleasure. But the facts of history do not support any of these ideas in toto nor do they reject any of them. All seem to contribute to the march of history but a unified theory has not been advanced. The best summary to date is part scientific and part common sense, namely, that all humans do seek and strive for physical and mental well-being in their person and social well-being in association with other humans. And, conversely, humans also seek to avoid ill-being. History records this seeking to attain and to avoid, both for persons and peoples.

DATES IN HISTORY

Time and events are the constituent parts of history. They are separate entities but are commonly joined in such terms as Stone-Age, Industrial-

Times, Agricultural-Season, and Primitive-Period. One marks date and duration, the other shows extent of achievement.

The action of events can be sketched with accuracy but time dates and periods cannot, they can only be given approximately. This is so because great events do not occur on the spur of the moment, on a specific day in a neat package. Even that greatest time keeper of all, the calendar, is off by four years. The calendar is divided by the birth of Christ as zero year but as Christ was actually born in 4 B.C., all B.C. and A.D. dates are off by this amount. We say that Columbus discovered America on October 12, 1492. He did indeed sight some land on that date but the discovery process required many years. "Man travels to the moon in three days" is correct for time of flight but the effort to do so started about the time of the ancient Greeks.

When we turn to marking the date of great events in human history such as the settlement of China or the beginning of capitalism, dates become even more vague, hazy and inexact. Thus the period of a civilization cannot be expressed exactly because of long periods of growth, decline or fusion with other cultures. We say that the Roman Empire ended in 476 A.D. when the last emperor, Romulus Augustulus was deposed. That was indeed the date that the empire toppled over and fell to the ground but by 476 A.D. the Roman Empire as such had long since ceased to exist. Nevertheless, events must be marked by time and they do follow one another in sequential order. The times given below, then, are approximated to the event, encapsulated in the several civilizations.

PERIODS OF HISTORY

There is no standard that marks the ages of man with accuracy. The most widely used divisions are the several Stone Ages, Primitive, Ancient, Medieval and Modern times. These terms are totally meaningless, apply only to the West, have little or no meaning in the East. Moreover, the division changes its base from tools used (Stone Age) to descriptive terms (Ancient, Modern), an undesirable switch, but generally accepted.

The proper division of history would seem to be by the technology of man, meaning the tools of production. This provides a single base, it applies to all of the civilizations East and West, to all time segments. It is technology that marks the critical stages of all of man's activities for it is through the technology of agriculture and industry that he sustains his life here on earth and provides the tools to do the job. Even kings, dynasties and generals, who occupy so much of history books, require technology as a base to attain these exalted heights. Technology provides a universal reference that expresses man's progress, his steady climb from primitive living to a sophisticated existence.

A general division would be such as this:

Palaeolithic Period. The Old Stone Age ending about 8000 B.C.

Neolithic Period. The New Stone Age ending about 4000 B.C., and the time when written history began.

Animal - Metal Age. Ending about 1500 A.D. Use of copper began 3500 B.C., Bronze age began 3000 B.C., the Iron Age began about 1500 B.C. During all this time the principal power of production was animals — the ox, the horse and camel.

Machine Age. Extensive use of machines began about 1700 A.D. with the Industrial Revolution. Subsequent terms have been used such as scientific revolution, technological revolution, atomic age and space age but the most accurate general term is Machine Age. It wasn't science or atoms that replaced man and the horse, it was the machine. Atoms are smashed and energy is harnessed in order to run machines. Man and the horse never did produce sufficiently but the machine is a true horn of plenty for mankind, pouring out a boundless and ceaseless flow of goods that grows bigger, more abundant, even better, every year.

In this book the divisions of history follow along classical lines, as follows:

1. Primitive Era, divided equally into Early and New Stone Age.
2. Middle Era, divided into Ancient and Medieval periods.
3. Modern Era, divided (a) 1500 to 1700 A.D., and (b) 1700 to 2100 A.D.

This method of division applies equally to the East and the West alike even though the 'Modern Era' did not get under way in the East until 1900 A.D., more or less. The division is also made to show the time of origin and time of ceasing of the several civilizations. Otherwise, each civilization is traced across these time periods.

Chapter 5

The Primitive Era

THE DISTANT PERIOD

Only animals roam the earth.
500,000 to 30,000 B.C., man emerges.
Homo Erectus, man who stands upright appears.
At first, is crude featured, heavy-boned, hairy, ape-like.
His technology is wooden clubs, rough stones, shells.

THE PRIMITIVE ERA, 30,000 to 4000 B.C.

Modern man has developed by 30,000 B.C.
Is fine featured, agile in movement, smooth skinned.
Had developed into three race groups:
Caucasian (white), Negroid (black), and Mongoloid (Yellow).

Early Stone Age, 30,000 to 8000 B.C.

Civilization

Man is semi-civilized.
Is a wanderer, not settled in villages.
Uses spoken language.
Shelters in caves, in lean-to.

Technology

Hunts and fishes.
Gathers vegetables, berries.
Discovers fire.
Craftsman in tools of stone, wood, shells, bone, hand-ax, chisel, awl, scapers.
Power use: Mostly man, some animals.

New Stone Age, 8000 to 4000 B.C.

Civilization.

Man is civilized by 8000 B.C.

Lives in villages and towns.
Shelter is mud hut, wooden house.
By 4000 B.C., all of the ten life institutions of man are established: Family, Language, Education, Religion, Government, Economics, Science, Technology, Art, War.

Technology.

Food is grown in cultivated plots.
Animals are domesticated: Pig, sheep, oxen, cattle, goats.
The wheel is in use.
Is a craftsman in pottery, weaves cloth, has masonry buildings.
Tools are finely made, uses polished stone, wood, bone, flint, ivory.
Power use: Man, animals, wind, water.

A BOLD LINE ACROSS THE PATHWAY OF HISTORY

At the end of the Late Stone Age, at or about 4000 B.C., mankind crossed the bold line from barbarian to that of a fully civilized being. From here on, for the next 6,000 years, down to the present day, mankind will live according to the pattern these primitive people designed and developed. They set a pattern and a life-style that has not changed and we live it even so today. The life-style has been improved with new foods, better housing, different tools, faster travel, even greater wars, but there has been no new institution of life nor changes in human nature since these primitive times.

We may summarize the three great life patterns bestowed by primitive man under three titles, as follows:

Man creature becomes modern man. To change from an animal-like creature into the finely chiseled features of modern man and the division into white, black and yellow was a process covering a half-million years. According to Charles Darwin it was a process of nature, an evolutionary change. By 30,000 B.C. our savage forebears had formed and shaped into what we now call modern man. We, you and I, are that man-creature, with the same shape, same structure, same bodily make-up. There have been no changes in the past 32,000 years.

Modern man becomes civilized. Between 30,000 and 8000 B.C., man gained two enormous achievements that qualified him to be called civilized. The first was his settled manner of living by planting and harvesting crops, having domesticated animals, building homes and using improved tools. Second was his social association of living in ordered groups, in towns and villages. We still live after this manner today, having only more people, larger towns called cities, better structures and power tools.

Civilized man develops a system of behavior. Between 8000 and 4000 B.C., man learned how to live in the social relationship of civilization, that is, how to conduct the business of living in large groups, in an organized and orderly manner. He had worked out a system of setting goals to be attained and the means for doing so. And, most importantly, man had invented writing, a method by which to record his activities. We call these systems of behavior 'institutions' and live by them still today, the very same institutions of our forebears, only more refined, more highly developed and more technical in structure.

The ten institutions are examined in detail in Part III but are listed here to show how these early peoples solved their problems of becoming civilized, a pattern we still use today.

Solving the problem of social association.
By a Family, a Spoken Language, Education of the young, a Government, an Economic System, and War.

Solving the problem of converting nature to man's use.
By Science, by Technology.

Solving the problem of relating to a supreme being.
By Religion.

Solving the problem of expression of self.
By Art.

This is the crucial heritage we have received from our far-distant, primitive forebears. As they performed these tasks before the writing of history began we do not know who they were exactly nor how they devised these ten vital institutions. We do know that it was a long time span of effort, a slow hit and miss developing process, a trial and error affair. It could not be otherwise for just to stay alive required a genius of action in the body, the mind and in spirit. Modern man can emulate by passing on to succeeding generations a more improved, a more perfected set of institutions.

Chapter 6

The Middle Era

The period of the Middle Era extends from 4000 B.C., the first beginnings of civilization in Egypt and India, down to 1500 B.C., the beginning of the Industrial Age. This includes the two historic periods of the western world called the Ancient Period, from 4000 B.C. to 500 A.D., when the Roman Empire fell, and the Medieval period from 500 A.D. down to 1500 A.D.

The Ancient and Medieval periods are not listed specifically because the terms have no meaning in the East and have only superficial meaning in the West. When the Roman Empire fell it did mark a change in the political affairs of Europe but it did not change the way of life in the use of tools or the means of sustaining life. Mankind still went on with the ox, the plow and an agricultural industry, plus a few crafts. As for the East, the fall of Rome had no significance, affected no change whatsoever. Hence the omission of Ancient and Medieval periods.

ANCIENT EGYPT

The Egyptians as a people were dwelling together as early as 4200 B.C. but founding of the ancient civilization is set at 3400 B.C.

Place. In North Africa, along the Nile River.

Government. Ruled by dynasties of kings and pharoahs.

Economy. Agriculture, mining and quarrying.

Religion. Many deities in the form of nature gods, sacred animals and semi-god persons.

Arts and Crafts. Crafts were in copper and bronze, the making of tools and weapons. The great period in art and architecture was from 2700 to 2200 B.C., during which time the pyramids, temples and tombs were built.

The Book of the Dead was a work of literature.

Egyptians were using a calendar about 4241 B.C.

Ceased. The Ancient period ended at 30 B.C. with the death of

Cleopatra, the last queen, who committed suicide, and Egypt became a Roman province. Egyptians have continued as a people, as an entity, down to the present day with these notable changes:

1. In 642 A.D. the Islamic religion became dominant, replacing the olden religious forms.
2. After centuries of rule by foreign nations, Egypt became a republic in 1953 A.D.

The chief industry remains agriculture, followed by mining and manufacturing.

MIDDLE EAST CIVILIZATIONS

Early in the Middle Era four separate civilizations flourished at the eastern end of the Mediterranean Sea in what is variously called Mesopotamia, Babylonia or the Fertile Crescent. It is the land that lies between the Tigris and Euphrates Rivers, although Persia extended eastward into Asia.

THE SUMERIAN

Founded about 4000 B.C. and flourishing by 3500 B.C., this is sometimes called the world's first civilization.

Government. Kings of various cities, with a central state.

Economy. Agricultural.

Religion. A mythology of gods but a central religion for all.

Arts and Crafts. Invented a system of writing, in cuneiform; the Sumerians engaged in banking, using a written contract; were fine craftsmen in gold, wood, copper and silver; noted for their pottery and jewelry; in architecture, were one of the first peoples to construct vaults, domes and arches; constructed canals for irrigation.

Ceased. At about 2000 B.C.

THE BABYLONIAN

This civilization began about 4000 B.C., was founded as an empire c.1775 B.C.

Government. Kings and a ruling class.

Economy. Skilled in agriculture.

Religion. Gods of mythology.

Arts and Crafts. Skilled in jewelry and pottery making; wheeled carts were in use about 2500 B.C.; erected large temples and towers; engaged in astronomy and mathematics.

One of the great law codes of mankind was issued here in the 1700's B.C., the Hammurabi Code of laws.

Literature. The Epic of Creation is a story of how the world was created when heaven and earth are formed out of the dragon Chaos. Another writing is called the Epic of Gilgamesh in which only Gilgamesh and his companions are saved in a ship while all of the rest of the world drowns in a flood.

Ceased. The date is fixed at 538 B.C. when Cyrus the Great conquered this area.

THE PHOENICIAN

Early settlement of these people was about 2700 B.C. and by 1500 B.C. they were known as Phoenicians.

Government. A king and a ruling class.

Economy. Basic industry was agriculture but the Phoenician state was directly on the eastern shore of the Mediterranean Sea and they became skilled sailors, sea traders and ship builders.

Religion. Mythological, especially gods and goddesses of fertility.

Arts and Crafts. The Phoenicians were skilled craftsmen in metal working, dyed cloth and glassware, and highly achieved as architects and builders.

The great contribution to human culture that Phoenicia made was the development of the alphabet, now used by the western world.

The Cedars of Lebanon used to build King Solomon's Temple in Jerusalem came from Phoenicia.

Ceased. Babylon was conquered by Alexander the Great in 332 B.C. and eventually became a Roman province in 64 B.C.

THE PERSIAN

The beginning time is set at about 1000 B.C. and by 546 B.C. the Persian civilization was flourishing as an empire. Persia is known today as Iran.

The ancient Persians were war-like people, noted for the wars and conquests under such leaders as Cyrus the Great and Darius I.

Government. By kings and a ruling class.

Economy. Agricultural.

Religion. Zoroastrianism.

Arts and Crafts. Skilled workers in gold and silver; skilled in architecture in the building of cities, temples, palaces and mosques; artistic in the weaving of fabrics and rugs.

Ceased. Persia was conquered by Alexander the Great in 332 B.C. The Persians, however, have continued as an ethnic people down to the present time. Today it is a nation, Iran, and the religion is Islam, which came with the Arab invasion in the 7th century A.D.

INDIA

The early people who lived in what is India today, at about 3500 B.C., were known as the Dravidian people. About 2000 B.C. the Aryan people invaded this area, settled, and developed the Indian civilization.

Place. The present state of India and Pakistan, in south central Asia.

Government. In the beginning there were a number of small states governed by independent rulers. A powerful leader arose in King Asoa, c.273 B.C., who united the country, building roads, hospitals and he issued a set of laws.

There was little change in the rule by single leaders until, beginning about 1600 A.D. a large part of India was regulated by the British East India Company, lasting until 1858 A.D. when the British Government assumed control. In 1947 A.D. a republic was formed with a constitution and democratic (representative) form of government.

Religion. The traditional religion was Hinduism, later came Buddhism, Jainism and Islamism.

Arts and Crafts. India is noted for its fine sculptures, statues of Buddha, temples, bronze work, the pagoda type building.

In architecture, one of the most beautiful buildings in the world is the Taj Mahal, a mausoleum completed in 1645 A.D.

Literature. The great Vedic poems and the Upanishads are among the world's great literature.

Invasions. From 500 A.D. to 1500 A.D. India experienced a constant succession of invasions including the Huns, Arabs, Persians, Muslims and Tartars. All had an affect upon the ancient Indian culture but the mixture absorbed from these invaders did not alter the Indian way of life which was agrarian, craftsmanship and trading. But the Muslim invasions of the 7th and 8th centuries did bestow a new and major religion.

The Indian way of life. From early times the Indian way had three inherent elements, sometimes called the three pillars of Indian society, as follows:

1. The autonomous village. The villages are made-up of family groups and each village is largely self-governing.
2. The joint-family. The large families, descendants of a common ancestor, lived as a commune, jointly sharing in food, worship, and property ownership. These large families were ruled by a family patriarch.
3. The caste system. Five classes of persons are distinguished: Priests (Brahmans); warriors (Kshatryas); traders and merchants (Vaisyas); farmers and workers (Sudras); and, the untouchables (Pariahs).

These three 'pillars' of Indian life continue so today but are much modified in the new republic.

Economy. This is still largely agrarian but industrial manufacturing and consumer goods are beginning to form a part of the economy.

CIIINA

Tradition sets the beginning date for Chinese history at c.2825 B.C. The first dynasty was the Hsia, beginning about 2205 B.C.

Place. Eastern Asia.

Government. Early rule was by dynasties, with an emperor. China is named after one of the dynasties, the Ch'in, and during the rule of this dynasty the Great Wall of China was built, later extended, finally reaching a length of 1,400 miles.

During the 1200's B.C. the Mongols from the north invaded China and two great Mongol lords became rulers of China, Genghis Khan and Kublia Khan, the latter described by Marco Polo who journeyed to China from Venice.

Dynasties continued to rule until 1912 A.D. when the Manchu dynasty was overthrown and a republic established. In 1949 A.D. a new republic was formed, called the People's Republic and a communist type of government instituted.

Economy. China's economy is largely agrarian but large centers of manufacturing are growing and mining of coal and ore is extensive.

Religion. The chief religions are Buddhism, Confucianism, Taoism and Islamism.

Arts and Crafts. Painting and music have been highly developed arts from ancient times. The Chinese are masters in porcelain work and in the pagoda type building. Printing, paper, gunpowder and silk were all first invented and used in China.

The Chinese have produced fine art work from early times in bronze, pottery, vases and urns, jade and ivory, and lacquer on wood.

Philosophy. Three of the world's great philosophies of life originated in China, all within a period of 300 years, as follows:

1. Taoism, by Lao Tzu, about 500 B.C., who taught that life is best understood by intuitive contemplation in order to discover the true nature of living.
2. Confucius, 551-497 B.C., who taught a human-directed philosophy of moral goodness, clear thinking, family devotion, self-discipline and peace.
3. Mencius, or Mong K'o, c.370-290 B.C., who taught an ethical code of good conduct, with welfare of the people under a benevolent royal authority.

The Chinese are the oldest continuous ethnic group on earth. They have never been conquered and overrun by a foreign people, they have held to their basic philosophy and beliefs over the centuries and continued in their basic pattern of life of the large family group. Today near the end of the 20th century, the first change in life style has begun with a turning to industrial production.

JEWISH

The Jews were originally desert tribesmen that entered Palestine about 1200 B.C. where they settled and this became their homeland.

Place. Along the eastern edge of the Mediterranean Sea, originally called Palestine and now named Israel.

Economy. At time of settlement, pastoral and agrarian.

Religion. Belief in one supreme deity, Jehovah or Yahwah.

Literature. The Torah and the Talmud. Over the centuries Jewish scholars have contributed greatly to both prose and poetry but acknowledgement of such work is not assigned to them as Jew but rather as citizens of the country in which they live such as Alexandria in Egypt, Roman, Spanish, American and Russian.

Additional. Jews are today and always have been a distinct entity only because of their beliefs and conduct, not because they are a separate civilization. They were a united people living in a homeland only from 1200 B.C., when Moses led them out of Egypt, until 70 A.D. when the Romans destroyed their temple in Jerusalem and Palestine became a Roman province. Since then the Jews have lived in every nation of the world but always as citizens of their nation of residence. They have a separate identity, that is as Jews, only because of their religious beliefs and ethical conduct. Their civil life conforms to the laws of the nation in which they live.

A homeland for these people was established in Israel, in 1948 A.D., but only a small percentage of the world's Jews live there today.

ANCIENT GREECE

Helenic tribes occupied the Grecian area about 1800 B.C. and by 800 B.C. had formed into city-states. The Grecian classical period was from 800 B.C. to 300 B.C.

Place. Eastern Mediterranean Sea.

Government. Early rule was by kings and elders, followed by separate city-states. The first form of democracy was established in the city-state of Athens.

Economy. Largely agrarian with hand crafts and sea trading.

Religion. Grecian religion related to the nature gods and spirits that were held to be immortal humans such as Zeus, Apollo, Aphrodite and Hera.

Arts and Crafts. In the fine arts, sculpture and painting. In architecture the Greeks were master builders of temples and public buildings such as the Parthenon and Erectheum.

Scientific Inquiry. The Greeks were the first to examine nature in a truly scientific sense, that is, a dispassionate inquiry into the causes and the processes of nature. For example: Thales, (c.640-546 B.C.), was founder in geometry and astrology; Pythagorus, (c.582-500 B.C.), taught that the basis of the world is number; Heraclitus, (c.535-475 B.C.), taught that only change is real; Aristotle, (384-322 B.C.), was a prolific writer in science with treatises on physics, biology, psychology, astronomy and metaphysics.

Medicine. Hippocrates taught diagnosis and care of the body and wrote the Hippocratic Oath, still in use today.

Literature and philosophy. Herodotus wrote the first great history and is called "the father of history;" Socrates, born 469 B.C., taught that knowledge is virtue; Plato, born 427 B.C., wrote extensively on the theory of Ideas, Forms and the Ideal; Aristotle, in addition to his scientific works, wrote treatises on Politics, Ethics, Rhetoric, Poetics and Logic. His book on ethics is still valid and in use today.

Sports. The Greeks were lovers of sports contests and the Olympic Games originated here in 776 B.C.

Ceased. Greece became a Roman Province in 146 B.C.

JAPAN

The original people of Japan were the Ainu. Folklore tells that the first ruler was Jimmu Tenno, who was a descendant of the Sun Goddess and became Emperor in 660 B.C.

Place. The Island of Japan, in the far western Pacific Ocean, off the coast of Asia.

Government. In early times rule was largely by military families or clans such as the Fuliwara clan, the Minamoto family and Ashikaga family, each ruled by a feudal lord or shogun. Central rule was by an Emperor until 1945 at which time the government was changed to a constitutional monarchy with a prime minister and a parliament of two houses called a Diet.

Economy. Until the twentieth century, largely agrarian and especially rice growing, and fishing as the second industry. In recent years there has been extensive mining and manufacture. Today, Japan is one of the most highly industrialized nations in the world with high skills and high productivity in manufactured products.

Religion. Shinto and Buddhism, with some Christianity.

Arts and Crafts. The Japanese have always had high skill and talent in poetry, painting, drama and sculpture. Their porcelain ware is of highest quality. Bronze and metal work, ivory and wood carving are also well known skills.

Numerous temples and shrines of delicate design exist throughout the country.

Painting on silk is one of the high arts.

Conduct. The Japanese have always been strict in their manners and observation of customs and remarkably devoted to family life.

War. Japan was the site of the first atomic bombing of a city when a nuclear bomb was exploded over the city Hiroshima during World War II.

ROMAN EMPIRE

The Etruscans were the early settlers in the Rome area and Roman bands began to invade about 900 B.C. The Etruscans were overcome and the Roman Republic was established 509 B.C.

Place. The central city was Rome, in what is now Italy, but the empire eventually encircled the Mediterranean Sea.

Government. A republican form of goverment. Public affairs were discussed in a Senate but Roman power always resided in an emperor, ruling nobles and the army.

Economy. The Romans had a well developed agriculture of grain, cattle and wines. Crops were rotated and irrigated. There was extensive mining of marble, iron and silver. Important products were pottery, wood, dyes and glass.

Religion. A mythology of gods was worshiped including Jupiter, God of the Earth; Vesta, Goddess of the Home; Mars, God of War; Ceres, God of Harvest; Hercules, God of Trade; Neptune, God of the Sea.

Arts and Crafts. In fine arts: Scupture and painting.

In architecture: The construction of roads, buildings, coliseums, bridges and aqueducts. Some bridges, now 2,000 years old are still in use.

In numerals: Roman numerals were the standard in Europe before the adoption of Arabic numerals. In the Roman system, number was made from seven basic figures: I (1); V (5); X (10); L (50); C (100); D (500); M (1,000).

In recreation: Numerous holidays provided entertainment for the whole population with chariot races, gladiators fighting lions in the Coliseum and warrior-to-warrior combat.

In law: Many of the laws of the western world were developed and codified by the Romans. Two major concepts that were developed were: First, that of Universality which asserts that all men have basic characteristics in which they are similar and alike; and secondly, that of Equity, which asserts that while the law is firm and must be obeyed as written, still some flexibility must be exercised in the interpretation of the law.

In war: Rome developed the first army of professional soldiers and with this power conquered the known western world. Most of these conquered people were subject to Roman law but were allowed a wide latitude in administering their own affairs.

Ceased. The last Roman emperor, Romulus Augustulus, was deposed in 476 A.D. Most historians mark this as the beginning of the Medieval Period in Europe.

BYZANTINE EMPIRE

The Roman Empire stretched along an east-west axis, as does the Mediterranean Sea, which the empire encircled. In time, this empire was referred to as the eastern and western parts. In 330 A.D., the Emperor Constantine transferred his capital from Rome in the western section to Constantinople in the eastern section. This city was originally named Byzantine. We know this city today as Instanbul, Turkey. When the Western section of the Roman Empire fell in 476 A.D., the eastern section continued on for another 1,000 years as the Byzantine Empire.

Place. Around the eastern part of the Mediterranean Sea, including what is now Turkey and Greece.

Government. A central government with an emperor who was supreme ruler of state and church.

Economy. Common to the times. Agrarian, herdsmen and trading. Extensive trade intercourse was carried on with the Orient.

Arts and Crafts. A combining of western Christian art with Far East art in painting, mosaics, decorations and ornaments. There was exceptional skill in glass and ornamental stones. In architecture the Byzantines erected elaborate churches with onion shaped domes, arches and decorations.

Law. Most of the Roman laws were codified and issued in a digest during the reign of Justinian in the 500's A.D. Much of the legal systems of the western nations today are based on or derived in large measure from the Digest of Justinian.

Ceased. In 1453 A.D., with the fall of Contantinople. The conquerors were Seljuk and the Ottoman Turks, who were Moslems. The Eastern Orthodox Church (Greek Catholic) continues today in many countries.

EUROPE

Europe is the direct descendant of the Roman Empire, which ended c.500 A.D., the date that marks the beginning of the European civilization. Near the close of the Roman rule two invasions added new peoples to the European population. One was the Huns from Asia and the other was the Germanic tribes from the far north of Europe, the Angles, Jutes, Franks, Vandals and Visigoths.

Place. The far western extension of the continent of Asia.

Government. Europe is not a state but rather a geographical area with a number of separate states and governments but all of a similar character in religion, economy and manner of life. The governmental systems have been four in number, as follows:

1. Feudal system. This consisted of three parts: The Lords and knights who were land holders, the clergy, and the workers.
2. The kings. During the Feudal period the kings were weak, with limited power. By 1500 A.D. the king ruler had gained extensive power and royal status.
3. Parliaments. The first parliaments were assembled in Britain and France in the 1200's A.D. where, for the first time, the affairs of state could be discussed in open forum.
4. Nation states. With parliaments and peoples' representatives in assembly, the ethnic groups began to take on the character of nationalities and national states as we know them today, such as English, Spanish, French.

Economy. A two-part economy marked the early period.

1. The Manorial System. In this system the lord owned the manor house and the land, while the serfs or peasants worked the land. The land was split into fields, so many fields for the lord, so many fields for the workers. The serfs tilled all of the fields and supplied the manor house with its needs.
2. Merchants and craftsmen. These people formed something of a middle class in supplying the needed housewares, clothing, tools and utilities for daily living.

Today, the whole of Europe is classified as an industrial/agricultural economy.

Religion. Christianity has always been the dominant religion of Europe. The early period was totally Catholic but after the Protestant separation in the 1500's, both Catholic and Protestant religion flourished.

Aside from a religion as such, the Roman Catholic Church performed two secular functions of far reaching value to western man, during this period. First, the church was the only body to maintain law and order in the early part of the Medieval Period and in the latter part, when kings and monarchs began to rule, the church also served as a guide to stabilize both kings and people. Secondly, the church monasteries were the centers of learning and also the repositories of western man's accumulated knowledge that enabled the first universities to begin in Europe.

The Crusades between 1099 and 1270 A.D. were church inspired and supported the actions although they were led by knights and barons. The object was to recover the Holy Land from the Moslems. There were eight Crusades that marched across Europe and into the Middle East.

Arts and Crafts.

In fine arts: Painting, sculpture, music, dancing and drama all flourished during this time.

In architecture: Great cathedrals, public buildings and highways were constructed.

In education: The first universities were opened: at Bologna in the 12th century, which granted doctor degrees; Paris University, granted the first charter in 1200 A.D.; Oxford University began in the 12th century.

In law: Four great concepts and procedures of law came out of Medieval Europe, as follows:

(a) The Magna Carta, in 1215 A.D., which curbed royal power, separated church from state, and guaranteed the basic rights of free men.
(b) Representative government, the essence of democracy.
(c) The idea that law should govern people, and not kings, not unseen gods, not other people, not dictators.
(d) The jury system to try violators of the law. This is used today almost universally.

In explorations: First ventures were to the west coast of Africa in the 1300's, then discovery of America by Columbus in 1492, then Ferdinand Magellan's voyage around the world in 1519-1522. These explorations are sometimes referred to as the first shrinking of the world and the airplane as the second shrinking.

In war: Many wars, devastating, cruel, and costly have marked the progress of the European peoples, most notably the eight Crusades, the Hundred Years' War, The Thirty Years' War, the Napoleon wars, Franco-German wars, and in modern times the two World Wars.

ISLAMIC CIVILIZATION

The people we know today as Arabs were originally Bedouin tribesmen, herdsmen and tradesmen of the desert. It was from these people that Mohammed came and formulated his great religion of Islam. Mohammed was born in 570 A.D., in the city of Mecca, and the founding of his religion is given as 622 A.D.

Place. The Islamic religion was established in Arabia but soon spread westward across north Africa and into Spain and then eastward into Asia, especially Pakistan, India and Indonesia.

Economy. Islamism is a religion and way of life and not a central state with an economic system. Until recent time, most Islamic peoples have been herdsmen, farmers, skilled craftsmen and traders. The Moslem people are noted for their method of agriculture and use of fertilizers and irrigation, for extensive trading and their talent as merchants in the bazaar section of cities.

Government. As noted above, the Arab-Islamic civilization is not a unified society or a nation as such but rather a religion, a moral code and a way of life for millions of persons in many countries. These people are called Moslems because they are distinct in their beliefs, their code of conduct and the folkways that make-up their cultural living.

Religion. The name is Islamism and the followers are called Moslems. The holy book is the Koran, with faith in Allah as the only God and Mohammed as his prophet.

Arts and Crafts.

In architecture: The Islamic people constructed great mosques with their domes and minarets known as Moorish palaces and Turkish mosques.

In crafts: Persian rugs, pottery, metalware, glassware, mosaics in tile.

Science. Astronomy, medicine and mathematics were highly developed by the early Islamic scholars. One enormous achievement of benefit to the whole world was the invention of the Arabic numerals 1, 2, 3, 4, 5, 6, 7, 8, 9, 0.

Philosophy. Much of the Greek writings were lost to the western world and unknown during most of the Medieval period but were kept alive by Islamic scholars and eventually passed back into Europe from these Moslem people. One of the greatest scholars was Al-Gazel who studied Greek philosophy, wrote about it and extended it.

THE AMERICAS

The North and South American 'civilizations' are not a descendant of the European but rather a direct transplant. These lands were explored, conquered and settled by European peoples, the English, French, Spaniards, Portuguese and German-Dutch. The basic institutions of government, law, religion, arts and science were direct importations by these people. And, as the early settlers were persons from the several European countries, the folkways, manners and life-style were a mere extension of the country from which the settlers came. This may be contrasted with India which, although totally under British control at one time, still retained and continues today in its own long-time cultural ways.

The brief listing below of the New World lands is, therefore, something in the order of the continuation of European civilization.

NORTH AMERICA

Discovered by Columbus in 1492 A.D. and at the time populated by Indians who were not organized or united in any union.

Government. Originally the settlements were colonists of several European countries and under European rule. In time, as the colonies grew in size and in population they eventually separated from the foreign rule and became independent nations known as Canada, United States and Mexico. Each of these nations control their way of life with democratic, representative forms of government.

Economy. Originally agricultural, fishing and crafts but after independence, Canada and the United States developed gradually in industrial production.

Religion. Catholic and Protestant religions are dominant with a third major religion in Judaism.

Arts and Literature. These have flourished in all three nations, with high emphasis on education.

SOUTH AMERICA

Often called Latin America, South America carries the same discovery date as North America. When discovered by Columbus the land was populated by Indian tribes not organized in any extensive union except as noted below under "Ancient America."

Government. Beginning about 1500 A.D. the entire continent of South America came under Portuguese and Spanish rule and remained so for 300 years. Agitation for independence from foreign rule began about 1800 A.D. and by 1900 all nations were essentially free of foreign rule. The ideal sought by each country was a democratic form of government but few have achieved this goal in full. In the greater number of states the rule has been by powerful groups, dictators or military juntas although all constitutions specify a representative form of government.

Economy. At the beginning the industry was agricultural and mining. Today, some states are well along in industrialization while others are adapting slowly. Oil in some areas has stimulated economic growth.

AUSTRALIA AND NEW ZEALAND

Like North and South America, Australia and New Zealand were discovered and settled by European peoples and their basic institutions of government, religion and art are similar to that of the European, largely British. However, the population is sparse, with much open land, and the life style is different from that of the crowded cities of Europe.

EARLY AMERICAS

The civilizations described below were located in Central and South America and were in full flourish when the Spaniards arrived. The Indians of North America developed adequate cultural ways for their livelihood but did not have a unified form of living such as the Incas and Mayas, noted below.

MAYA EMPIRE

Beginning. This civilization formed about 1000 B.C. in Yucatan in

Central America.

Religion. Priests administered the religion, with deities of the sky and of the earth. They worshiped nature gods: The Moon god, Sun god, Corn god, Wind god.

Government. By a priesthood theocracy. The Mayas lived in separate city-states and were not united into a single nation under one ruler such as the Incas were.

Economy. The Mayas were farmers and the major crop was corn. They were also craftsmen in working gold and copper.

Architecture. These people built many temples in the form of pyramids.

Arts and Crafts. The Mayas engaged in sculpture, they developed a calendar, studied astronomy of planets and stars and used the zero in mathematics.

Ceased. With the arrival of the Spaniards in the early 1500's A.D.

INCA EMPIRE

Beginning. About 1000 A.D. in what is now Ecuador and Peru. Their settlements were located high in the Andes Mountains and they were known as the Empire of the Sun.

Religion. A priesthood and they worshiped gods of nature.

Government. These people had a monarchy, ruled by a king and a theocracy for the king was considered a semi-god who came from the sun.

Government. The Incas were skilled farmers who raised beans, tomatoes, corn and potatoes. There was extensive mining of metals: gold, tin, silver and copper.

Arts and Crafts. The Incas were experienced goldsmiths and silversmiths and produced intricate pieces in these metals.

Ceased. Conquered by Spaniards under Francisco Pizarro in 1532 A.D.

AZTEC EMPIRE

Beginning. About 1300 A.D., in what is now Mexico.

Religion. The religion was administered by priests, with the worship of numerous gods of animals, serpents, gods of war and of the sun. These people sacrificed to their gods, including young men, women and children, many of whom were prisoners of war.

Government. The Aztecs were ruled by an emperor and the ruler at the time of Spanish conquest was Emperor Montezuma.

Economy. Extensive farming and raising of cattle.

Architecture. These people were skilled in building temples, pyramids and aqueducts.

Arts and Crafts. The Aztecs were skilled in sculpture, metalwork, weaving, picture writing and music.

Ceased. With the coming of the Spaniards under Hernando Cortes in 1519 A.D.

LOWER AFRICA
(Including the Modern Era)

During Ancient and Medieval times, lower Africa, also called sub-Saharan Africa, had no organized societies with regulated government and economy such as the European states. Northern Africa experienced the Egyptian, Roman and Islamic civilizations but lower Africa was not touched by these cultures. The northern desert area, the Sahara Desert, was a region that divided the continent.

The inhabitants of lower Africa were people of the Negro race, divided into such various peoples as the Bantu, Hottentot, Nubian, Bushmen, Swahili, Zulu and Pigmies. Organization was mostly on a tribal basis although several empires did come into existence, the Ghana Empire about 1000 A.D., the Mali Empire about 1200 A.D., the Songhai Empire about 1500 A.D. These empires were a loose confederation of tribes without a formal structure or central government.

Beginning about 1500 A.D. European explorers entered lower Africa and their governments began to lay claims or rights to various sections and then to exploit them for economic reasons.

About 1900 A.D. the native Africans began to dispute these claims and to reject foreign domination. At the beginning of the century about 80 percent of Africa was dominated or controlled by foreign nations but by 1970 the whole was divided into about forty independent nations, self-ruled and free of foreign power.

Government. All of the nations are independent republics although true democracy has not been fully attained by all for some of the nations are controlled by a power elite.

Economy. Agriculture, in the form of plot farming and cattle raising, has dominated the economy of Africa from early times. Mining is now an extensive industry with extraction of coal, copper, gold and diamonds. Oil is produced in many places.

Religion. Islam is the largest single religion, followed by Christianity. In out-lying and lesser populated places there are still tribal religions with worship of nature gods and man gods.

Arts and Crafts. There is much native art work in sculpture of wood and metal. Rhythmic music is a highly developed art with dancing to accompany it. Literature consists largely of folklore.

Other. Africa is noted as the source of the slave trade, the sale of enslaved persons by African rulers for shipment to North and South America where they worked on large plantations as slaves. It is estimated that in the 300 year period from 1550 to 1865 A.D., that ten million slaves were shipped to the western hemisphere.

Chapter 7

The Modern Era

The beginning of the Modern Era is centered at the year 1500 A.D. because of four major actions that changed the course of mankind and life for all human beings. These activities were:

1. The world explorations that began in the late 1400's;
2. The scientific inquiries that began in the late 1400's;
3. The flow of inventions that began in the 1400's such as Gutenberg's movable type;
4. The beginning of industrial production in the 1600's.

These endeavors of man began in Europe but now, after 500 years they have enveloped the world both East and West. The explorations were a one-time event but the scientific inquiries, the inventions and the industrial production, continue to expand in size and in intesity.

In this chapter we shall review this period of history as a list of achievements by man rather than a list of civilizations as in the previous chapter. This is so because there have been no new civilizations and no new religions begun in this period, only a continuation of those previously shown. There have been wars, political and territorial changes but no new people have emerged and all cultures tend toward the industrial way. Moreover, scientific inquiries and technological methods are not the property of any one nation or peoples except as originators of these enterprises. Each scientific inquiry and each technological method, when completed, becomes a cluster of information, an explanation of How this happened, How that occurred. This information soon becomes public property the world around and all begin to employ it to their use. In this broad sense, then, there is only one civilization of man today, a scientific/industrial one, with political and cultural divisions that suite each particular nation.

THE SECOND BOLD LINE ACROSS THE PATHWAY OF HISTORY

There is no expanation for the change that took place in the minds and hearts of western man about 1500 A.D. Something weaned him away from the stagnation of Medieval times into a Rennaissance of learning and action that has culminated in a new type of civilization for mankind, variously called scientific, industrial or technological. Whatever the name or whatever the cause, all we know for sure is that a magic flute sounded, man heard and man followed. Not blindly as in the fairy tale but with intelligence and reason. An abrupt right turn was made in the course of life for all mankind as men began to view the worlds of nature, of man and of God, with new eyes. Earth men crossed a bold line separating the past from the future, to begin a new kind of life and living on earth.

Let us summarize in brief the endeavors of man on each side of the two bold lines of history that we have drawn in this book.

1. The first line was drawn at the year 4000 B.C. Prior to this time the great activity of man was the effort to become civilized and to establish the ten great life institutions.

2. After 4000 B.C. the important action was the founding of the major civilizations and religions and then developing these into a high estate until 1500 A.D., at the same time producing the needed goods with animal power and by hand craft.

3. After 1500 A.D. the great activity has been the preoccupation with science, technology, economic and industrial development and the production of needed goods by machine.

This latter surge of action has been going on for the past 500 years and is still in progress, ever and always at an escalated pace. The knowledge that has been accumulated fills the libraries of the world and the products of achievement fill the coffers of man, while the sum of it all is beyond the comprehension of the mind. But some understanding must be had and in this concise book we shall summarize the period in two parts, first with a brief comment on the major achievements of the era and secondly with a time chart of specific achievements, largely scientific and technological.

MAJOR ACHIEVEMENTS OF THE MODERN ERA

From Ideal to Real. Prior to 1500 A.D. the central interest of western man was spiritual, believing that the accumulation of material things was secondary to the first order of a soul salvation. Beginning at this time, however, the effort turned toward a material salvation also. The ideal life of self denial and reward hereafter, so well defined by religion and philosophy, began to give way to an envisioned life of well-being here on earth. As we know quite well today, the cause of this turning toward the real world was the result of the scientific inquiry and then the technological production of goods that began at this time. Man's soul was not and has not been abandoned but his body needs and life-style needs have been provided with a sufficiency undreamed of at the turning point of 1500 A.D.

The Nation. The concept of 'nation' came into being about the middle of the 1800's and is today the dominant term to designate a people, their culture, their political structure. What was formerly referred to as the country of Italy or the Russian civilization is now known as the nation of Italy and the Russian nation.

One World. From the political standpoint the world is sharply divided into separate nations, each with its own fierce patriots, each with its own zealous citizens. But mankind is not split into isolated societies, each living aside from the other, each with its own peculiar manners, its own particular customes, as in the past. The phrase "all the world is one," although not a certified reality has come to have a real meaning as we may note in the following.

1. First is the incredible speed of transportation in which oceans are crossed and continents spanned in a few hours, not weeks or months.
2. Communication is hardly a matter of time, it now is instantaneous. An earthquake in Japan is known as quickly in London as in Tokyo; the election of an American president is known in the Australian "out back" at the same time that the American citizen is informed.
3. The industrial spirit. The aim of the entire world is to gain a high quantity of consumer goods, either by direct production or through trade. No matter the political base: Communist, Capitalist or Socialist; no matter the religious belief: one god, many gods, no god; no matter the cultural custom — the aim and the goal is high technology and mass of goods.
4. The industrial tie-in. The interlocked system of trade between nations has an enormous influence, is a huge factor in the concept of one world. For example, the dire need of oil from Arabia to operate the machines of Europe, the need of the Japanese to export to the world their high production of goods and their critical need to import raw materials.

The Governance of Man. Kingdoms and monarchs have virtually disappeared from the affairs of mankind and have been repalced by the nation and representative government. The representation is a mixed variety, with some nations having dictators, but in all nations the voice of the people is part of, if not the whole of, government.

Population Increase. At the beginning of the modern period only two continents were fully known, Europe and Asia, and these were lightly populated. The continents of (lower) Africa, North and South America and Australia were still undiscovered and only sparsely populated by native groups. Now, five hundred years later, all the world is fully inhabited with high density in relation to needed supplies and the density rate is increasing. Aside from the natural increase by birth, much of this population gain is the result of the achievements in medicine, in the prevention of disease and the prolonging of the individual life span.

Mode of Living. The products of industrial technology have conferred on mankind an entirely new mode of life from that of former times. The home shelter, food, clothing, home furnishings, the lesser effort of labor, the leisure of recreation, the opportunity to travel far — all these have made the manner of living a "modern way of life," a new universe for the individual. The benefits are not distributed equally to all but the modern way was totally unknown at 1500 A.D., even to the rulers and the wealthy.

Exploration. The discovery of the Americas and Australia and the opening of lower Africa was not merely finding of new land, it also poured into the world the raw wealth of these four continents. And, some say, a new spirit of freedom was born in man as a result of the explorations and the securing of the wealth.

Increase of Knowledge. There is no way to measure the quantity of knowledge in the world but several rough approximates have been made to show the growth. Here is one of them:

At the year 1 A.D., all of the world's knowledge could be put in one book.

At the year 1000 A.D., still only one book required.

At the year 1500 A.D., still only one book to record the world's knowledge.

At the year 1700 A.D., add one book, making a total of two.

At the year 1900, add three books, total five books.

At the year 1950, add five books, total ten books.

At the year 1960, add ten more books, total twenty books.

At the year 1970, add ten more books, total thirty books.

At the year 1980, add twenty books, a total of fifty books to record the accumulated knowledge of mankind.

In other words, the modern period and especially the 20th century has seen an increase of knowledge of unprecedented magnitude.

Scientific Discoveries. Science, in the strict sense of the word, performs only one activity, namely, the investigation of nature. The discoveries of Kepler, Newton and Einstein were scientific and are not to be compared with the mechanical, electrical and technological uses that were made of these discoveries. These latter are resultant discernments, employed to convert nature to the uses of man. They are the practical aspects of scientific findings. The scientist seeks out the structure and function of natural things and the laws that regulate them, irrespective of resultant uses. Both the method and the spirit of such inquiry into nature was unknown to earlier times. The Greeks came near to it but scientific man did not appear until the Modern Period.

Inventions. The deliberate invention of mechanical devices began about 1700 A.D. and the pace increased with the passage of time. A partial listing is given below.

Technology. Technology is that branch of human endeavor that converts the things of nature into products that man can use. There are two instruments in the world that can perform the manipulative work of technology, that is, the moulding, shaping, forming and finishing of usable objects, and they are human hands and a machine. Horsepower, electricity and steam do not make products, they are energy sources. A horse cannot make a chair nor can a spurt of electricity weave fabric. Such operations are reserved to human hands or a machine.

Technology in the modern period has passed through three stages, as follows:

1. Man operated machines. The early machines had to be attended constantly by a person, to start it, stop it, feed materials and remove the finished product.
2. Automated machines. The second period saw machines that were automatic in that they required only the supervision of a human, with the feeding of raw materials and the removal of the products being a continuous process. Much or most of the machines today are automated.
3. Servo-mechanisms or serving machines. This new direction of technology is generally referred to as cybernetics, a Greek word that means steersman. In its modern use the word refers to the field of study and technology begun by Norbert Wiener and others.

A serving machine tells another machine what to do rather than a human being performing this duty. The computer is an example. While the computer itself cannot think and must have the basic instructions inserted, called a program, thereafter the computer will give directions, solve problems and correct errors.

Medical Treatment of Disease. A longer life and a healthier life has blessed modern man through the discovery and application of miracle medicines, new procedures in the treatment of disease, new techniques in operation, even the replacement of body parts with transplanted or mechanical organs.

The Atom. Perhaps the most spectacular achievement of modern man has been the conversion of mass into energy by fission and fusion of the atom. Whatever the benefits in peace or the horrors in war, the crucial fact is that with nuclear action man has opened a new source of energy to do his work and to supply his wants and needs. He has created, has brought into the world, a thing that did not exist on earth heretofore.

War. War in all of its negative aspects has kept pace with all of the positive 'progress' of man. It is not nation-states that become embroiled in war, it is the whole world; it is not thousands who die, but millions; it is not only the soldier at the front who faces battle, but the home population of women and children as well; and atom bullets that dissolve all substance, human and material, are used in addition to lead and steel.

Space. The exploration of outer space with both satellites and man in space machines is one of the highest triumphs of man since he appeared on earth. Thus far the only practical use has been for communication and experiments but the future holds a multitude of benefits in science, technology, medicine and economics, all for the well-being of mankind. Some forecasters even anticipate the regions of space as a living area for man.

CHARTS OF ACHIEVEMENTS

••••• *SCIENCE* •••••

1543 — Heliocentric theory of the universe, Copernicus.

1609 — Laws of planetary motion, Kepler.

1614 — Logarithms invented, John Napier.

1628 — Circulation of the blood, Harvey.

1662 — Royal Society of London founded.

1666 — French Academy of Science founded.

1687 — Velocity of light discovered, Roemer.

1687 — Newtonian mathematics, Laws of motion, Newton.

1690 — Wave theory of light, Huygens.

1735 — Classification of plants and animals, Linnaeus.

1803 — Atomic theory, Dalton.

1831 — Electro-magnetic induction demonstrated, Faraday.

1822-1895 — Pasteur, proved the germ theory.

1896 — Radioactivity, Becquerel.

1898 — Radium discovered, Marie and Pierre Curie.

1900 — Quantum theory, Planck.

1905 — Special theory of relativity, Einstein.

c.1916 — General theory of relativity, Einstein.

1932 — Unified field theory, Einstein.

••••• INVENTIONS, TECHNOLOGY •••••

1500's – Musket gun.

1590 – Microscope, Jansen.

1593 – Thermometer, Galileo.

1608 – Telescope, Lippershey.

1609 – Telescope, Galileo.

1643 – Barometer, Torricelli.

1663 – First newspaper, in England, Public Intelligence.

1696 – Steam engine, Savery.

1705 – Steam engine, Newcomen.

1752 – Lightning, demonstrate lightening and electricity the same, Franklin.

c.1765 – Spinning jenny, Hargreaves.

1769 – Steam engine, Watts.

1769 – Spinning mill, Arkwright.

1770 – Steam car, Cugnot.

1785 – Loom, Cartwright.

1793 – Cotton gin, Whitney.

1796 – Lithography, Senefelder.

1800 – Flow of electricity discovered, Volta.

1801 – Arc light.

1801 – Paper making machine, Fourdrinier brothers.

1804 – First locomotive, Trevithick.

1807 – Steamboat, Fulton and Livingston.

1811 – Breechloader gun, Thornton.

1819 – Stethoscope, Laennel.

1836 – Revolver, Colt.

1837 – Telegraph, Morse.

1839 – Photography, Daguerrer.

1840 – Incandescent light, Grove.

1846 – Sewing machine, Howe.

1859 – Drake oil well, Penna.

1861 – Machine gun, Gatling.

1861 – Passenger elevator.

1866 – Open hearth steel.

••••• *INVENTIONS, TECHNOLOGY* •••••

1868 — Typewriter, Soule, Glidden.

1876 — Telephone, Bell.

1877 — Phonograph, Edison.

1883 — First skyscraper, Chicago.

1884 — Machine gun, Maxim.

1884 — Modern bicycle, Starley.

1885 — Automobile, Benz.

1885 — Motorcycle, Daimler.

1886 — Internal combustion engine, Daimler.

1891 — Submarine, Holland.

1891 — Zipper, Judson.

1892 — A. C. Motor, Tesla.

1895 — Diesel engine, Rudolf Diesel.

1895 — Motion pictures.

1895 — Wireless telegraph, Marconi.

1895 — X-rays, Roentgen.

1902 — Air conditioning, Carrier.

1903 — First airplane flight, Wright brothers.

1904 — Sound moving pictures.

1920 — Commercial radio broadcasting begun.

1922 — Radar, Taylor, Young.

1923 — Television, Zworykin.

1926 — Television, Baird.

1929 — Modern rocket, Goddard.

1930 — Jet-aircraft engine, Whittle.

1939 — Jet engine aircraft, Heinkel Co.

1948 — Transistor.

1945 — Atom bomb tested.

1952 — Hydrogen bomb tested.

1954 — Atomic submarine.

1957— First earth satellite, Russia.

1961 — First manned space craft to orbit the earth, Russia.

1969 — First man on the moon, United States.

••••• *UNIVERSAL CONDUCT GUIDES* •••••
(Middle and Modern Eras)

In the East

Teachings of Confucius.
Teachings of the Buddha.
The Vedic Scriptures and the Upanishads.

In the West

Nicomachean Ethics by Aristotle.
Hebraiac monotheism and Ten Commandments.
The Roman Laws.
Magna Carta.
American Constitution.
United Nations' codes.

All of the major religions, East and West, include moral codes.

THE THREE ERAS

In trying to assess the relative importance of the three periods of history reviewed above, the criterion should be the measure of progress in each, the quantity of improvement in the condition of the human race. But such a yardstick does not exist in firm units. The theory of progress asserts that humankind is advancing, is improving. This is an excellent idea but there is more hope in it than reality, for the facts to support the case are weak or non-existent. There have been great changes in life-style for part of mankind and none at all for the other part. And as for life feelings, such as hate and fear, these still operate with their old time force in the affairs of man, causing the same well known episodes of un-brotherly love. Progress to date seems to be a halting march of two steps forward, then one back, then repeat, resulting in a sum total of much change but little forward (or upward) improvement for all.

A better assessment is made if we separate the whole into two parts. In the first, the material element, there is no question of advancement and improvement. The multitude of inventions and new products, the great increase in wealth, the inquiry into the processes of nature, the control of the forces of nature — all these have been a benefit of untold munificence to mankind, and hence a contribution to an improved life-style for the individual. The good has not been 100 percent for among the many new things have been harmful drugs, injurious machines and toxic wastes.

The second area, that of bio-social living, remains at a constant level as we may note in the following:

- The body organism of man remains unchanged in the past 50,000

years;
- The mentality for social living remains unchanged in the past 6,000 years as is shown in such institutions as family, religion and war;
- In some ways man may have regressed when we consider the great crimes committed to acquire wealth, the subjection of the weak and helpless peoples by the powerful, the two World Wars in one generation, the use of nuclear devices in war.

There is one respect in which the idea of progress is valid and it rests in this: Each succeeding generation and period has the advantage of beginning on the accumulated knowledge, wisdom and wealth of the preceding periods. As Sir Isaac Newton expressed it, if he could see farther than some, it was because he stood on the shoulders of giants. So it is with society, each generation has the advantage of standing on the shoulders of those who have labored in the vineyard of life, leaving their experiences of success and failure as a foundation on which to begin anew, as a guide to follow. Any add-on of value by the new generation must certainly be progress. The age-old hopes of peace on earth, unity of mankind, freedom and equality are still unrealized but the goals are probably nearer today than in former times. At least their fulfillment now lies within the ability and the power of mankind.

PART III

CULTURE OF MAN

Chapter 8

The Culture of Man

The whole world of humankind is divided into two parts, the people themselves, who are called society, and the manner of their living which is called culture. These two terms have very different meanings and we must mark the distinction.

Society. The term 'society' refers to people themselves, not their handiwork. The society might be a tribal group, an ethnic group, a religious organization or a political association. We know societies by such names as ancient Greeks, Romans, Eskimo, French, Japanese, Russian. Each of these peoples have a culture of laws, tools and manner of living but the people themselves are distinguished from their cultural ways.

Culture. Culture includes anything and everything that pertains to human beings such as beliefs, knowledge, morals, religion, tools, technology, language and folkways. E.B. Tylor, the anthropologist, who first introduced the word 'culture,' said that it was all of the knowledge, art, laws, customs and habits acquired by man. You will note in this definition that there is no mention of society, only the products of society. It is the culture of a people that serves all their needs and wants such as food, clothing, shelter and protection from danger and it provides a people with a meaning to life, of that which is significant and worthwhile.

One important reason for drawing the above distinction is because people and societies die but their culture does not. The Greeks, Romans and Sumerians are examples. Although these people have ceased to be, we still use their cultural things today such as laws, ethics and art. This distinction is important to any one individual in his or her life time and to each generation as a whole for both use the past culture in their life ways and also add to the accumulated mass as a result of their life-living.

As the range of culture extends across the whole of man's activities it embraces an enormous mass of data, so much so that it cannot be grasped or understood unless we divide it into several parts. And of course this is also necessary for humans to organize and have order in their manner of living. This separation into parts or categories was made long ago by our distant forebears and the grouping is known as institutions. It is institutions that we shall examine in Part III of this book.

MEANING OF INSTITUTION

The word 'institution' has come to have three general meanings. In common everyday use of language we speak of a hospital, a university or a museum as an institution. In a restricted sense they are such for they function under such norms as education and medicine, are orgainzed into a pattern of social behavior. They are, however, a single enterprise.

Sometimes the word is loosely applied to a field of study or a discipline such as the institution of philosophy or of physics. Again, this is correct but is a constriction on the whole term 'institution.'

In this book the term is used in its greater sense, that is, to mean a life-institution, such as the family, government and religion. These are the highest forms of organized behavior known to man, the established ways by which a whole society lives and behaves. An institution is a system of behavior that regulates the life of a society, a nation or a group, fixing the specific rules of conduct of life for millions of people in order that they might live in a unified, united way. This is the broad meaning of the term 'institution.'

Institutions serve many purposes and consequently have been described in a multitude of ways, such as: A culture area for man; a pattern of behavior; a system of norms and regulations; a repository of culture; and system of social behavior; tools for socialization; agent of culture and the social controller. But by whatever sub-name they are known their essential character is the same, namely, a life-institution by which man as a whole and societies as a group operate and conduct their manner of living.

Institutions are not invented on the spur of the moment nor are they devised to meet some specific, single purpose. All of the institutions were developed over long periods of history, by many societies, in all parts of the world. People living in a group found that certain rules of action and rules of restraint were not simply necessary for associating but were good in themselves as a means to pleasant living. In time, these rules and regulations came to be standard, the correct way to live, to behave, to conduct the business of living. In the farther passage of time the action, the beliefs, became a fixed way, a "folkway" and were written down and spelled out in exact terms. They became a way to conduct a government, an economic system, a war and a religion. In short, they became institutions.

THE SOURCE OF INSTITUTIONS

In this modern age institutions are a polished system and accepted as the ordinary way of life but it was not so in the beginning. Early man, who first developed the life-institutions, faced life forces that out of dire necessity had to be confronted and overcome in order to avoid death, maintain life and to associate with his fellowmen. It was in this process of living that the several institutions were devised, not at a meeting of the committee but over centuries of trial and error. We shall here list the ten institutions from the standpoint of these essential needs.

Need for Social Association

1. To procreate, to renew the race.
   Solution: THE FAMILY. A safe environment in which to give birth, raise the young and start them in life.
2. To communicate with one another in an intelligent manner.
   Solution: A SPOKEN LANGUAGE. Instead of gutteral sounds and gestures, a language with an alphabet, to be spoken.
3. To learn and teach others, to disseminate knowledge.
   Solution: EDUCATION. Instructions to the young in crafts, personal care, use of tools, mathematics and social manners.
4. To regulate and control social conduct of groups by authority.
   Solution: GOVERNMENT. The establishing of rules and laws for social interaction, with duties defined and the penalty for disobeying.
5. To produce the necessities of life.
   Solution: AN ECONOMIC SYSTEM. a regulated production of the needs of life and then a trade or exchange of products.
6. To defend from the enemy and to prosecute a foe.
   Solution: WAR. Organized fighting, divide and conquer.

Need to Convert Nature to Man's Use

7. To understand and discover about nature.
   Solution: SCIENCE. The chemistry of fire was learned, weather predicted by nature signs, crops planted by weather conditions and rise and fall of rivers, grains and soil studied, astronomy of moon and sun was learned.
8. To make better tools, increase production, devise better methods of working.
   Solution. TECHNOLOGY. This is the production of goods: The method, the tools and the power. In filling this need the wheel was invented, the bow and arrow, the ship, plow and polished tools; the

horse was harnessed to the plow; cotton, wool and flax were spun; cloth woven; the houses built of brick and stone instead of mud and thatched.

Need to Relate to Supreme Beings.

9. To relate with the great forces of the world, the unknown and unseen. *Solution: RELIGION.* An organized ritual and system of belief toward a god, a supreme being.

Need to Express the Self

10. An expression of the self in joy and sorrow, an interpretation of life. *Solution. ART.* Man early learned to draw, paint, sculpture and make craft objects and decorations for enjoyment.

STRUCTURE OF INSTITUTIONS

Although institutions are as diverse as their titles imply, such as religion, war and the family, nevertheless they have a similarity in their structure and method of organization. This structure has three parts, as follows:

The People. There must be people of course and they are divided into members of the organization and the officials or officers, those who administer and operate the affairs of the institution.

The Departments. The German sociologist, Max Weber, was the first to propose the name 'bureaucracy' to describe all groups, all institutions. It means that institutions are too large to be operated as a single enterprise and must be broken down into sections, into bureaus. For example, a government is divided into executive, legislative and judicial departments and these are then farther divided into sections or bureaus. It is the same in facotries with their sales, clerical and production departments and in the military with army, navy and air force. In the army the division continues into infantry, tank, artillery, supplies and engineer 'bureaus.' As Max Weber pointed out, it is within these bureaus that institutions perform their real operations, each with its rights, responsibilities and duties, including relating to other bureaus or departments.

Whatever the term employed — bureau, department or unit — the fact is that all institutions, world-wide, are so divided. Whether the organization is a government, a factory, a school system, a labor union, or a church, it must be and is separated into sections in order to be administered efficiently. And it is here within the department or bureau that the individual finds his concrete place, his position, in the institution and consequently in society as a whole.

The Property. All organizations must have the necessary facilities to operate and this is found in the property, the physical part of an institution. We know this property as buildings, machines, tools and necessary supplies to perform the functions which the organization is intended to do.

FUNCTION OF THE INSTITUTION

An institution operates as a system, that is, an organized process in which there is a flow of work. This 'flow' has three parts called the input, thru put, and output, in a continuous order. For example, a government is a system in which the laws are put in by a legislature, they are put thru the people as a guide to conduct, and the output is orderly living, beneficial living. The family is a system where money and labor is put in, there is a thru put of care and management, and an output of new humans, healthy and educated persons, a life enjoyment. A shoe factory is a system that takes in leather, cuts and sews the leather and puts out shoe.

A system is distinguished from a single enterprise in that it is set-up to repeat the process of in-put, thru-put, and out-put on a continuous basis. Thus, a journey from New York to Rome is a single enterprise that terminates when the journey is completed. In a club, a church or a political organization, which do not use raw materials such as a factory does, the system flow is after this manner:

1. In-put. This consists of the information passed to all members, together with supplies and money to operate.
2. Thru-put. This is the work that is performed, setting of goals, achieving those goals.
3. Out-put. This may be benefits to the members only, it may be beneficial information for the world at large, it may be goods and services such as medical aid.

The great and solid fact about institutions is that their contents may change but the institution itself does not, for it goes on and on in time. The ten institutions we shall review below were in existence 5,000 years ago but their content today is far otherwise than in days of yore. Institutions are something like music in which the notes, the rhythm and the melody takes many forms but it is still the basic and fixed staff and scale and notes. For example, war today is far different from the wars of Alexander or Napolean but the institution of war endures. The brilliant brain or Aristotle could not have imagined the character of education today but the institution continues. And as for the institution of science, it virtually outdates itself every twenty-five years but the basic elements continue.

It is this self-renewing that characterizes the institution. Customs change, cultures change, the generations of people die and are replaced but the institutions go on. This is the great value of institutions to mankind.

Chapter 9

The Beliefs of Man

We have seen in Part II the concrete actions of mankind in building the great civilizations and erecting the institutions to control these civilizations. In this chapter we shall consider the beliefs of man that inspired those lofty works.

No vast work of the magnitude of erecting a civilization is accomplished haphazardly, without aim or purpose. Instead, men and women must have inspiration, must hold definite ideas about the reality of the world, that is, about God, nature and man. They must believe that their actions are proper, just, and done according to the laws of god and the rules of nature, or at least in harmony with these great forces. Man acts as he does because he believes he is dealing with reality, with the real world as it is, and he performs his actions according to his beliefs about that reality.

The beliefs that man has held about reality down through the ages and across the centuries are grouped into five categories for review. They are belief-systems and are: Magic, Mythology, God-centered, Nature-centered and Man-centered. These five belief-systems have been the blue print for behavior for both society as a whole and for the individual from the beginning of human time.

The five belief-systems have been as necessary to mankind as the physical means to sustain life. Just as man does not live by bread alone he cannot live without ideas and beliefs about how to live, how to conduct his life activities. Without a belief to orient life, to point the way, to show the light, man would not know the way to go, how to behave, what was good and what bad, what was worthy or what unworthy. Without some belief about the "world out there," about nature and society, man would have no means to guide his behavior outward into that world, nor inward toward himself. Now the belief may not be accurate (the earth is flat), but it does serve as a guide, as a rule for behavior, until a better idea is put forth (the earth is round), by which to guide the way. A belief, then, is a working basis for action, for steering the way in the world of reality. All action, both great and small, is based on this formula: First an idea or belief about what the world is like, then an idea about what action to take toward that world, and then take the action.

THEORY AND BELIEF

There is little to distinguish between theory and belief for they both serve the same purpose, namely, a basis for behavior but in strict logic the terms are separated. A theory is formed from observed facts. For example, apples are seen to fall from a tree to the ground. The question arises: Why do they fall downward instead of upward? Man forms the idea (theory) that some force pulls the apples downward. Experiments are made and the theory is extended that a magnetic "pull" causes the apples to fall not just downward but rather toward the center of the earth by a force which is called gravity. This is theory forming rather than proposing a simple belief that it was a desire of an unseen god that wished the apples to fall downward.

Some theories are not so cut and dried, cannot even be tested and proved. An example is Sigmund Freud's division of the mind into id, ego and superego. No one has ever located any such elements in the human mind as a factual certainty, nevertheless the theory of them has served to produce a whole new dimension in the science of psychiatry, and provide new insight into man's mind and to his behavior.

Other examples of well-known theories are: Artistotle's belief that all things are made of air, water and land; Democritus' theory that all things consist of tiny atoms; Darwin's theory of evolution; Einstein's theory of relativity.

Beliefs, like theories, are held to be truths about reality but with less strictness of proof or no proof at all, being simply a mental conviction. Nevertheless they are the foundation for most human action as we see in such beliefs as: The sun will rise tomorrow and so I can plan a regular day's activitiy; love of fellowman is a better attitude than hate; hard work and effort will produce beneficial results.

In the five belief-systems given below, the first two, Magic and Mythology were strictly beliefs, without proof. The last three are a combination of belief and theory.

MAGIC

What science is to modern man, magic was to primitive man. The scientist today, after diligent inquiry into the workings of nature, converts the things of nature to the benefit of mankind. In former time the shaman, using mysterious methods known to himself, also attempted to convert nature to the benefit of his people. Although the techniques of science and magic differ in the extreme, the objective was the same, namely, to control nature.

The person who administered magic was a shaman or witch doctor, a person with special qualities and abilities. He was held in high esteem by his people for he had powers to render good or inflict evil.

The general belief was that with the proper method nature could be manipulated to the advantage of the people or the harm of an enemy. If the proper procedure was followed, the shaman could alter the course of nature. To bring needed rain you held a rain dance and made certain incantations and if it didn't rain as a result, then the dance was done improperly, otherwise it would have rained. If you wished to cause pain or even death in your enemy you simply constructed an image of him and stuck it full of pins or quills but the image must have something from the person such as hair, a cloth, spittle or a fingernail.

One belief in magic was that the name of a person was a part of that person, woven into the fabric of the person so that to know a person's name was the means to control the person, even from a distance. Accordingly, your true name must always be hidden and kept secret so that no one could gain control over that which was part of you.

One of the chief jobs of the shaman or witch doctor was the treatment of disease and illness. Some illnesses were actually treated with herbs and drugs but most treatment was manipulated by magical methods or sorcery. This was so because it was believed that most diseases were caused by an evil object or evil power that gathered into the body, or else a spirit and demon had entered, or even that the patient's spirit itself had escaped and must be brought back.

Treatment had to fit the case, of course, but it consisted of such actions as trying to squeeze the foreign thing out of the body, or forcing it out with noxious smoke, or starving it out. If such treatment failed then exorcism was used, that is, a special ceremony, incantations and commands. If these also failed then the demon might be frozen out, burned out, or even cut out surgically.

Alchemy was also a form of magic such as the making of a love potion to capture m'lady or turning base metal into a precious metal like gold and silver.

Taboo was part of magic but more in the order of a code of conduct, a negative one of don't do this, don't do that — or else. If you followed the taboos all would go well and life might be serene but to break a taboo was serious business and would result in severe punishment, usually from all of the people of the village. This was so because violating a taboo by one person would bring down bad luck or even catastrophe upon all of the people.

In this modern day we tend to believe that magic was used to deceive the people. Not so. Primitive man believed in magic fully and faithfully and the shaman made a sincere and honest effort to control and maneuver nature, in full belief that it was for the benefit of the people, the good of the tribe. Even today we are not entirely immune to the powers of magic for we knock on wood, avoid walking under a ladder, shy off from number 13, avoid black cats, and express our hope with a chicken wishbone. This is magic, that is, the remote control of events, even though we call it superstition.

Magic has little meaning to modern man but we should not forget that for thousands of years, in all parts of the world, our forebears survived and lived with the same devotion to magic that we exhibit toward science today. It was not looked upon as trickery, not pulling rabbits out of a hat, but rather a code for behavior by which to deal with the natural world.

MYTHOLOGY

The word myth has the meaning of a legend or a tale of folklore but in ancient times legends about the gods and their powers were sincerely believed in. Mythology is very similar to religion in that it is concerned with supernatural events and beings. The beings, or gods, are seen as real persons both in form and in actions, but they are persons with supernatural powers.

The gods and goddesses are not some far-away beings but are rather close by, have regular contact with humans and take part in all human activities from birth to death. The gods have power over various parts of nature such as the sun, earth, sea and agriculture and they also have direct power over human things such as love, hunting, drinking, war and peace. Because of their close association with human beings, the gods can be influenced to either help or hurt mankind according to the mood of the god or depending on the appeasement made by pleading and sacrifice.

The best known mythologies to western man are those of Egypt, Rome, Greece and Norse, each with their own set or group of gods. Each group was peculiar to the people who believed in them, still all were similar in their root character, in the roles they played in human and natural events. These roles included an explanation of the creation of the world and of man, each god had his or her own particular part of nature to control and all of the mythologies had their gods go out as heroes to do battle, to do good or evil, and all of the gods had controversies among themselves.

First we shall review the tales of creation of the world and man and follow this with a list of the major gods and goddesses together with the role or responsibility assigned to each.

Creation of the world.

1. Roman and Greek version. There was nothing but a vast and mighty hole and out of it came the barren earth, then came mountains and the sea, then light and darkness, then love. When free from the hole, these things joined into a fruitful earth, with day and night made from the darkness and light.
2. Norse version. Again there was a formidable hole or abyss with darkness in the north and fire and light in the south. There came a great blast in the fire and it caused Ymir, the mighty giant, to appear, then came the gods led by Odin. In time these gods slew Ymir and made the earth from his body: Land from his flesh, the seas from his blood, the heaven from his skull, the forests from his hair. Then, taking sparks from the fire world the gods put the sun, moon and stars in the heaven.

Creation of man.

1. In the Greek-Roman myth, the god Promethus molded a piece of clay into the image of the gods and then breathed life into it.
2. In the Norse version, Odin took an ash tree to make a man and an elm tree to make a woman and then from these two started the race of man.

There are many other mythologies, in India, Japan, North America Indians, and Aztecs, although their gods are not as numerous as in the four lists below:

THE GODS AND THEIR ROLE

Greek Gods	Roman Gods	Their Role
Zeus	Jupiter	Ruler of gods
Hera	Juno	Queen of gods
Apollo	Apollo	God of sun and youth
Poseidon	Neptune	God of the sea
Pluto	Pluto	God of the underworld
Artemus	Diana	Goddess of moon and hunting
Hestia	Vesta	Goddess of the home
Aphrodite	Venus	Goddess of love and beauty
Eros	Cupid	God of love
Kronos	Saturn	God of time
Dionysus	Bacchus	God of wine
Demeter	Ceres	Goddess of agriculture
Athena	Minerva	Goddess of wisdom
Ares	Mars	God of war
Hermes	Mercury	Messenger of the gods

Norse Gods		Gods of Egypt	
Odin	King of gods, god of war and heaven	Horus	God of heaven
Frigga	Wife of Odin, queen of gods, queen of earth	Osiris	God of vegetation and dead
Balder	God of peace	Ra	God of sun
Loki	Mischief maker	Isis	Wife of Osiris
Freya	Goddess of beauty and love	Seth	God of evil
Heimdall	Guard to the gods	Shu	God of air
Thor	God of nature	Tefnut	God of rain
Tyr	God of the brave	Geb	God of earth
Sif	Goddess of love	Nut	Goddess of the sky
		Ammon	God of the wind
		Mendes	God of rural life

The belief in mythology, in the nearness of the gods who participated in the affairs of man was very real to the societies who held the mythologies. Like magic, they were part of the real world of man, they were beliefs that directed the living of those societies.

THE THREE MODERN BELIEFS

The following three systems of belief will be stated in a brief summary form for two reasons. First, they are well known to the average person for we are living within and under their guidance at the present time. Secondly, each of these realities — God (religion), nature (science), and man himself — are treated at length under these titles in separate chapters.

The demarcation line between one belief and another is a fuzzy and watery one. This is so because each overlaps the other. The two most distinct and separate realities that we know are man and nature. As the one thinks and is a socializing being, and the other does not, the separation is sharp and clear. But beyond that it is not, for man is also a thing of nature in that he lives, requires nourishment, has growth, lives a limited time and then dies, just like a tree or a horse. Accordingly, when we classify the realities and the beliefs into God, Nature and Man, we must remember that these only signify the predominant content of the reality and therefore the dominant belief about that reality. A good example of this is the utter preoccupation of man with science and nature, which partially refutes religion, while still holding fast to a religious God.

The Rule of God is Supreme. This is the belief that there is a real God, that the laws of God are all-inclusive, that they directly guide the affairs of man and also of nature. This idea was the first great unified system of belief about reality and it was developed by many civilizations, most notably the Hebraic version of monotheism. It was and is still today centered in the supernatural realm, in the belief in a supreme being, a God who rules the universe. He is not present in person but in spirit to guide man and animals and things of nature and consequently He controls man's fate and destiny, enmass and individuallv

In the western world this belief is the common property of Jews, Christians and Moslems. There are differences in doctrine and ritual but not in this fundamental belief that there is a God who is all-knowing, all-powerful, all-good, all-helpful to mankind and also who punishes for disobedience.

In the Far East the major beliefs have always been more earth-bound, more in the order of a moral code for living rather than a supreme command from another world. There is belief in a Supreme One, a Divine Intelligence, but it is the conduct and behavior and attitude of the person that dominates the philosophy and teachings of Confucius, Buddhism and Hinduism.

While religious belief centers on a supreme being who dwells apart from man, in the practice of religion there is always close relationship between God and man. If there is belief in God, prayer, good moral living and supplication, God will guide man in the true pathways of life and dispense a benevolent bounty to all who obey His rules. It is belief in a moral, never-changing God, not in a fickle being, not a man-made image, not a myth, not a totem.

The Rule of Nature is Supreme. As far back as Aristotle, who held that the world constituted the genuine reality of existence, men have looked upon nature as the real world. And then, beginning about 1500 A.D., with the discoveries of science, the Industrial Revolution, and the idea that kings did not rule by divine right, Nature became the central focus as the 'real' reality. Francis Bacon set the tone with his great book Novum Organum which discussed scientific methods, and also his statement that "nature to be commanded must be obeyed." Man began to turn from heaven as the sole source of life giving to the material world for both sustenance and salvation. Man came to believe that material well-being did not originate in heaven but rather on earth, in Nature; that sickness was not inflicted by sinning but rather by a little germ; that cure of sickness was not by prayer or magic but by nature through herbal medicines, food and rest. And then with Darwin's theory that man himself was not created on the spur of the moment but rather evolved over a long period of time from lower forms of nature and is therefore a product of nature alone, farther lessened the dominant view of man created.

This belief in the primacy of nature has led mankind, through the scientific method, to inquire into every department of nature, the physical and the biological, and even into outer space, seeking to learn and to know the laws of nature. Man has centered his intelligence and his actions on nature as the source of his survival and well-being, rather than looking heavenward for these things as a gift.

The Rule of Man is Supreme. The belief that man can control the physical world, the world of nature, is of most recent origin, too new to be widely accepted but still a theory that is gaining momentum. The source of this idea is the marriage of two special activities of mankind beginning about the mid-twentieth century, namely, Science and Technology, a union that has begun to change the character of man and to partially refute the dictum of Bacon by stating that man can command nature to obey him.

The theory (if such it is), asserts that nature operates by specific and immutable laws and not according to the whim of a god; that man can search out and discover these laws; that once the laws are known man can alter them sufficiently to convert the things of nature to his own use and benefit.

A devotion to this belief during the past 100 years has literally altered the course of direction of mankind and the life style of the individual. In the realm of pure science the discoveries are too highly complex for the average mind to grasp and all that the layman can do is marvel over such events as the smashing of the atom, generating electricity from atomic sources, discovering stars in other worlds, of finding life in a bubbling smudge.

Technology is often referred to as applied science and here the layman can see and come to know the end result of the scientific inquiries. Technology means to work with high skill, using tools and ideas as the basic raw materials. This man has done in every field of human activity and produced a flood of goods and products that boggles the mind and benumbs the brain to contemplate. For example: the automobile, the airplane, the telephone and television which have shrunk the world space area from months away to minutes away; new medicines and germ killers have increased the normal life time by one fourth and the expectation of surviving early childhood by a like amount; where food, clothing and home shelter were once an enormous problem to solve, they are now purchaseable over the counter from the local merchant.

This belief in the primacy of man, in the superiority of man, over all other forces in the world continues to grow and enlarge in the whole of human society. About half the world today has an industrial economy or is so oriented and the other half is dependent almost wholly on an agricultural economy. The industrial part has found a degree of prosperity that is considered a superior way of life. In the agrarian part, there is much prosperity and also much poverty. In both parts, for those who have and for those who have not but expect to have, the true course is believed to be more science, more technology, a greater knowledge of nature and more products for consuming.

THE ENDURING BELIEFS

Except in isolated places, magic and mythology have passed from the human scene, but in the days of their use they filled a vital need of mankind for they answered the eternal question of man: What is reality and how does it operate? As belief systems they were valid for the times, as a true explanation of reality they were not.

The immediate successor to magic and mythology was religion which endeavors to explain reality in a supreme-God, human-Man partnership. Until the advent of science the whole of reality could be and was explained in religious terms because that which could not be explained by logical reasoning was attributed to the wisdom of God. For men with inquiring minds this explanation was not sufficient and so began the method of scientific inquiry, under whose regime we live today.

The energetic mind of man has now begun to ask the question: If religion replaced myth will science replace religion? There is no evidence to date that this will come to pass and the prospect seems dim indeed. Each is a separate sphere of reality, the one dealing with the concretes of nature, the other with such indefinite forms as the immensity of humanity, the majesty of the universe, the greater forces of nature, behavior and destiny of man. Now the religious answer to these enormous things may not be accurate but the mass of mankind believes that it is, namely that a Supreme Being is concerned with man and nature. And the individual human, when he or she comes to a condition of utter helplessness and despair can find no relief in science but can find comfort in religion. Science can only be recreated, but religion, so far as the mind of man is concerned, can create. All signs point to the triad of beliefs — in God/Nature/Man — as the guide for man into a long and distant future.

Chapter 10

Man in Association

Just as man is a biological animal even so is he a social animal for there is no record, no knowledge, of persons having ever lived apart from their fellowman. This social association occurs in two major forms, first in a close, friendly relationship such as the family and intimate friends, and secondly in large groups such a a large industrial firm, a national citizenship or in an institution. The small group, will be reviewed in Book II, and the large group will be considered in this chapter.

LARGE GROUP ASSOCIATION

The social association of great masses of people such as nations, political bodies and societies are regulated and controlled in five distinct categories, as follows:

By Institutions. We have examined institutions in a previous chapter and will only note here that it is through and by institutions that large group associations take place. Institutions themselves are super-groups such as a school system, a political party or an entire nation. Each of these have their rules and regulations to govern their actions, their system of Do's and Don'ts. These control the group as well as the individuals who live within the arena of the institution. A society or a large group cannot behave as a whole because it is too massive, too huge, and so it must be directed and regulated by rules, by laws. These rules and laws form the directing power of an institution, are in fact, the institution, per se.

By Norms of Conduct. The word 'norm' means a rule, a regulating standard by which to guide the conduct of human beings in their social association. In small groups the norm is folkways and mores, in large groups the regulation is by law. Or, to state this another way, the norm for behavior is a set of laws. These laws, or norms, define the manner and method by which a group, or persons within a group, may conduct social associations. And, as all know, where that conduct does not conform to the rules there are penalities for disobeying the regulations.

The structure of law is reviewed in the chapter on Government. Here we shall merely note the two major classes of rules that pertain to social regulation.

Custom Law or Permissive Law. These are the regulations that pertain to both civil and criminal laws. These rules state that which is permitted (you may worship as you please), and that which is not permitted (you may not steal, may not commit treason). They also state the penalties for violation of a law: You must pay a fine, you will be imprisoned, you will lose your rights of citizenship.

Regulatory or Practical Laws. These are the rules that pertain to business operations, consumer protection and industrial regulations. They include also the safety rules for such as motor vehicle operation, strength of materials, safety in the products that people buy, fire protection rules. The intent in criminal law is to enforce compliance under threat of punishment, while the intent of regulatory law is to guide and control for the benefits that will accrue.

Media Association. The media, usually called mass media, is not a social group nor an institution but it has come to function as a powerful influence in the affairs and behavior of modern man, for by word and sight it enters into the life of men, women and children, twenty-four hours a day. In times past the public was instructed and influenced only by personal contact or the printed word, both of modest impact, but with the advent of mass media there is an endless stream of sight and sound impinged upon the mind. It is a direct association with all of the world both by the individual and the group.

The media consists of the press, radio and television, and to some extent the telephone, all common and known to all persons. They are instruments for the dissemination of news, information and entertainment to the general public. Each in its own way exerts a persuasive influence on human actions through the instantaneous revelation of events, their prolonged or repeated spread of information, through their emotional appeal. Through the media the individual gains a relationship with all the world, with all of humanity, and through the media the thoughts, beliefs and actions of the individual are influenced, even controlled.

METHODS OF ASSOCIATION

Humans associate, have a social relationship, by three methods: They either cooperate or compete in an action or else they oppose each other in an action. These are the three methods of association both by the individual within the group and between groups themselves. These are the processes of behavior that all perform at work, at play and in all activities of life.

Cooperation. This is a common term familiar to all and means people working together, playing together, acting in unison, in a harmonious manner, striving together to achieve a common goal. Here are common expressions that exemplify cooperation: We completed the project without a difference, our team played as one, we get along well together, we all pitched in and finished the job on time. This is social association by cooperation.

Competition. This is striving against, a behaving in opposition. Competition is not warfare for a person may even compete against himself, that is, strive to attain a higher goal than previously attained, try to make a better golf score than the last time around the links.

Competition occurs in every area of life, in the home where children strive to be the superior one, in the school for higher grades, in the factory and office for an elevated position or perhaps for greater output, in politics for power and in business for wealth.

Although competition is carried on within the bounds of law and social values it is not always a friendly game. Individuals and groups compete against one another to win and for keeps and the loser may and often does suffer personal or financial defeat. Methods of action may be rough and merciless but in competion there is always some element of equality in the chance to win for both opponents.

Conflict. Conflict is forceful opposition in which a person, a group or a nation will employ some means of forcing defeat upon the opponent. Conflict usually flares where there is deep and prolonged difference although the cause of action may occur suddenly. The causes are legion ranging from religious through economic causes, political doctrines, racial distinctions and personal hatred. Man in all ages has always sought a harmony in human relations and deplored conflict but it is as present and as widespread today as it has always been.

THE INDIVIDUAL IN INSTITUTIONAL RELATIONS

The individual relates to an institution in a distant manner because an institution exists largely as a set of rules and norms and so there is no direct, intimate contact. For example we do not rub elbows with our government but rather associate through laws that represent the government, and we associate with the economic system in our employment, market supplies and market prices.

Personal association with an institution takes place in three broad areas, as follows:

By influence and power. We cannot see a governmental structure nor a distant factory producing goods nor the medical discoveries that cure disease, for they are distant from our presence but still we will obey the authority of the law, purchase and use the factory products and accept the medicines to cure our illness. This is the dominant manner in which institutions affect individuals.

By contact with a local branch. It is locally, in our home community, that we experience a direct, personal contact with instititutions, that we satisfy their demands upon and power over us. This is accomplished through such representatives of an institution as the policeman, the tax collector, the church leader, the store manager.

The Institution as an Arena. For the individual an institution is something of a life-arena in which the separate parts of living are conducted. Each encloses a segment of life in which the individual lives and behaves for a bit and then moves to another, and so around the ring. This is apparent from the title of the different institutions such as school, family, church and government. Each is a separate slice of the pie of life in which the individual performs his necessary duties and then moves on to the next.

GROUP VALUES

Group relations contain values that extend beyond their surface apparency. Perhaps the most important is the exchange of values between groups and members and the group itself. As the group exists to benefit the members, the members extract that benefit and the members then in turn contribute back into the whole group their value in efforts. It is a reciprocity of actions that escalates both members and the whole group in an upward exchange of meaningful values to both parties.

A summary list of group values would include the following:

- The institution lends an adhesive quality to life. Without some regulatory power such as the consent of the governed and the consequent laws to control behavior, groups could not adhere, would fly asunder like a smashed atom. And without a group association, individuals could not exist except in a disordered, blundering fashion.
- Groups have social power as we see in such forms as the enacted laws of government, the established right of authority in religion and the influence of knowledge to be taught as possessed by a university.
- Groups regulate behavior in that they set the rules for behavior and the members, in conforming to such regulations, have an established pattern by which to behave, to act.
- As groups regulate behavior, just so are they the agents of socialization, the process by which a person is taught and instructed in how to conform to the mores of society.
- All groups and institutions are transmitters of knowledge from one time unit to a succeeding one. Men die but their culture lives on is a truism of sociology. The ten life-institutions that we shall review

in this section of the book have been the vehicles by which past wisdom has been conveyed down to the present. If modern man is more intelligent and lives a higher form of life than that of the past it is because of the building, layer by layer, on the culture of the past, transmitted through groups and institutions.

- Groups extend individual behavior. One person alone is extremely limited in his or her area of achievement but as a member of a group the possibilities are multiplied in high proportion. The simplest example is the acquiring of a spouse, who is not only a sexual partner but also an increasing of ability to attain higher goals.
- Groups limit activities. this is the converse of the above which stated that groups extend behavior, for they also limit activities to that of their stated purpose. They do not seek to restrict in toto but only to avoid wrong behavior. Just as they say "thou shalt," just so do they say "thou shalt not."
- It is in the group that the individual gains or loses the enriching qualities of life such as freedom, equality, justice and welfare. These values of worth are not available to the individual outside of the group for the group both gives them and takes them away. In fact, a person alone does not need to seek freedom and equality for he posseses them by right of singleness. Robinson Crusoe had these qualities in abundance because there was no one to say him yea or nay.

It is the existence of groups that allows man to be civilized, to be a social being. Man may make the institutions but the institutions make man human, for they are the stream that conveys humanity down through the years, bearing on their crest and in their depth the wisdom to do so.

Chapter 11
The Family

The word 'family' requires no definition for it is familiar to all as that group of persons living together in a house and known as father, mother and children. The world around, in all societies and down through time, these three persons have been known as a family group.

In this chapter we shall view the family as an institution, as a unit in the orderly arrangements of the affairs of mankind. Here the family takes its place beside the other institutions such as government, church and school, as a place of organized behavior in the general scheme of human living. (In Book II we shall consider the family as part of Personal Living.)

The family as an institution has many distinctions and here is a list of some of them:

- It is the most important institution of man for it is the fountainhead of the human race.
- It is the oldest institution and came first in the order of organized social living.
- It is the most enduring, or as Margaret Mead has said, it is the toughest institution that mankind has.
- The family is identical in make-up in all societies, ancient and modern, as noted above.
- It has the most members throughout the world.
- It is the strongest in binding power.
- It is the basic institution.
- It is the incubator of culture.
- It is the cradle of man, of society.
- It is the fundamental strength of every society.

Such is the character of the family institution.

TYPES OF FAMILIES

Family types are seen from two viewpoints, that of marriage and that of kinship.

According to marriage. Two types of marriages have always existed in human society, the monogamous and the polygamous. There are other types such as group marriage and associational agreements but these are incidental and small in number.

1. Monogamy. This means one spouse at a time and is far and away the most prevalent type of marriage-family, both yesteryear and today. When two persons cannot agree in their married state, then a divorce is obtained and the two are legally separated and free to marry again, by law. But a second partner cannot be taken until the first is separated by a legal decree. A joint or mutual agreement to separate, without legal permission, is not sufficient, is not permitted.
2. Polygamy. This means more than one wife or more than one husband, at the same time. Polygamy is still practiced in some countries but is less prevalent than in times past. It was more common in ancient times when the composition of society was largely tribal and the large family or multi-family produced its own food, clothing and shelter.

According to kinship. The family has two forms when considered according to kinship.

1. The nuclear family. This is a family household that is made-up of a husband, a wife and children. It is also called the biological family, the basic family and the universal family because it is the most common type. It is a two-generation family group.
2. The extended family. This is a household that includes the nuclear family plus relatives of the family such as uncles, aunts, cousins, grandparents and in-laws. It is not necessary that all live within the same house but all will live nearby and function as a whole, as a unit.

THE FAMILY IN HISTORY

The basic form and function of the family has not changed since the earliest times. There is the male and female as sexual partners who become parents upon the arrival of children and all living together as a social unit, fulfilling the needs of life. Other forms of behavior have changed many times, such as that required by law, religion and economic methods but the family has remained unchanged.

Although the family form has been constant the style of life has undergone enormous change beginning about 1700 A.D. with the Industrial Revolution and then greatly accelerated in the twentieth century. In the beginning the family filled its basic needs of food, clothing, shelter and medication by growing the food, making the clothing and house, finding herbs to treat illness. Making tools, teaching the young, caring for the aged were normal family functions. For thousands of years the family acted in this fashion as a self-contained unit.

The first change came with the Industrial Revolution when the head of the household went to a factory or a mines and began to work for a wage. Now, instead of planting a garden he would buy his foods at a store, and mother, instead of weaving home spuns would buy the family clothing at a store. This transition moved at a modest pace for two hundred years until about 1900 A.D.

The speed-up of change in family life began in the early twentieth century and then, sparked by two World Wars, new insights into nature through science and new techniques in the production of goods, a whole new manner of life for the family took place. The essence of this change in the family as an institution has been to transfer the old-time responsibilities of the family to other parties such as the government, the school, the doctor, and the professional farmer. The following list will sketch this change-over of responsibilities and duties from the family to outside agencies.

Production of necessities. As noted above, foods, clothing, tools and home shelter, once the direct activity of the family are now purchased over the counter at the store or ordered by mail.

Education. Except for the earliest training of the child, schools now educate the young and the old. The educational levels to be attained are set by governmental regulations and in most countries attendance at school is compulsary.

Medicine, health care. Except for minor first aid treatment, doctors, nurses and hospitals now render the medical care of the family.

Welfare. In former times the aged and ailing were cared for by the family but this is now the chore of agencies, by charitable organizations or the government, or else by direct payment to a professional welfare agency.

Protection. Nearly all protection from crime, disaster, assault and public danger is now the responsibility of governmental agencies.

This great change in the status of the family is well described in the term 'consumer.' People and families are not identified as producers today, (only factories produce), but as consumers. Where John once made shoes for his family and Tom grew potatoes, they no longer do so, even though John works in a shoe factory and Tom works on a farm. They are now wage earners and receive money for their labor and then go to the store and buy shoes and potatoes for the family, then wear the shoes and eat the potatoes as 'consumers.'

FAMILY FUNCTIONS TODAY

The role that the modern family fills in an industrial society may be summarized under the following points.

Reproduction of the race. While the actual production of a new member of the human race is the sexual union of male and female, a family setting is still the site for this activity.

Early care of the young. Some children do become parentless at the very beginning of life and agencies take over their care but the normal and natural setting is for the family to nourish and protect the very young and so it is done throughout the world.

Early teaching of the young. The first teachings include instructing the child to care for himself or herself, to learn, to respond to others, to engage in life pursuits, to associate in play and cooperative efforts.

Socialization. This includes the guiding of the child in relations with other persons, first within the home and then with other persons outside the home, both children and adults, including how to act toward and how to respond.

Enculturation. While this might include all aspects of life in general, its specific reference is to learning the material side of living and the behavioral rules of life. It is the first training of the child in the culture to which he or she must conform, teaching them the established ways of the group and the society in which they live.

Pass on the cultural heritage. As the parent teaches the child in the manner of social living, so the child in turn will teach his or her children, passing on the cultural ways from generation to generation.

THE DIFFERENT INSTITUTION

The family has one great distinction that sets it apart from all other institutions. Governments, schools and industry are legal groups, an assemblage of rules and regulations, but the family is not so constructed. A family is a blood group, a biological assemblage, with love, affection, warmth, closeness and self-sacrifice as the binding qualities. No other group has this adhesive character, not even the church, because no one can infuse into the human being the affective response between mother and child, parent and children, and children for one another. It is a bond that is welded in shared joy and sorrow, in sickness and health, in birth and death. The scientist speaks of forces in nature such as rays and particles and waves that cannot be seen. There is a force in humans, too, and it is family affection. It, too, cannot be seen but as in nature, it is there. The accolade "greatest of all institutions" in not too much.

Chapter 12
Language

Would you care to guess which is the greatest invention of mankind? The wheel? airplane? sending pictures through the air as in television? It is none of these, it is language, the ability of one person to communicate intelligently with another. Animals communicate by barking and chirping, even babies talk by cooing but these sounds are not language even though they have a meaning to them. Only man has a language.

Would you care to guess which is the second most important invention of man? It is the extension of language, the ability to write, to send a message with little swirls and swishings made by a pen or pencil. Man can communicate with picture drawings but only in simple matters. To express ideas and reasoned thought requires language-writing.

Language is an institution of man because of its central position in all that mankind does, both individuals and the group. It is the core instrument in all human relations, all communication between persons, between one nation and another and between each generation of man through the long ages of history. Language is the number one tool of culture for without this means of communication between persons, there could be no society or culture except in a rude, crude form.

ORIGIN OF LANGUAGE

The origin of spoken language is buried in a distant past of perhaps a half million years but growing from age to age as the need to communicate increased. As new objects were discovered or certain ideas became fixed and were used repeatedly, man invented vocal sounds to identify these things, sounds that we now call language. We know of and about this growth through the many tales, myths, customs and rules that were passed from generation to generation and then verified by pictures and artifacts that remain. And of course it is possible to infer the fact of language, for man could not have lived in groups as he did, discovering, inventing and constructing for thousands of years without a language to conduct the necessary sound relations for these chores of cooperative living.

Written language began 6,000 years ago at about 4000 B.C. Since then the chronicle of man has been recorded with exactness.

There are approximately 2,600 languages that are assigned to families or groups such as the Indo-European, Semitic, Polynesian, Sino, Mongolian and various Indian languages. All of these languages have a similar structure with an alphabet of letters such as A, B and C, with a vocabulary of words made up from these letters and a grammar of rules for constructing sentences. These are the language parts that each child must learn in his native nation in order to gain proficiency in the three arts of language: Reading, speaking and writing.

THE GRAMMAR OF LANGUAGE

As noted above, grammar refers to the several parts of language, the basic divisions that are studied in order to understand a language, of which there are three parts as follows.

Alphabet. The alphabet is the single letters of language such as A, B, C and X, Y, Z. the number of such letters varies in each language. For example, the English alphabet has 26 letters and the Hawaiian only 12. The Chinese alphabet is not letters but rather symbols or pictographs. Thus, to express the idea of a male human in the English alphabet, the letters m-a-n are combined into a word. In the Chinese language, 'man' is expressed with one symbol, similar to the English Y, inverted.

Words. Words are the letters, gathered into one unit, called the vocabulary. A word has two essential uses, the first is a noun, in which it stands for an object (a building), an event (building destroyed), or an idea (red). The second use is as a verb, in which it expresses action, as: The building is burning.

Sentences. When words are put together into a meaningful statement they are called a sentence. Thus, the child is sleeping and the sun is shining express meaningful facts. "Freedom for all persons" expresses an idea sentence.

LANGUAGE IN ACTION

The two forms in which language is used, spoken and written, operate as follows.

Spoken language. Spoken sounds transmit knowledge from one person to another either in their immediate presence or by a recording device such as telephone, radio or tape. The sound is made with the tongue, mouth and larynx and there are approximately fifty different sounds that can be made with these voice parts. It is with these sounds that the human being forms his or her words and sentences into meaningful utterances such as speech, songs, and imitations. And these meaningful sounds, in turn, are the instrument with which human beings conduct the business of life in daily conversation, in teaching, in meetings, and dedications.

Written language. Like spoken language, writing transmits knowledge and it also stores it. Some knowledge is stored in the human mind but the quantity is limited and the quality is often fickle, while there is no limit to the storehouse of writing and the content is firm. The storage takes many forms, such as books, tapes, paper documents and magnetic disks. The voice record on film or records is a form of written language. The history of mankind, the record of discoveries and inventions, the bookkeeping records of a business firm and our own personal journals are all language in written form.

TWO USES OF LANGUAGE

The use of language is endless but two aspects of it are enlightening to our purpose here.

Language and the individual. Language is not only an instrument to express and communicate, it is also the means by which we learn. Some learning is achieved by direct experience such as burning the finger on a flame of fire or being robbed because of carelessness, but such learning is quite limited. To learn about the world and life we must read or listen to spoken words. Without language we could assemble only a few facts and ideas.

We also do the major part of our thinking through language, because thinking is largely a talking to one's self. Some writers assert that it is through and by our vocabulary that we do all of our precise thinking and therefore it is important to acquire a large vocabulary for then we are able to extend the range and content of our thinking. And, in consequence, more ably solve the problems of life and guide and direct our courses of living.

Learning and thinking have an inward direction while the outward direction of language is to express our thoughts, feelings and ideas. Without a language we could not say how we feel, what we have seen, what we intend to do tomorrow or how we expect to build a new addition to the house.

Language and the group. Language, both spoken and written, is the means by which human relations are conducted, the tool for socializing. We do relate to others by hitting them, by trading with them, and loving and hating them but even these relations spring from language in thinking, writing and speaking. Without language there could be no order, no coherence, in human relations and consequently only the crudest form of group conduct.

It is in this second aspect of language that it assumes the character of an institution for here it spreads across and within the whole of humanity. Through language the news of the world is told, trade and economic matters are arranged, the mysteries of nature are revealed, the business of government conducted, the successes and failures of man are recorded.

Language, then, is the institution par excellent, the master key to social behavior. All other institutions are subsidiary and derivative because they require a language to exist and to function.

Chapter 13
Education

To educate means to teach, to train, to develop, to improve. In common usage it means to convey information and instruction to a person in order that the receiver will acquire new knowledge. For example, the child goes to school to learn the rules of mathematics and the story of man's history, and the scientist is forever educating himself as he searches for new information about nature.

There are two main objectives in education, two particular reasons why a person acquires an education at all. The first is to aid the individual in developing his or her mental abilities in thinking and reasoning. And then from out of this basic aim to think and reason there flows the secondary level of values in the development of character, learning of motor skills, artistic expression, and social abilities. To say it otherwise, an education is acquired to help the person in attaining the many goals of life.

The second purpose in education in an extension of the first, namely to change human behavior. It is designated 'change human behavior' because with new knowledge a person then has the ability to act in new ways, in a new manner. The child who successfully completes elementary schooling will forever act and behave in a manner quite differently than if he or she had not attended school at all. And the arena of life where new knowledge is formally taught is the institution of education.

EDUCATION IN EARLY TIMES

Formal instruction began about 4,000 years ago and it is worthy of note that two major elements of that education, as set down by the early schools, have not changed in any large degree. First is the division of knowledge into such categories as art, philosophy, science, religion, mathematics, etc. And secondly is the division of students into age groups approximately as their mental capabilities permitted them to acquire additional information, which was in multiples of six years. For example, the starting age was six years, the next unit seven to twelve years, the next thirteen to eighteen, etc. This is still the approximate age divisions today, usually called primary or elementary, middle, and higher grades.

Ancient Grecian education. Primary education consisted of the three R's of reading, 'riting and 'rithmetic; middle schooling was devoted to geometry, drawing and music; higher education was in art, philosophy, rhetoric, medicine, astronomy, and other sciences.

Roman education. The Romans copied and imitated many Greek subjects, with a few additions, most notably that of law. Elementary subjects were reading, writing and arithmentic; middle schooling was in grammar, literature and dialectics; higher education was in law, medicine, architecture, mathematics and rhetoric.

Middle Ages. During this period much of the education in Europe was conducted by the Catholic Church in monasteries. Also during this time much of the Greek learning was lost to the European world and not available for teaching but it was kept and studied by Islamic scholars in Africa and the Near East.

Elementary studies were in reading, writing, arithmetic and the catechism; next came music, Latin, religion and poetry in the middle schooling; higher education was given in the seven liberal arts of Grammar, Rhetoric, Dialectic (logic), Arithmetic, Geometry, Astronomy and Music, plus instruction in ethics or metaphysics and theology.

The Universities. Probably the first of the higher learning schools was the University of Alexandria in Egypt which housed an enormous library of information. This is where Euclid worked and formulated his system of geometry about 300 B.C.

European universities began about 700 A.D. in Spain where the Moors had established such a school. The University of Bologna, in Italy, was chartered in 1158 A.D. and followed shortly by the universities of Paris and Oxford.

The universities taught in all branches of the four great categories of knowledge of the time: Arts, law, medicine and theology.

Education in the East. In the far East the practical arts were not taught as extensively as in the West. The tendency was to form schools of thought and teach within these groups, following largely the political and moral teachings of great individuals such as Confucius, c.500 B.C.; Gautama (Buddha), c.500 B.C.; Lao-tse, c. 500 B.C.; and Mencius, c.300 B.C. However, there were universities in India in ancient times but learning in them was limited to a certain class of persons, not the public.

THE NEW WAY

The beginning of modern education in the West started in 1543 A.D. when Copernicus published his theory of the universe as we know it today. It was not the theory itself that was the turning point but rather the method used in arriving at the theory, namely, the inductive method of observing, gathering facts, testing them and then stating a conclusion about the facts. Then in 1620 A.D. Francis Bacon published his Novum Organum in which the inductive method of reasoning was clearly stated and this is the method of science.

At about this same time, in 1617, the educator Wolfgang Ratke layed down some rules of education as follows. These regulations are still valid today.

- Education should proceed from the simple to the complex.
- The order of nature should be followed.
- Things should come before rules. (That is, observe and study first and then make rules, which is of course the inductive way.)
- Teach students to analyze, not construct.
- Individual inquiry is to replace authority (church and state).
- Books and methods are to be uniform.

By Vocation and Manual Training. This type of education goes by many names: The Practical Arts, the Industrial Arts and the Technical Arts. These are modern words but this type of education is very old. For example, six thousand years ago the people along the Nile River in Egypt were making brick and stone buildings (masonry), growing barley, wheat and flax (agriculture), raising cattle for food and work (cattle breeding), and teaching these trades to the young. Two thousand years B.C. the Hebrew scribes taught poetry, tent making, agriculture and trade. Architecture and engineering were taught in the schools of Athens and Alexandria. A thousand years ago English guilds were teaching apprentice groups within their particular guild.

Teaching in the practical arts in a formal method started in the latter part of the 19th century. Two of the earliest systems were developed by Victor Della Vos, in Russia, and by Johann Pestalozzi, in Switzerland. These early schools provided model shops and complete farms as the setting for teaching. Many art and industrial schools today teach not only the manual work to be performed but supplement this with academic subjects such as mathematics, drawing, chemistry and bookkeeping.

Other types of education. Massive quantities of knowledge are dispensed today outside of the regular school system and vocational training schools although the subjects taught are both academic and practical. Many religious bodies teach their own members, industrial firms have intensive training for employees, the military teach vocational and university courses and there is much self-study instruction by mail. There are schools for do-it-yourself, art and craft instruction, hobby training, teaching the feeble minded, the handicapped, the deaf and the blind. With the advent of television and magnetic tapes, formal-type instruction is now being taught in the home.

NEW AND OLD KNOWLEDGE

During the past one hundred years, and especially during the last fifty years, the society of man has acquired an enormous stock of new information and we are prone to equate this with a giant increase in man's knowledge. But this is an inaccurate conclusion. The contribution has been largely in the fields of science, technology and economics and it has been mostly a learning in-depth rather than in extension. The foundations were layed and much of the superstructure built in these institutions before the twentieth century had arrived. What man has done is dig and probe deeper and deeper into them and it is from this endeavor that mountains of information have sprung and new ways of living revealed.

It is far otherwise in the arts and the humanities because little new information has been uncovered. Theology, ethics, law and the arts of the dance, painting, sculpture and music, or in sum, the field of human behavior, remains largely unchanged since the days of the Ancient Greeks and Romans. Their rules of practice, manner of execution and content of material remain very much the same today as in the past. Personal conduct is as difficult to regulate and control as it has always been except that mannerisms are more refined, perhaps sophisticated.

EDUCATION OF THE INDIVIDUAL

In a very true and real sense, education for the individual never stops, has no limits and is not confined to learning from the pages of a book. After graduating from the school institution, each person must go on to that great and extended institution of living, where the values of the first are put to practical use in the second. In the scientific and technological world of today, a modest education is an absolute necessity just for normal survival, while for any degree of success or attainment of high station, the individual must extend his or her educational efforts to a higher level, to the equivalence of an academic degree.

Chapter 14
Religion

The oldest institution in the world, by necessity, is the family, needed to reproduce the race. The oldest institution in the world, by choice, is religion, filling the need to relate to a Supreme Being. Long before there were such organized units for living as government, education, industry, art and science, there was religion. In today's world the term 'religion' means church and God but for people in early times religion encased the whole and total of life and living, here on earth and then in a life hereafter.

If there is any rank in institutions by importance, then religion would seem to follow the one of first order, the family. Although food to stay alive was critical, supreme powers were invoked to produce that food. Religion was the instrument that first put life in order for mankind for it explained his presence on earth, provided him with the rules of conduct and held out a hope and promise for a better life after the pain and sorrow of life on earth. Early man gained an insight into the three great orders of life, through religion: How to live toward a supreme being (God), how to live toward his fellowmen (man), and how to live toward things (nature). Religion continues to furnish an explanation of these three orders of life to great masses of mankind, even today. To early man this explanation was an absolute necessity, for modern man it still fills that basic need for hope and comfort in time of tragedy and loss, in time of despair.

THE KNOWLEDGE OF GOD

To untold millions of humans God is seen as a concrete real, although man has no knowledge of God as such, that is, in a scientific sense in which a person is known or a tree has being. These are concrete objectives that can be seen, felt, analyzed for their content, and observed as to their action and behavior. But we know God under a different set of elements or condition, summarized briefly in two parts, as follows.

A religious consciousness. A sense of religion is implicit in man, an instinctive feeling, an innate sense of a Supreme Being, an Ultimate One. As noted above, even before men called this being 'God', they had a conscious awareness of Him, or It, or a Supreme Something.

By second evidence. Of the many exhibits of a God-presence here are the four usually mentioned:

By reason. The order of the universe and the constancy of nature must be directed by a God.

By history. All humans, at all time, have related to a God.

By morality. The high concepts of justice, freedom, absolute good, in their purest state, are God-parts, personified.

By experience. An unceasing faith, a surety of belief, a certainty of hope, a conviction by insight and a dependency on ultimate aid, all these could only be God inspired.

The great dissertation by St. Thomas Aquinas listed five reasons for the existence of God: Prime Mover, first cause, pure act, necessary Being and summit of all being.

TYPES OF RELIGION

Religion exists in many varieties but three classifications identify the three major forms. These groups coincide roughly with the progressive changes in mankind from primitive times to the present, as noted in a previous chapter.

Magic — the primitive religion. In magic there is always a priest, shaman or medicine man who can communicate with spirits, who can manipulate supernatural forces. His abilities were most extensive: Cure illness, assure fertility of a female, increase the crops, bring more game near to hand, cause rain to fall or to stop falling, protect the people from harm and the warrior in battle, with a charm.

The shaman, it was believed, also had power to harm others: Cause death and disease at a distance, make enemy women infertile, cause loss of stock and crops, and bring down disasterous storms.

Magic was believed in and practiced for thousands of years and the tribal priest or shaman was both respected and feared in his community for the supernatural powers that he possessed.

Modern religions. All of today's great religions are grounded in faith and belief in a super force or being but with a different basis for that belief. Four notable distinctions exist:

1. Monotheism - One God, the belief of Judaism, Christianity and Islamism.
2. Polytheism - Many Gods, as in Hinduism.
3. Ethical religions - as in Confusianism, Buddhaism and Taoism.

4. Ancestral/Natural religion - as in Shintoism.

Deism - Humanism. This is sometimes called natural religion to distinguish it from revealed religion, or else the religion of reason, not revelation. It is not an organized religion such as Christianity, but rather a set of beliefs, a point of view, that has come into being with the new learning of science, some of which contradicts the Hebrew and Christian Bible teachings. It leans heavily toward a practical ethics and away from metaphysical speculation. Most of the established faiths now hold a point of view that is less firm today than in the past about the absoluteness of their scriptures.

The Deism-Humanism beliefs follow along these lines: There is a God but He does not mingle or meddle in the affairs of man; man is a rational being and works out his own destiny and it is not fixed by God; as man is rational he has learned that the processes of nature are regulated by physical laws, not by the will or wish of a God; religion is a practical matter of good conduct and right moral living, not the aspiration to a life in heaven or a hereafter. Deism-Humanism is Western in origin but the moral-human tone is similar to the great religions of the East.

FUNCTION OF RELIGION

Just as religion has a dual relationship of man-to-God and man-to-man, just so does it function in a two-pronged manner, first in a conduct of sacred affairs and secondly in a conduct of secular affairs. This separation is not sharply defined in church systems but the distinction is there and may be reviewed as an aid in understanding religion as an institution.

First function - sacred.

1. Belief in the tenets and doctrines is the first requisite in religion, is indeed the source of it. In most religions it includes belief in a Supreme Being, or God, who is all-powerful; in many religions there is belief in life after death.
2. A scripture or sacred writings. All of the ritual and rules of conduct are contained in these.
3. Doctrines. These are the formal statements of the principal parts of the basic writings.
4. A ritual. This includes prayer, a church ceremony or worship, Holy Days to be observed, fasting and restrictions of eating, and events of celebration such as Christmas, Passover and Ramadan.

Secondary function - secular. This is largely a code of conduct for members of the religion, derived from the sacred writings, and defining right and wrong conduct.

1. Teaching, with instruction in religion and manner of daily living.

2. A code of conduct, a civil behavior for the members.
3. Manner of marriage, burial, and birth ceremonies.
4. An application of church principles to all secular life such as Max Weber's Protestant Ethic of frugal living, thrift, the virtue of work.

ORGANIZATION

While religion is a spiritual realm, it exists and operates entirely in the domain of the material world of people, property, wealth and nature. In this respect then, each religion is organized like any other social or business entity and consists in the following four general divisions.

1. A leader such as a priest, rabbi or a preacher;
2. Property, such as the building for worship: a church, synagogue, temple or cathedral. Many churches also have auxiliary buildings for schools, recreation and social activities;
3. Workers, such as teachers, clerical help, maintenance personnel;
4. A source of worldly income, such as money, gifts and investments.

THE MAJOR RELIGIONS

Thus far we have considered religion as an institution in the affairs of mankind and shall now review in brief the several religions themselves.

Hinduism

Beginning. About 3500 B.C. and considered to be the oldest living religion.

Place. India.

Founder. No individual person.

Books. The Vedas, the ancient sacred literature of Vedic poems and prayers; Brahmanas, the rituals of sacrifice and prayer; Upanishads, a philosophy of God, man, nature and immortality; Bhagavad-Gita, an epic poem teaching devotion and faith.

Beliefs. Hinduism is not entirely a religion but rather a philosophy in thinking and ethics in behavior, teaching a way of life, a way of living here on earth.

Hindus believe in and worship many gods who represent world qualities such as Beauty, Wisdom, Learning and Truth. They are each an aspect of Brahma, the world-soul, the Absolute.

The supreme world spirit is Brahman, who is infinite, eternal and perfect, the Divine Intelligence. The three parts of Brahman are: Brahma, the Creator; Vishnu, the Preserver and God of love; and Siva, the Destroyer.

There are many sects and cults in Hinduism, each teaching their own manner of living, with social divisions into castes and classes, but all relating to a universal soul.

Place today. India, Pakistan, Ceylon, Siam, South Africa.

Shintoism

Beginning. Prehistoric time.

Place. Ancient Japan.

Founder. Unknown.

Books. Kojiki, the record of olden times; Nihongi, the chronicles of Japan; and Tengishiki, hymns and prayers.

Beliefs. Shinto (Shen-Tao) means The Way of the God Spirits or Gods. It is a modified religion involving many rituals and customs.

Originally Shintoism was a form of nature worship whose gods were the forests and rivers, the waterfalls and the sea. With the passage of time it also included patriotism as part of the Way and referred to the emperor as a descendant of the sun goddess. There is much stress on the traditional rituals and the old customs of Japan.

Place today. Largely in Japan and other parts of Asia.

Judaism

Judaism is the oldest of the monotheistic religions, the belief in one God, in one supreme being.

Beginning. Established in the 13th century B.C.

Place. Palestine (now Israel).

Founder. Moses, about 1900 B.C. and Abraham, in the 1200's B.C.

Books, writings.

1. The Torah, the Law, the first five books of the Bible. Contains the basic laws of Judaism and the ten commandments.
2. The prophets.
3. Poetic writings: Proverbs and Psalms.
4. The Talmud. The Jewish writings after the Bible, with comments on Judaism, religious laws and civil laws.

Beliefs. The central belief is in one God, Jehovah or Yahweh, and in the ethical conduct of daily living. Jews are strict in observing the law as written in the Torah: In manner of dress, food to eat and moral behavior.

The Ten Commandments are a condensed statement of Jewish belief (and are also part of the Christian code), as follows:

1. There are no other Gods than Jehovah.
2. There shall be no worship of idols or images.
3. The name of Jehovah shall not be taken in vain.
4. Rest every seventh day of the week.

5. Honor thy father and thy mother.
6. Never commit murder.
7. Never commit adultery.
8. Never steal.
9. Never swear or give false testimony.
10. Never envy other people nor covet what they have.

Jews observe the Sabbath from sundown Friday to sundown Saturday. Holy days and feasts are: Rosh Hashanah, the Jewish New Year; Yom Kippur, the day of Atonement, with fasting for 24 hours; Passover, feast of deliverance.

Place today. In all parts of the world, but largely in Europe, the Near East and North America.

Jainism

Beginning. 500's B.C.

Place. India.

Founder. Tradition claims that Jainism was originated by saints but two persons are recognized as founders, Mahavira and Jina.

Books. The Agaman or Angas.

Belief. The central doctrine or belief is a reverence for life, of non-violence and non-injury, because everything in the universe is eternal. Human actions are to be guided by right faith, right knowledge and right conduct. And right conduct means:

1. Do no kill or hurt.
2. Do not steal.
3. Do not lie.
4. Do not live an unchaste life.
5. Do not covet and desire things.

ZOROASTERANISM

Beginning. At about 500 B.C.

Place. Ancient Persia (now Iran).

Founder. Zoroaster (Zarathustra).

Books. The Zend Avesta.

Belief. This faith depicts a struggle between the forces of good and evil. Man must choose between truth and falsehood, light and darkness, moral right and wrong, high and low life standards. The highest virtues are pure thoughts, pure words, pure deeds and pure (good) health. To lie or cheat or deceive another person are the greatest of evils.

Place today. Iran (formerly Persia) and India.

Buddhism

Beginning. 500's B.C.

Place. India.

Founder. Guatama Buddha, The Enlightened One, lived 563-483 B.C. His real name was Siddhartha Gautama.

Books. The Tripitaka, the three baskets. Two later writings are also part of the sacred literature: Lotus of the Good Law and Paradise Scriptures.

Beliefs. Buddhism is part religion, part philosophy and part ethical rules. Two of the most common teachings are as follows:

A. The Four Truths of Sorrow.

1. Suffering exists in the world and is part thereof.
2. Suffering has a cause, namely, the desire for pleasure, for possessions.
3. Suffering and sorrow will cease and be overcome by suppressing desire.
4. The path to end desire and therefore end sorrow and suffering is eight-fold.

B. The Noble Eight-Fold Path taught by the Buddha. These are the eight stages that lead to Nirvana, the ideal state of being, the Ultimate Reality, the Perfect Knowledge.

1. Right Understanding. Seek and know the truth.
2. Right Resolution. A determined effort to attain wisdom.
3. Right Speech. Use only kind words, not slander or bitter words.
4. Right Conduct. Love and understanding should guide all actions.
5. Right Living. Choose an occupation and means to livelihood that is pure.
6. Right Effort. The deeds and aims must be in harmony.
7. Right Meditation. Thinking must be clear with the mind at peace.
8. Right Rapture. This is Nirvana, the highest consciousness.

Place today. Largely in India, Ceylon, Burma, China, Japan and Korea.

Confucianism

Beginning. 500 B.C.

Place. China.

Founder. K'ung Ch'in, Confucius.

Books. Analects, Five Kings (or Ching).

Belief. Confucianism is not a religion in the sense that it involves worship and ritual but is rather a code of ethics and education, an instruction in the proper way to live. The central message may be seen in his great rule of: Do not do to others what you do not want them to do to you. Some important teachings are:

- Jen: To strive for goodness within the self.
- Li: Filial relations and respect for age.

- Chun-sui: Friendly relations with all persons.
- Te: To lead others by virtuous character, not by force.
- Wen: Forever seeking high moral character.

The duties, responsibilities and manners to be observed toward family members and friends was greatly emphasized. Confuscius taught that persons should always strive for a higher degree of living through self-respect, sincerity in deeds, honesty in all dealings, earnestness and benevolence.

Place today. China, India and some Western world. Many who follow the teachings of Confucius are also Buddhist and Taoists, for there are no sects or central organization.

Taoism

Beginning. 550 B.C.

Place. China.

Founder. Lao-Tzu (Lao-Tse)

Books. Tao Te Ching (The Way and It's Power).

Belief. Tao means the Way, the Way of Nature, the Cosmic Order. The Way is eternal and real but difficult to know, it cannot be seen, only felt. One may attain the Way although it is deep and obscure.

Taoism teaches that man should live in harmony with the forces of the universe. He should seek to find peace of mind and to enjoy a fruitful life. He should not struggle for wealth and great position but instead work in the service of others.

Place today. In China and Korea. Taoists may also be Buddhists or follow the teachings of Confucius, who also taught the Way but emphasized the moral life of truth and right conduct.

Christianity

Beginning. 30 A.D.

Place. Palestine (now Israel).

Founder. Jesus Christ, lived from 4 B.C. to 30 A.D.

Books. The Holy Bible, consisting of the Old and New Testaments.

Belief. Christianity is derived from Judaism which teaches a single God. Christianity teaches a trinity God of Father, Jesus the son of God, and a Holy Spirit.

Christians believe in a life hereafter which is attained by belief in the trinity Godhead, baptism into the faith with confession of sin, and lead a moral life based on the Golden Rule of: Do unto others as you would have them do unto you.

Holy dates. Christians observe and celebrate four major holy dates each year, as follows:

- Christmas, the birthday of Christ.

- Lent, as a season of penitence.
- Good Friday, day of Christ's crucifixion.
- Easter, day of Christ's resurrection from the dead.

Ten Commandments. Listed above in the section on Judaism, these commandments are also part of the Christian code of conduct.

Place today. Throughout the world but is predominant in Europe, North and South America and Australia.

CHRISTIAN DIVISIONS

All Christians hold the fundamental belief in Christ and his mission on earth but are split into three major groups according to certain interpretations of that mission, as follows.

1. Roman Catholicism. Catholics believe that God sent his son Jesus to establish the Catholic church, appoint apostles to teach and guide, and appoint St. Peter as head of the church. This mission of Jesus continues today through the pope and his bishops.
2. Eastern Orthodox Church. Also known as the Greek Orthodox Church or Greek Catholic Church, is a loose confederation of church groups centered in eastern Europe, Asia and Egypt, although there are churches throughout the world. Belief is similar to that of Roman Catholicism in worship, mass, baptism, confirmation and communion but do not recognize the pope as supreme head of the Christian churches. Members are helped in their faith with icons, pictures of Jesus, Mary and the Saints.
3. Protestanism. This division of Christianity was originally part of the Roman Catholic Church but as the name implies, broke off in protest.

Beginning. 1500 A.D.

Place. Germany

Founder. Martin Luther, a Catholic priest. Luther posted 95 theses on a church door October 31, 1517 A.D., protesting many of the practices of the church and calling for reform.

Books. The Holy Bible. The Protestant version differs slightly but not essentially from the Catholic version.

Belief. There is no difference in the fundamental faith of Catholics and Protestants for each believe in the Trinity, baptism, forgiveness of sin, a life hereafter and the importance of good moral conduct here on earth. The essential difference is in the administration of the religion. Catholics rely on the Church as the final authority in all matters of faith while Protestants believe that the Bible alone is the ultimate source of instruction about God and the salvation of man.

Place today. World wide.

Islam (frequently called Mohammedanism)

Beginning. 600 A.D.
Place. Arabia.
Founder. Mohammed ibn Abdullah, lived 570 - 632 A.D. The religion of Islam is monotheistic and the followers are called Moslems, those who submit to God.
Books. The Koran (Quran), Hadith (tradition).
Belief. The Koran teaches:

1. The absolute unity of Allah, that god is just and God is merciful, that Mohammed is the prophet of God, as was Abraham and Jesus.
2. There are strict rules that forbid stealing, lying, adultery and murder. The great moral virtues to be sought are: Kindness, patience, honesty, courage, honor and generosity.
3. Strict duties are imposed on believers:
   - Profess faith in Allah.
   - Ritual prayers, facing Mecca five times each day.
   - Almsgiving.
   - Fasting, in Ramadan, the 9th month of the Moslem year.
   - A pilgrimage to Mecca at least once in a life time.

Place today. North Africa, Middle East, Pakistan, Indonesia in particular, but there are believers world wide.

Chapter 15
Government

Government is that institution by which man controls his society and directs its destiny. Without government man could not live as a society for there would be no organization, no guidance to his living and he would exist in utter chaos and confusions. It seems correct to say that without government the highest state of attainment that mankind could reach would be to live in isolated, pastoral tribes, never in great cities, never achieving the great goals of scientific inventions and high technology. One of the prime failures of the American Indians, who possessed a continent, was to organize a government.

To govern means to rule, to direct people in their activities by right of authority. Thus, a government is a person or a group of persons, who rule large numbers of people such as a nation. This ruling body is known by such names as a congress, a parliament, a diet or a supreme soviet and directs and controls the nation through laws.

Where does this "right to govern," this "right of authority" come from? Who gives this right? In times past kings and great families inherited the right, some even claiming that they had a "divine right." In the modern world of today the right is given by the ballot, that is, by the consent of the people themselves which they express by the ballot vote, which designates the persons they wish to have govern them. At election time the people in every district cast a vote for their national leader and also the representative from the district who will represent them in their national government. These representatives then assemble at the seat of government and proceed to make laws and regulations to guide the nation.

This form of selecting representatives to govern is quite similar throughout the world, both East and West, and under all three major systems of government, democracy, socialism and communism. The form of selecting national party leaders and the governing party, however, is different in the three systems.

Types of Government. Government is a political affair and the usual division is as follows:

Monarchy. Rule by a king, tsar, emperor, rajah or pharoah.

Aristocracy. Rule by a privileged upper class, a nobility.

Oligarcy. Power is in a small group such as the Thirty Tyrants of ancient Greece.

Dictatorship. Rule is by one strong leader with a close group of supporters.

Democracy. The spirit of democracy was expressed by Thomas Jefferson who said that all authority belongs to the people but rule by democracy is accomplished through two or more political parties, one of which rules for a limited time.

Communism. This is rule by a single party whose leaders perpetuate themselves.

HISTORY

Government by benevolence came first with a patriarch as head of a group of families or a tribe such as Moses and the Israelites, the Indian tribes of the American West, desert and African tribes of today. This person acts as chief of the clan, with ruling authority, with a body of elders to advise.

Government by power or force has been the norm through most of man's history by such ruling heads as kings, pharoahs, generals and conquerors. This has been so the world around, in East and West.

The first real government, as we understand the term today, came into being in Greece, about 500 years before Christ, in the form of a democracy. This was a government whose purpose was to guide and direct the people in constructive activities, not simply to rule over them. The place was Athens, one of the Greek city-states, where their customs and rules were formulated into laws for guidance. Both Plato and Aristotle wrote extensively on political matters and Plato's "Republic" and "Laws" are well known.

But the democratic form did not spread out from this good beginning. Nearly two thousand years were to pass before the roots of "rule by the people" secured firm ground and then another five hundred years to spread around the world.

The coming of parliamentary government may be traced to the Middle Ages following a dispute between King John and the Lords of England which resulted in the Magna Carta, drawn in 1215 A.D. Unlike a simple code of conduct such as that of Hammurabi, this was the first time that the rights and the duties were spelled out in a legal contract between those who rule and those who are ruled. It was truly named the "great charter" because it is still a very real part of the English and American legal systems.

But this good beginning, like that of Greece, was slow to develop. Kings and nobles still continued to rule, many by "divine right," until the 18th century when the American and French revolutions began the conversion from noble rule to common rule. There are still nations that are ruled by dictators and single power groups, nevertheless all nations, including the dictator ones, now operate under a written constitution that defines the rights, duties and privileges of the people. Some promise more than they deliver but they at least imply that the common citizen does have rights and is entitled to recognition before the law, is not a beast or a non-entity.

THE FUNCTION OF GOVERNMENT

The governing of a large mass of people has a three-way thrust, the political guidance, the making of laws and the administration of those laws. These are the essential duties of a government and always have been, whether the form is democracy, communism, aristocracy or dictatorship. It is these three aspects of government that classify it as an institution and which we shall now review.

Government as a political agent. The political aspect of government may be defined as that part which proposes the objective of the government and also the party that sets forth the objectives. For example, the political overtone of the American government is one of democracy which constantly seeks the great goals of freedom from restraint, equality in rights, protection from oppression. The political party aspiring to administer the government assures the people that, if elected, the people will have these high objectives for their enjoyment.

Political parties exist because there is more than one way to reach the great goals of freedom, equality and prosperity. Party #1 will claim they have the best method and Party #2 will claim that their way is the better. In the United States these parties are called Democrat and Republican.

All forms of government have this political side including the ancient ones of Greece and Rome. Even the king and the dictator have some plan or program for the nation, for regulating the condition of the people. In today's governments this political aspect is usually put forth as the nation's domestic policy, the foreign policy, economic policy, military aim or welfare policy. These 'policies' taken as a whole are the political part of government.

Governments are usually dressed with the title of Democracy, Socialism or Communism but their mode of operation may be classified into four major groups, as follows.

1. Single person system. Kings and dictators govern here.
2. Single party system. Here the government is dominated by a single group as the Nazi in Germany or the Communists in Russia. The

people have representation in government but all conform to the single philosophy of the party.

3. Two-party system. Britain and the United States have this form. In general the one party tends to be conservative in outlook and limit government controls of industry while the other party tends to liberalism or progressive action by extending government controls of industry and promoting civil enterprise.
4. Multi-party system. Some nations have four or five parties contending for control of the government, each seeking to administer according to its philosophy or policies. France, Italy and Japan each have several parties.

Government as Law Maker. This is patently clear on the face of it. As a people must have rules, regulations and laws by which to conduct the affairs of life and the business of living, it is the government that fills this need. In a body assembled the representatives of the people propose and pass the laws that will direct and control the nation.

Government as Administrator. Clearly the laws that are passed must be administered and this is the third function of a nation's government. Although the laws are made at a central place, the nation's capital, administration must be carried out from many locations at the three levels of national, regional and local offices, as follows:

1. National government. At this level there are three principle divisions.

   Legislative Branch. This unit makes the laws of the land. Although state and local governments make many regulatory laws for their own particular needs, nevertheless these laws must stay within the bounds of the national laws.

   Executive Branch. This unit administers the laws, puts them to work for the nation and enforces compliance with them. The head of this branch is known as President, Prime Minister, Secretary or sometimes just Leader. This person is also the leader of the party that is in power, that is in control of the government.

   Judicial Branch. This element of government we know as the courts and judges, who are charged with interpreting the laws and prosecuting violators of the laws.
2. Regional Government. Regional sections of a nation are known as a state (State of Ohio) or a province (Province of Ontario). The head of a regional government is designated as a governor, prime minister or administrator. To the average citizen it is the regional government that is most readily seen for it is at this level that the national laws are administered and enforced, where some tangible contact is made with government. A few exceptions exist such as national taxes, service in the armed forces and national welfare programs but even these have their regional representatives.

3. Community Government. This is the city, town or village government with a mayor and council to direct the local affairs. To a large degree the town or community government merely administer the state or provincial laws that regulate schools, criminal acts, health and safety rules. Local governments do have power to impose taxes and pass law regulations as they pertain to the local scene.

THE INDIVIDUAL AND GOVERNMENT

For the individual the government provides an arena of life that has two major domains. In the first the government acts as a protector from the threat and danger. Within the bounds of our homeland we have a feeling of security and therefore a sense of freedom to move about and live our lives in a safe environment. While this is very much an act of physical protection it also conveys a mental feeling of contentment and security.

In the second domain we see the government as a guider and director of our life and living. The rules and regulations that specify our rights and our duties act as stabilizing forces to our lives that otherwise would be one of confusion and even constant disaster. Some of these laws are sometimes distasteful and restrictive but these we accept along with those which bestow a benevolent guidance of "you may do this" and "you may do that," pointing the way to an ordered way of life.

Chapter 16
Economics

Economics is that department of human culture that regulates the business world that supplies mankind with his needs and wants. It is a fundamental institution in that the means for life and existence eminate from here and consequently the well-being and happiness of men and women. Economics is often called the science of wealth and welfare but we know it best as the commercial world of buying and selling, of growing foods, of mining and manufacturing and a flowing river of consumer goods from automobiles to tooth picks, from candy to space ships.

Economics is concerned with the means to produce goods and not the actual production of them, for this is the province of technology and industry, to be described in a following chapter. Instead, economics is that part of the business world that provides money to build plants and dig mines, that provides the machines to do a job, the labor to do the actual work and the selling of the products that are produced. We may distinguish the two fields by saying that Economics regulates the production and consumption of goods while Technology and Industry employ the skill and does the actual production of the goods.

HISTORY OF ECONOMIC SYSTEMS

Economics has been a present fact in the life of mankind since Day One because it is 'economic things' that supplies man with his material well-being. As a system by which man has attained that well-being we may divide history into three periods, as follows.

Ancient Times. Down to about 500 A.D., agriculture was the only industry, with the family and clan producing all of their food and other needs. The Greeks, Romans and Oriental peoples grew their own foods, raised cattle, made their own clothing, built their furniture, and erected their own shelter. Aside from trading there was little more to the state of economics and style of living over the years, either for the common people or the nobility except that upper classes may have had better clothing and a more secure shelter. There were of course brilliant works in buildings, aquaducts, and pyramids but these were isolated events and not a direct part of an economic system.

Medieval Times. Two systems existed in Europe during the Middle Period, down to 1700 A.D. Although the term 'Medieval' applies to Europe the economic methods in the East were similar.

The Manorial System. After the fall of the Roman Empire the land in Europe and North Africa came under the ownership of lords and nobles and consisted of large estates called manors. The manor was actually a village with the great manor house as the central building, farm buildings and the houses of the villagers. The lord was the ruler of all and the villagers were serfs. Serfs were not slaves but they were not entirely free because of their need to be attached to a manor to earn a living for the lords and nobles owned the means of sustaining life: The land, tools and the animals.

The land was divided into strips for tilling, some strips for the serfs on which to grow their own food, some strips for the Lord which the serfs planted and cultivated for the manor house. The whole was a self-sustaining community with little if any intercourse with other people. This system ended about 1450 A.D.

The Domestic System. This method was something of an entree to the Industrial Revolution which followed. As the towns grew and extensive crafts began to rise in the towns, the first beginnings of an economic exchange came into being from three angles:

(a) The guilds needed outside workers to make their products and they paid these workers in cash, not bread and potatoes;
(b) The workers began to buy their needs with the cash;
(c) The lords, in need of cash, began to sell their serfs freedom for cash and to grow cash crops such as grain, wool and flax, which further prompted the decline of the manor system.

Under the domestic system the arrangement was that persons would make goods in their cottages for a factor or middleman, at piece-rate wages. The workers did not own the raw materials or the tools they used, they merely made the products for a pittance and then done subsistence farming for their food.

The Industrial System. The beginning of the Industrial System may be fixed at about 1700 A.D. with the coming of steam and water power to operate machines. For the worker it would be little more than an extension of the Domestic System in which, instead of making goods by hand at an isolated location, he would now go to a central place, a factory, and begin to produce goods with a machine. And this is still the method by which goods are produced in the industrial system except that the power, energy, machines, resources and environment is greatly improved over the early beginnings.

THE ELEMENTS OF ECONOMICS

Aside from all the theories about political economy there are certain basic elements that inhere in every economic system whether capitalist, communist or socialist. Moreover, these elements inhere in each industry whether manorial, giant industrial plant or small farm. There are four such parts, as follows.

Capital. This consists in the tools and machinery plus the power to operate them. It also includes the land and the buildings in which to perform the work plus the insurance against accidental loss of the property. The business terms for capital are:

(a) Investment - The money and funds required to begin and to operate the enterprise;
(b) Banking - An agency for handling the money flow;
(c) Insurance - Protection against loss from accident or disaster.

Production. In the actual process of production, two major parts are indentified:

(a) Raw materials - All basic materials come from the land and the sea by mining, agriculture and fishing and these are processed and fabricated into a finished product.
(b) Labor - Labor consists in the persons who do the work and have such titles as manager, machine operator, salesman, truck driver, and bookkeeper.

Distribution. After goods are made or grown they must be sold and delivered, an operation grouped into three parts:

(a) Marketing - This is the selling, the buying and the financing of goods.
(b) Transportation - The movement of goods by water, rail, automobile and airplane.
(c) Commerce - This is the exchange process of imports and exports, between parties and countries.

Consumption. To consume products and goods means the use that is made of these goods which is usually identified by one of two values:

(a) Single value - The food we eat, the opera we see and the airplane flight are used only once and having served their purposes are not, cannot, be used again. These have short term consumption.
(b) Re-use value - These are goods that can be used over and over again such as furniture, household appliances, musical instruments, automobiles and eye glasses. These have re-use value and long term consumption.

INDUSTRIAL SYSTEMS

The industrialized nations of the world today manage their industrial or economic systems under one of three philosophies or theories. None of these systems are air tight for each is tainted with the ideas and practices of the other and this is so because in actual practice the hard fisted world of producing and selling goods does not conduct itself as the worldly philosophers would have it. For example, here is a core idea in economics about the ownership of property: Individuals (private firms) should own all production property, the state should own it, an elite class should own it, peoples co-operatives should own it. All of these are in force today around the world, none of them work in toto to the exclusion of the other and no golden mean has as yet been found.

Three economic systems are prevalent today, as noted below. It is well to bear in mind that there are really only two basic systems, that of capitalism and socialism. Communism is just one form of socialism. In fact, Marx himself called his system 'scientific socialism.'

Capitalism. Under this method of business, sometimes called the free enterprise system, production is for a profit. The ownership of property and the means of producing goods is in the hands of private persons or companies. Under this system the government should exercise a minimum of control or authority, only enough to keep order within the system.

Socialism. Many persons prefer the term 'collectivism' meaning multiple ownership although this applies to capitalism because of stock purchase by many people.

Under this system production is according to use and not primarily for profit. Here the state has ownership of resources and utilities but private individuals may own all other facilities for production of goods.

Communism. This is another form of socialism but all resources and all production facilities are owned by the state with a few cooperatives operating some industries. There is no private ownership and there are strict regulations for all workers who are paid on a wage scale within the limits of state fixed boundaries. Individuals own their private possessions. All economic planning for the entire nation is done by a central bureau.

ECONOMIC MAN

Humans are described by many names such as social animal or religious creatures but fundamentally we are very much an economic being. The first order of life is to find a way to live and to stay alive, all a matter of economics, and after that we become social, religious, artistic, war-like or peace-like. But foremost the economic needs must be satisfied.

As an economic being humans have occupied two positions down through the ages of time, one as producer of goods and the other as consumer of goods. These positions have changed radically as we shall note here.

The person as producer. Prior to 1500 A.D. the entire world economy was agricultural with a few craft products, and the whole was produced by hand or animal power. A person could not produce more than he or his family would consume because his only facility was muscle power. Beyond bare necessities he could not go and therefore had no luxuries to consume.

The discoveries and inventions of the 16th and 17th centuries that erupted in the Industrial Revolution of the 1700's completely changed the status of the person from that of producer only to that of consumer also. The cause, as all know, was the introduction of machine power to replace muscle power.

The person as consumer. When the individual began to work as an employee, for a wage, he also began to buy the goods he needed instead of making them himself. He switched from a producer of his food, clothing, furniture, even his doctoring, to a buyer of these things, or, a consumer of goods only, not a producer of them.

This new economic status of mankind, of men and women, as that of consumer, is central to the institution of economics today. Great nations, giant firms and the local retail store all vie mightily for the patronage of the consumer, the common man and woman. And the horn of plenty that pours forth the consumer goods is not the poetic basket of fruit and vegetables but rather the ugly machine which knows no surcease.

Chapter 17
Science

The term 'science' has come to have a broad meaning in modern times, so much so that one hardly knows where it begins and where it ends. Mother now cooks the family meal in a scientific way, junior conducts scientific experiments in the sixth grade, and even the pleasant art of fishing has been replaced by the science of fishing. So it is necessary that we separate the gem from the dross in order to understand with some accuracy the institution of science.

In the true meaning, science is concerned with the laws of nature, seeking to understand such things as light, motion, the atom, the living cell, mass and energy. The trained scientist examines these parts of nature in order to learn how they exist in nature, their structure and function, what is the cause of their actions and motions, what are the effects of these parts of nature. Then, after intensive inquiry and testing, the scientist formulates laws to explain the workings of nature and uses these laws to predict natural events. An example is the motion of the earth, sun and planets. These are laws of nature: The earth turns on its axis once in every twenty-four hours; the moon circles the earth once each month; the earth circles the sun once each 365 days. Knowing these facts, these laws, it is then possible to predict that at certain seasons in the northern hemisphere the weather will be cold, with snow and freezing of water pipes unless care is taken.

When a new law of nature has been learned, when a new door has been opened into the secrets of nature, then the work of the scientist is completed. Now much further use will be made of that knowledge and many benefits may accrue to mankind but the scientific part, as such, is over. The practical uses that follow is not scientific inquiry but rather technology, the converting of nature's bounties to the uses of man. Some call this development of nature's resources applied science, and so it is, but it is not pure science and the term 'technology' is more accurately applied. Sometimes the dividing line is quite indistinct as in the production of the atom bomb and the journey of man into space, where both the scientist and the engineer worked side by side. But science as such is concerned with inquiry and prediction, not invention and production.

HISTORY OF SCIENCE

Before the modern period began at about 1500 A.D. there was very little progress in science. About 580 B.C., Thales of Miletus asked the question "of what is the world made?" and about 400 B.C. Democritus taught that matter consisted of atoms, of tiny particles. At this same early period Hippocrates taught that diseases have natural causes, was not inflicted by gods. Euclid and Pythagoras had developed geometry by 300 B.C. Ptolemy, at about 100 A.D. taught a system of the universe, with motion of the earth, sun and planets. This was scientific thinking but not scientific fact for Ptolemy had the sun circling the earth, as it appears to do when seen by the naked eye.

Except for these early and excellent beginnings, science died aborning. The Romans, Egyptians and Medieval Ages contributed nothing to science as we know it today but of course they were not concerned with it. There was excellent technology in buildings, aqueducts, bridges and structures like pyramids and great cathedrals because their interest was with man and his relation to God, not with matter, energy and light.

It is proper to date the beginning of modern science at 1543 A.D. when Nicholas Copernicus published his book on Celestial Spheres, although experiments began many years before. The following events are highlights in scientific discoveries and will exemplify the progress in pure science.

1543 — Copernicus: Proved the earth moves around the sun.
c.1600 — Galileo: Use of the telescope and the scientific method of observing, measuring, experiment and then stating a theory.
1628 -- Harvey: Discovered circulation of the blood.
1687 — Sir Isaac Newton: The laws of medicine.
1803 — Dalton: The atomic theory.
1858 — Darwin: Theory of evolution.
1860 — Maxwell: Electro-magnetic theory.
1876 — Pasteur: Microorganisms cause disease.
1895 — Roentgen: Discovers X-rays.
1900 — Planck: The quantum theory.
1905 — Einstein: Special theory of relativity.
1911 — Rutherford and Bohr: Theory of atomic structure.
1941 — Fermi and others: Nuclear chain reaction.

THE SCIENTIFIC METHOD

A brief description is not sufficient to explain the work of the scientist as he makes his inquiry into the workings of nature, for it is a strict and long-term discipline. As an example, the first stage is called observation and this might go on for one year, for twenty years, for a life time or even into succeeding generations, as in the case of the atom, the cell, the heavenly bodies. But a rough idea may be obtained from an enumeration of the several stages of the method.

1. Observation. This is the detailed examination of the phenomenon being investigated such as the atom, disease or ocean tides.
2. Formulate a theory, that is, make an expression of what appears to be happening. This is not a guess but an opinion based on observed facts, combined with previous knowledge, of what appears to be the exact truth.
3. This is a further statement, a conclusion, of what has been happening plus a prediction of what will happen in the future.
4. Experiment, test the theory. No idea about the workings of nature has validity unless or until it has been tested. Every scientist considers his theories faulty until they have been shown otherwise and he does this by experiment. The usual method is to construct a model, a working miniature of his theory. We have all seen pictures of these models, of the little balls to represent the atom parts, of the molecule, of blood circulating through the veins and arteries. A model may be a verbal description, a drawing or a working model such as toy automobiles, buildings and mechanical men.
5. Re-examine the hypothesis in the light of the experiments. If there are faults or errors then the process begins all over again and a new theory is made and a new model constructed.
6. When repeated tests show the theory to be approximately as its true counterpart in nature, then the scientist will draw a final conclusion, state a law or rule for this phenomenon.

The scientific method is inductive, it demands the gathering of many facts before a conclusion is drawn. Deductive resoning is not suited to the scientific method as we may note by the following examples:

Ancient Wisdom	*Scientific Fact*
The earth is flat.	The earth is round.
The sun moves around the earth.	The earth moves around the sun.
Disease is caused by myasmia and displeasure of the gods.	Germs and bacteria cause disease and illness.
The brain is bloodless and cold. (Aristotle)	The brain consumes 20% of the blood, is seat of knowledge.
The brain is a cooling devise for the heart.	The brain is for thinking, for reasoning.

THE FIELDS OF SCIENCE

The sciences are grouped in different ways and some overlap such as mathematics which is part of all of the sciences, but a list review will aid in understanding the institution of science and its broad aspects. The Physical and Biological Sciences given separately below are sometimes grouped as the Natural Sciences.

ABSTRACT SCIENCE.

- Mathematics: The study of quantity, magnitude, form and numbers.
- Logic: The study of reasoning and inference, deductive and inductive forms.

PHYSICS. This is often called the basic science, the fundamental discipline, and for two reasons. In the first place it deals with the basic stuff of nature such as matter and energy, waves and particles, and secondly because the content extends to or is part of the other disciplines. The major divisions are:

- Mechanics: The dynamics or motions of bodies, fluids, gasses and solids.
- Thermodynamics: Heat action.
- Optics: Light action.
- Electricity and magnetism, including electronics.
- Acoustics: Sound action.
- Nuclear physics: The atom and its nucleus.
- Solid state physics: Crystals and semi-conductors including transistors, rectifiers and solar batteries.
- Radiation: X-rays, radio waves and ultraviolet rays, alpha, beta, gamma rays.

Derived Fields.

- Astronomy: Study of the celestial bodies and usually identified as the oldest of the sciences.
- Geology: Study of the earth and its minerals (mineralogy).
- Oceanography: Study of oceans, tides, waves, currents.
- Meteorology: Study of weather conditions.

CHEMISTRY. Chemistry studies the structure and function of matter and is divided into two broad areas, as follows:

- Organic chemistry. This is the study of living things, of plants, animals and their parts. This is a science that affects humans most intimately because it examines the soil, the plants and animals and from these studies is derived the knowledge of agriculture, of medicine and of pharmaceuticals.
- Inorganic chemistry, the study of minerals. This discipline examines metals, clays and fuels of the earth and from this comes new

products for man to use: new types of metals, plastics products, cements, new fibres and fertilizers.

Derived Fields.

- Electrochemistry: Examines how electricity causes chemical change.
- Geochemistry: Studies the chemical composition of the earth's crust.
- Microchemistry: Examines minute quantities of matter.
- Physical chemistry: Studies the physical energy in substances.

BIOLOGY. This science studies living organisms from sub-microscopic bugs to human beings and elephants and includes plants from seeds to giant trees.

- Human biology includes anatomy and physiology. Studies include the structure and function of the human body, including disease and cure (medicine).
- Plant biology. Studies the grains and grasses, fruits and vegetables, plants and trees. Special fields are agriculture, floriculture, horticulture and forestry.
- Animal biology and zoology. The structure and function of animals, including their disease and medicines for treatment.

Derived Fields.

- Molecular biology (cystology): Study of the cell, often called the atom of living things.
- Microbiology: Study of microscopic life such as bacteria, molds and viruses.
- Morphology: The structure of organisms.
- Histology: The study of tissues.
- Embryology: The development of organisms.
- Physiology: How organisms function.
- Genetics: The study of heredity.
- Ecology: How organisms relate to their environment.
- Bacteriology: The study of bacteria.
- Paleontology: The study of fossils.

SOCIAL SCIENCES. This field of knowledge is concerned with the study of the behavior of man in all of his apects, political, economic, as an individual and in groups, in morals and folkways. It is the newest of the science groups and some even disallow the term 'science', claiming it is too young to have developed a true scientific method in the studying of humans. Nevertheless, giant strides have been made and much knowledge accumulated. The major fields of study include the following:

- Anthropology: Studies peoples, societies and their culture.
- Archaeology: The study of prehistoric man.

- Economics: Studies the earth's resources, converting them to human needs and the distribution of wealth.
- Philology: The study of languages and human records.
- Political science: The study of government, laws and customs.
- Psychology: Covers the mental processes of man and human behavior.
- Sociology: The social interaction of groups, peoples and societies.

SCIENCE AND THE INDIVIDUAL

Science takes its place as an arena within which the individual lives and behaves, just as he does within the institutions of government and religion. The latter are more visible, more immediate and more comprehensible to the average person because all persons participate in these areas of human behavior as a part of daily living while a science consists in a firm discipline of study and inquiry.

Where science becomes an arena of life for the individual is in the products of science which are used to enhance the life style of all humans. After a new door is opened into the secrets of nature, whatever is discovered is developed and turned into a practical use for humans and it is at this point that science takes on a real meaning for most men and women. The new thing — a food, a medicine, a process, a machine — becomes a real part of life, of human living. Alas, evils are also discovered such as the atom bomb and lethal chemicals but the benefits to date have far surpassed the evils. Science as an exclusive institution is for the genius, as a derived institution it is for all men and women.

Chapter 18
Technology

Technology is not a single field of knowledge such as government or economics and therefore it does not stand alone as an entity, as a unified discipline. It is rather, as the word signifies, a technic, a way of doing things, a manner of work, a system of enterprises.

In the particular meaning of the word, technology refers to the method and the means by which material things are produced, the application of mechanical means to the manufacture of goods but also the invention of new ways and new means to produce goods.

Benjamin Franklin described man as a tool-making animal, to which we might add that when the tools are put to use, man is then engaged in technology, for the essence of technology is to perform work with tools and machines. And this of course requires the necessary power and energy to operate these machines. So we may say then that technology is the process of obtaining raw energy such as coal and water, converting that energy to a controlled power to operate tools and machines. Or we may phrase the matter this way: Technology means to harness energy and then use it to supply the needs and wants of man.

Technology is often defined as applied science and truly the dividing line is thin and watery. Some say that they are tied by an umbilical cord and should always be expressed as 'science and technology.' Certainly the two are wedded and bedded together but each is a distinct and separate entity of knowledge and practice. The purpose of science is inquiry alone while technology is the practice of producing a product, of some utilitarian use, usually for the benefit of mankind.

Technology is also described as a practical art, a useful art. This is accurate to the degree that finesse is employed in the performance of doing or that beauty is incorporated in the product. The majestic buildings of Greece and the sublime cathedrals of the Medieval age were more than bricks, stone and mortar; the doctor who opens a human body must work with a professional art as well as a technical intelligence; shooting men into space and bringing them back is both high art and high technology.

Tools, which are the basics of technology, are often described as an extension of man's three principal qualities, as follows:

1. The senses. Such tools as eyeglasses, the telephone, telescope, radar, and microscope all extend and amplify man's natural senses.
2. Thinking and reasoning. The adding machine, calculator, mathematical systems, logic, abacus, cybernetics, the computer – these extend the mind.
3. Motor capacities. Most any tool for work extends man's abilities: Hammer, gears, the wheel, the lever, the level, machines, pulley, the wedge.

HISTORY

Only the word 'technology' is new for the practice goes back to the beginning of man. For example, there is evidence that fire bricks were in use about 10,000 B.C. When man began to write history at about 4000 B.C., he was already using the wheel, fire and the plow, he was erecting buildings, weaving cloth and making pottery, crop rotation was in practice. The Great Pyramids of Egypt were built in the 2500's B.C. Each of these is an example of technology, of man producing goods by technical means.

TYPES OF TECHNOLOGY

The whole of technology is greatly diversified and there is no formal classification, so for our purpose here, which is to show the extent of this institution, the fields have been grouped into six categories of Energy, Inventions, Engineering, Agriculture, Mining and Manufacturing.

ENERGY. This is the source of all technology. Energy is the ability to work, the force and power that moves machines and tools. Although gears, wheels and levers actually cause motion in a machine they are transmitters of energy, not a source of it. Major forms of energy follow:

- Man power and animal power.
- Wind, that turns the windmill or pushes on the ship sail.
- Water, that turns wheels and generators.
- Chemical energy, such as heat and steam from fire.
- Electrical energy, that drives machines, gives light, transmits sound.
- Atomic energy, from splitting of atoms to make electricity, to make bombs.
- Solar energy, the rays from the sun that are converted to heat, to light and electricity.
- Mechanical energy, the work that machines perform.

INVENTIONS. Invention, to invent, means to discover new devices and new methods of performing work. It means to create a new thing that did not exist before. It means not only new machines and products but also such un-machine things as a new language, a new alphabet. Here, however, we shall hold to technical things.

Everything that is man-made has had to be invented and so the history of invention goes back to a distant past. Among the first inventions would be the crude stone tools, the sewing of skins for clothing, erecting a rough shelter of tree limbs or mud. The lever, a prime machine, was early used to move huge rocks and tree branches. The next level of inventions would include the wheel, the plow and the use of fire, all of which are still in use today.

Many other basic devices were invented and in use before 1500 A.D., the beginning of the modern period. Among these were the following: (See also chart in Chapter 7, Modern Era).

- In China: Papermaking, block printing, silk cloth, porcelain, rockets, magnetic compass and gun powder.
- In Ancient Greece: The key, lathe, potters wheel, carpenters level.
- In Egypt and Mesopotamia: The wagon and chariots, irrigation, metal tools, writing, papyrus and the calendar.

Important inventions since 1500 A.D. Beginning with modern times, first slowly and then at a faster pace, a large quantity of inventions have appeared, some useful and beneficial to man, some harmful and destructive and some of mixed blessings. We shall review the noted inventions by century periods.

1400's:	Printing from movable type	
1500's:	Guns, microscope, thermometer	
1600's:	Pendulum clock, slide rule, telescope	
1700's:	Cotton Gin	Piano
	Electric Battery	Steam Boat
	Lithography	Steam Engine
	Hydraulic Press	
1800's:	Bicycle	Radio
	Airplane	Rayon
	Diesel Engine	Revolver
	Gasoline Engine	Reaper
	Incandescent Lamp	Steam Locomotive
	Linotype	Sewing Machine
	Machine Gun	Telephone
	Motion Pictures	Telegraph
	Photography	Typewriter
	Photoelectric Cell	Submarine
	X-Rays	

1900's:	Atom Bomb	Nylon
	Atomic Reactor	Radar
	Electron Tube	Stainless Steel
	Jet Engine	Transistor
	Lazer Light	Television
	Vacuum Tube	Computer

ENGINEERING. Originally the term 'engineering' meant to design and construct such projects as roads, buildings, dams, canals and bridges. Such works were grouped as either military or civilian according to need. But in today's world these are only classical branches of engineering for with the rise of high industrialization there was an accompanying need for extended engineering and as we shall note below, this enterprise of man now flows out in many directions.

In primitive times the engineering projects consisted in the construction of roads, of buildings and dams to aid in crop growth. Many projects of true engineering value were completed in Ancient and Medieval times such as the Great Wall of China, the Egyptian Pyramids and Sphinx, the Hanging Gardens of Babylon, the great roads, aqueducts and the Colosseum of the Romans, the cathedrals of the Catholic church, the Mayan temples.

After the Industrial Revolution engineering came to mean not only design and build but also to operate and maintain. Major branches of engineering are as follows:

- Agricultural: Farm buildings and machines, use of soil and water.
- Aeronautical: Aircraft design and construction.
- Automotive: Design of automobiles, tractors and motorcycles.
- Acoustical: Auditoriums, concert halls, opera house, sound equipment.
- Civil: Roads, bridges, dams, tunnels, railways, harbors, airports, entire cities.
- Communication: Telephone, telegraph, television, radiophone.
- Chemical: Plastics, fertilizers, acids, gasses, fuels.
- Electrical: Electrical machinery, power stations, transmission lines, electronics.
- Hydraulic: Water supplies and systems for cities, for industry.
- Heating and ventilation: Climate control in buildings.
- Hydroelectric: Plants to generate electrical power from water sources.
- Industrial: Production and management of plants.
- Illuminating: Lighting systems for buildings and cities.
- Mining: Extraction of minerals and fuels from the earth.
- Mechanical: Machine design, combustion engines and large machines such as power shovels and draglines.

- Military: The needs of war: Guns, transportation, defenses, troop supplies.
- Marine: Design and construction of ships and docks with facilities.
- Metallurgical: Extraction of metals from ores.
- Structural: Skyscrapers, factories, stadiums and towers.
- Sanitary: Sewage disposal, water treatment to kill germs.
- Traffic: Design of highways, flow of traffic.
- Atomic and nuclear: Reactors and nuclear power.

The two branches of technology reviewed above, Inventions and Engineering, have the character of being a single enterprise, a stand alone quality. Automobiles and telephones may be manufactured en masse but they are not mass engineered.

The following three branches of technology, Agriculture, Mining and Manufacturing, however, have the character of mass production for consumer use.

AGRICULTURE: Man first became a civilized creature when he became a farmer. We do not know the exact time when the conversion took place but the type of site and the approximate place is known. For Western man it was along the banks of the Tigris, Euphrates and Nile Rivers and for Eastern man it was the banks of the Indus River in India and the Hwang Ho River in China. The time was about 25,000 years ago. Prior to this time man was a hunter and roamed after animals but with the planting of crops he must needs stay home and take care of them. He became civilized and learned to live in a social relationship with other human beings.

The word 'agriculture' comes from the Latin and means to cultivate the field but in modern usage it also means to raise livestock, grow plants to make fibers for clothing, even gathering fish from the sea. The several branches, with representative kinds, follows:

Crop Growing.

Cereal crops: Barley, corn, oats, rice, wheat.
Coffee, tea and cocoa.
Fiber crops: Cotton, flax, hemp, jute, sisal.
Forage crops: Alfalfa, clover, hay, straw.
Fruit and Nut crops: Grapefruit, lemon, orange, dates, figs, olives, apples, berries, cherries, grapes, plums, almonds, chestnuts, pecans, walnuts.
Flowers: Roses, orchids, lilies, tulips, lilac.
Rubber: Rubber trees.
Sugar crops: Sugar cane, sugar beet.
Tobacco: Tobacco plant.
Vegetable crops: Potato, cabbage, bean, lettuce, tomato.

Animal Raising.
Cattle, bees, goats, horses, sheep, swine.
Poultry: Chickens, ducks, geese, turkey.
Dairy Farming.
Milk, butter, cheese, cream.
Forestry.
Timber, lumber, fuel.
Fisheries.
Salmon, tuna, oysters, lobster, shrimp, trout.

MINING. This is the branch of technology where man extracts from the earth the metals, minerals and fuels that are embedded in the earth. The substances are known as natural resources, are not man-made and are irreplaceable. Some natural resources can be replaced or re-grown such as trees, tillable land and fish but the minerals and fuels in the earth cannot. When these are consumed they are gone forever and man must then turn to some replacement of them such as atomic fuels or chemical substitutes such as plastics.

The stages of civilized development are often designated as Stone Age, Metal Age, Machine Age, Atomic Age. In this progression man was well into the metal age when he began to write history, about 4000 B.C., for men were mining gold, copper and iron and making products from them. About 1000 B.C. the Phoenicians were sailing all the way to Spain to get silver and to the British Isles to obtain tin.

Mining was a moderate industry across the ages of history down to the Industrial Revolution. The effort was directed toward obtaining the precious metals for jewelry and crafted objects, and mining was performed by hand power. But the Industrial Revolution required massive quantities of all metals for fabricating products and also the fuels to operate the factories. All the world then became the grounds for mining, not only on land but under the sea, and power machines began to do the mining, replacing the pick and shovel.

Types of Mining.
Metals: Gold, silver, lead, iron, aluminum, iron, tin, zinc, uranium.
Non-Metal Minerals: Quartz, feldspar, graphite, suphur, asbestos, diamonds.
Mineral Fuels: Petroleum, coal, natural gas.

MANUFACTURING. To manufacture means to make a product, to fabricate a thing. In agriculture the product is grown and in mining it is extracted from the earth, but in manufacturing the thing is man-made. The very meaning of the word indicates man-made: Manus, to use the hands and facre, to make. And so it was in olden times, made by hand, but today it is mostly machines that do the making while the old word lingers on.

History

In the chapter on Economics a brief history was inserted which we shall re-mention here and supplement.

The system of manufacturing that was in effect at the beginning of the Industrial Revolution, about 1700 A.D., is known as the Domestic System, meaning that the work was performed in the home and not in a factory.

This system is also known and better described by its second name, the Outwork System. Under this method of manufacturing the merchant or manufacturer would purchase all raw materials that were to be used, take these to the home of the worker and there the worker would fabricate or process the material into a product. For example, a merchant would take the cloth, buttons, thread and needles to a home, the woman of the house would then cut and sew these materials into a dress, the dress would be returned to the merchant and the woman would be paid for her work.

This outwork system was the prelude to the factory system. The worker still made the product but instead of doing so in his or her home, now reported to a factory building to do the work. But in addition the worker would now operate a machine to make the product instead of doing so by hand. This system of going to a factory to operate a machine to make a product is still in effect today, is the method by which the great flow of manufactured products pour forth from the mills and factories.

Industries and products. The types of products that are manufactured number several thousand but are grouped by industries, as follows:

Chemical: Drugs, soaps, toilet goods, plastics.
Electrical equipment: Motors, communication devices, electronic devices, cables.
Foods: Meat, vegetables, fruit, dairy products, bakery.
Furniture: For home, office and factory.
Fuels: Oil, gasoline, diesel.
Instruments: Photography, measuring, musical.
Lumber: Boards, pre-fabricated parts such as a truss.
Hardware: Tools, appliances, casings.
Leather: Shoes, purses, luggage.
Machinery: For: construction, office, refrigeration, farming, processing, engines.
Primary metals: Iron and steel in bars and sheets.
Printing and publishing: Books, newspapers, magazines, business forms.
Paper: Containers, boxes, bags.
Plastics: Pipes, gears, cabinets, bottles.
Rubber: Tires, tubes, gloves, boots, aprons.

Stone, Clay, Glass: Concrete, plaster, dishes, bricks, windows, pipes.
Sporting Goods: Clothing, balls, bats, skates.
Textiles: Clothing, fabrics, knitting, weaving.
Transportation: Automobiles, airplanes, boats, trains.
Tobacco: Cigarettes, cigars, chewing tobacco.
Toys.

THE MATERIAL CULTURE

Let us re-state in summary, then, that the institution of technology consists in six great domains of human endeavor: Energy, Invention, Engineering, Agriculture, Mining and Manufacturing. These contain the sum and substance of man's material culture.

When Samuel F.B. Morse, the inventor of the telegraph, sent his first message by wire, it was these historic words: What Hath God Wrought? We may ask this same question today about technology but replace one word: What Hath Man Wrought? And this is not a Platonic inquiry but is instead a hard and realistic question that poses a dual choice. With the awesome might of his technology man has reached a stage where he can provide a material salvation to all of mankind. Will he do so? And, this same might can effectively destroy mankind? Will man do so?

Chapter 19
Art

The word 'art' has no end of meanings and has come to mean all things to all persons. There is an art of war and an art of painting, an art of football and an art of dance, an art of love and an art of hate. Even the hammer used for driving a nail is now a work of art because it is not a stone and a stick tied together with a leather thong but is rather a unit of steel and wood of beautiful design and functional use.

But art as an institution does have an authentic meaning for it is concerned with the beautiful in nature and the works of man and also with the aesthetic feeling these works convey to the viewer or listener. This does not mean only exceptional skill such as that of Shakespeare and Michaelangelo for lesser humans also speak and paint artistically. The great artist uses the same materials that the lesser skilled use: Canvas, lines, paint and brush; and portrays the same subjects: Man and nature. What he has is greater skill in the use of them.

ART AS INSTITUTION

Art is not an organized entity such as a government or a school system but takes its place as an institution of man after the manner of language. It is a way of acting by human beings that is universal and time enduring. Every society the world around engages in song, dancing, drawing, carving (sculpture) and building (architecture). These are the property of all mankind. As for duration, one of the most impressive works of art in the world is "Bison Lying Down," painted on the walls of a cave in Spain 25,000 years ago. Robert Louis Stevenson said that art preceded science and philosophy, meaning that people made art and enjoyed the experience before they wondered about the cause and influence. In this view then, art is among the older institutions of man.

Art is a boundless domain that includes the whole of life, both nature and man, and even extends into heaven. Every object in the world and all the events of history are subjects of art, either to be shown as it is or shown how it might be, could be, or should be. Here the artist may take his or her flight of fancy in fictional depiction, drama, in pictures and the dance or inspire with musical tones. In art we find the feeling and spirit for life, the joy and happiness, the pity and pathos. Art depicts life but does so in softer tones.

Art is an institution also because of its historical value, not in the fact that it may teach history but in the manner in which it does so. The cold type of the history book can only relate facts of events and persons but art is profound and deeply impressive with warmth and feeling, a sense of being there, of being with. The beauty of the European cathedrals that lift their spiry arms to heaven and the Taj Mahal of India can only be known in person or in pictures, not in words, and the dress and costumes of the many peoples are poorly described in words but come alive in artful pictures.

THEORIES OF ART

Ever human is an artist in his or her own way and so untold billions have been acquainted with art but few agree as to its nature. Indeed, it seems to be the nature of art that none should agree in the matter for the secret would then be out and the mystic quality gone. However, many artists and commentators have expressed themselves concerning the nature of art and five ideas seem to predominate, as follows:

Art is merely a form. The idea here is that art is only a shape, a design, a configuration, an arrangement of parts. Thus it is in the dance, in buildings, in painting, in music. This form will have two qualities: It is pleasing and gives pleasure or else it is ugly and therefore un-pleasing or repulsive.

Art is an expression of emotion. Although concrete things are used in art such as paint and canvas, stones and wood, violins and the human voice, these are only vehicles on which art rides. The essence of art is emotion and this is what the artist expresses and what the viewer or listener receives — an emotional feeling.

Art is only a creative act. Whether or not there is an emotional feeling in art it is an accident. Art is merely an act of creation, the bringing into the world something that was not there before. In fact, you can create art within the mind, enjoy it or not, and then dispel it from the mind. Such an art piece would have no form, no concrete existence, and need not have emotional feeling accompany it, but is still an art creation.

Art exists as a "thing" in nature. In this view, man makes artistic things but he does not make "art." Art exists or inheres in nature, is an integral part of nature but it cannot be seen and so when men and women paint a picture, perform a dance, sculpture a statue, it is called art because each is trying to unveil this hidden part of nature, the "art" part.

Art is merely a symbol. When the school teacher tells her class that

2 plus x equals 4, she is using a symbol for something that is missing. If a certain concrete number is inserted where the symbol is, it will round out the whole to a pleasant completeness.

In a similar manner art is merely a symbol but one for ideas and feelings about nature, about man. For example, the tree is not only green it is artistically a beautiful color of green; the tree is not simply a vertical stick of wood, the shape and design of the trunk and branches form a pleasing combination; the music is not mere sound but is artistically made by the musician to impart a pleasant sound; the poetry is not a string of words but is combined to express an artistic vision of love, of combat, of success, of failure.

The above are theories but they are also an insight to the diversified and many-sided nature of art.

THE INGREDIENTS OF ART

Any work of art whether fine, useful or folk art will have three parts, as follows.

1. A material content. There must be a concrete substance in which or upon which to produce the work. Thus the painter requires paint and canvas, the musician needs an instrument and the singer a voice, the actor requires a costume, the dance must have music, the poet will require paper to place his work upon.
2. An artistic content. This is what the artist puts into the work. Many writers call this the physical content to distiguish it from the aesthetic part. This element is the artistic skill that the artist displays such as lines and color in painting, the shape and design of a building, the rhythm and motion of the dancer or the style and unity of prose and poetry.
3. An expressive content. This is what the work puts out, the message that is conveyed to the beholder of the work. Inasmuch as the art will affect the beholder's mind it will naturally convey a dual message as follows:
   a. A communication. This will be an intellectual judgment of the work, a conclusion as to what the art represents, what idea the artist tried to implant in the work, how well the work was executed. A slide rule is not used to draw the conclusions but rather a judgment is made according to the apparent effort of the artist. For example, the Pieta communicates pity and the Mona Lisa a wistful, pensive attitude and both in a profound, total sense.
   b. An arousal. This is the aesthetic part, the emotion that the work evokes in the beholder. Thus, as the Pieta depicts a pitiful scene it should arouse a feeling of pity in the viewer. Any emotion might be aroused such as a feeling of hate, a sense of beauty,

a feeling of immensity, even an impulse to action.

That which the artist puts into a work of art is seldom ever equivalent to that which the beholder receives. The level of communication will be the same of course, but the degree will not. For example, the artist will paint a landscape or a child according to his idea of majestic or beautiful and the viewer will interpret the landscape and the child according to his knowledge and experience of these subjects. There have even been works that evoked the opposite of that which the artist intended, works that instead of attracting have repelled.

These three ingredients of art, material, artistic and expressive content inhere in all art, are intrinisic to art.

GROUPING OF THE ARTS

There is no fixed or fundamental grouping of the arts but three categories may be used to better comprehend the all-inclusiveness of this institution, of which the first two are the classical divisions and the third a modern grouping.

The Seven Liberal Arts. The trivium of grammar, logic and rhetoric, and the quadrivium of geometry, astronomy, music and arithmetic.

The Fine Arts. The fine arts are so called because they are considered to be purely aesthetic, wholly expressive of beauty and pleasure, with an arousal of emotions and a stimulation of ideas and visions. The particular content of the fine arts may be briefly stated under two heads, Principles and Structure.

1. The Principles of Fine Art. Four main elements are to be noted:
   a. Balance. There must be symmetry for a pleasing effect, not mass in one place and scarcity in another.
   b. Proportion. Except in caricature the parts must be depicted as they are. The best example is the human figure.
   c. Rhythm. There must be a certain flowing of lines, or a flowing of motion in order to impart a contiguousness in shape.
   d. Dominance. Some part, some portion must dominate the whole such as an idea, an emotion, a shape, a form, a stark event.
2. Structure in Art. Every work of art must be built, must be constructed. This is the artistic part as distinguished from the aesthetic, as noted above. This structure must be done in a medium of which there are three, as follows.
   a. Space structure (form).
      (1) Painting: With lines for form and shape, and color.
      (2) Sculpture: With rhythm of lines, with ideal form.
      (3) Architecture: With design, form and perhaps color. Efficiency in use is also art.

b. Time structure (form)
   (1) Music: With tones, rhythm, harmony and melody.
   (2) Literature: With patterns of composition, style of presentation, idea content.
   (3) Poetry: Similar to literature plus the forms of couplet and sonnet. Poetry has rhythm, meter, metaphor.

c. Time-Space structure (form).
   (1) Dance: With dynamic motion in graceful patterns of bodily rhythm, in sequences.
   (2) Drama (acting): With mimic, imitation and re-enactment of real persons and life events.

Modern Art Groupings.

Liberal Arts. From Latin meaning the arts suitable to free men. In modern times it refers to philosophy, literature, history and language, or the humanities, to distiguish from scientific, professional and technological subjects.

Useful Arts, Applied Arts. Consists of tools and objects such as a boat, a spoon, shoes, automobiles, even actions such as an organized parade.

Decorative Arts. Interior decorating, fabrics, mosaics, tapestries.

Graphic Arts. Printing, design, prints such as wood block.

Craft Arts. Ceramics, carvings, jewelry, goldsmithing, pottery, leathercraft, furniture, metal ware, textiles.

Folk Art. This usually refers to traditional art, that which is practiced and displayed by people rather than the skilled artist. It includes song, dance, painting, musical instrument playing, carving, hobby decorations, story telling, folklore literature, poetry.

Professional Art. As practiced by the master: Doctor, lawyer, photographer.

Popular Art. This is work that is intended for viewing by a large audience and has mass appeal, such as the radio and television shows, theatre, circus acts, village festivals, carnivals.

ARENA OF ART

At every instant of the day, art is present in the life of the individual. Every frame of vision and every bracket of sound will carry their overtones of art, of aesthetic feeling. We are not always consciously aware of them but they will still attract or repel and we react to them accordingly. Whether the art is fine, useful or plain folk art, we live and exist in this arena of life, some even becoming artists themselves. Sir Thomas Browne said that nature hath made one world, and art another. We walk in both worlds at all times.

Chapter 20
War

"War," said Napoleon, that great maker of war, "is the business of barbarians." Lord Channing said that if you wish to visualize what hell is like, you will see it in a war. Front line fighters from every nation on earth are more explicit for they say that war is hell.

Despite this universal hatred of war by mankind the world around, war has been very much the business of man throughout his long history. It has been calculated that during the past 5,000 years of history only 78 of those years are known to have been free of war. During the other 4,922 years man has heard the sound and felt the dismal misery of war by club and arrow, gun and bomb.

War is that institution by which man tries to settle his disputes, by which people attempt to solve their differences. The very thought of peaceful negotiation is more abhorrent than war if victory seems possible or spoils beckon. The sorrows of defeat and the loss in life and property are too often overlooked. The opponents usually reckon the cost worth the effort.

It is worthy of note, however, that man has made a conscious effort to abolish the institution of war. Many groups promote this objective and nations affiliated in the League of Nations and then the United Nations have expressed their opposition to war as a means of settling disputes between nations. So far the efforts have been futile for the world's budgets swell with arms expenditures as man prepares to fight his wars not only on earth but in outer space as well. Founding of an Institution of Peaceful Settlement to replace the Institution of War, is still very much a visionary dream of mankind.

War as an institution may be divided into three categories to aid in understanding the scope and breadth of this human action, that of policy, armed forces and armed conflict.

POLICY OF WAR

Policy refers to the attitude or intent of a party or a government. With respect to war it has reference to the intent and action of the government, of a nation, which we may divide into two sections, as follows.

Policy of Aggression. Until the twentieth century most wars were outright acts of offensive aggression with the intent to conquer and take what was wanted with apologies to no one. Of course the attacked nation had to defend itself but the intent of the attacker was offensive. History is full of examples: The Romans, Napoleon, England and France in the Americas, the United States against the Indians, Japan in the East. Even the "holy crusades" of the Middle Ages, which lasted across a span of two hundred years, were pure forms of aggressive war.

The aggressor always justifies the action: The need for more territory and trade, for independence from an oppressive monarch, to restore rightful ownership, to save the souls of the heathens, to aid the progress of backward peoples, to make the world safe for democracy, the right of a superior people. All of these justifying reasons were in fact the policy of the aggressor and one that would result in a benefit to that aggressor.

Policy of Defense. About the middle of the twentieth century the nations began to identify their huge war expenditures as a policy of defense and the distasteful word 'war' was replaced with such designations as the Department of Defense.

A policy of armed defense carries several meanings. It means of course to defend the nation against invasion by an aggressor. It also means to attack another nation, not as an offensive action but rather to prevent that nation from attacking one's own country. In a third sense it means to defend or protect the trade and wealth that lies beyond the boundaries of a nation but which the nation claims as a part of its own. Modern wars fall largely into this third meaning, that of economic 'defense.'

ARMED FORCES

This second element of war consists in the people and implements or weapons needed to carry out a policy of war.

Personnel. These are the people who are trained to fight and are divided into army for land warfare, navy for sea warfare, and air force for air warfare. In today's technological wars many of these "fighters" have little actual acquaintance with guns and personal combat because they fight with mechanical and electronic weapons from a distance, such as rockets and missles.

Weaponry. Weapons are the instruments of war, the tools with which the conflict is waged. In times past these weapons were arrows and spears, hand guns and cannons, but modern wars have added such as air craft, chemicals, missiles, atom bombs and computers. These of course are the front line weapons but war is a total business and so the rear echelons include industrial plants, fuel such as oil, transportation and technical know-how.

ARMED CONFLICT

Conflict means the actual engagement of persons in forceful combat, using weapons to achieve a victory. With this premise in mind we may divide the wars of man into two parts, as follows.

Soldier wars. Before the twentieth century war was a matter of direct combat, of man to man, gun to gun, ship to ship fighting. Here the issues of battle and the outcome of the war was settled by a direct confrontation of soldiers and weapons. Women and children were only indirectly affected and were located far from the sound and fury of battle.

Total war. The first beginnings of a new type of war occurred in World War I with the use of long range artillery to shell distant cities, the use of airplanes to bomb whole areas and chemicals to spread death irregardless of the recipient whether combat soldier or unarmed citizen.

During World War II this new type of warfare was employed more extensively and more severely. First was the devastating air raids on whole cities such as London, Coventry, Berlin and Cologne. Then came the missile raids on England, the air raids on Japanese cities and the whole culminating in the dreadful atom bombs dropped on Hiroshima and Nagasaki. In these strikes of war there was no discrimination between soldiers and children, church and gun factory, between food for nourishment and fuel for war. The many claims that only war targets were bombed was a hollow phrase for the bomb simply fell and killed without regard to person or property.

MIGHT AND RIGHT

The old war banner of "might makes right" was right for the mighty only. That the cause for war might have been wrong, that there were two sides to the problem, each of equal merit, was not considered. The policy was to calculate the risk and if the fates spoke favorably, then exercise the might.

However much we disagree with the old way or with war itself, there was some merit in the reasoning if we allow that only trained men would be exposed to war and only the two parties at issue would participate. But in today's world this condition does not, cannot, exist. With high technology, economic interdependence between nations, plus the fact that the former peoples who were colonial dependencies of super-powers are now all free nations, all this has obliterated the "might makes right" and for the first time in history it is possible to say that "right makes might." This is so because if two nations today prepare to engage in war, the many neutral nations cannot stand idly by for they too will become involved from the effects of the war. They will have some "rights" in the matter, even though they are not a participant.

If peace and goodwill are ever to descend upon man it will be when the concept of nations and of nationality are replaced with a sense of friend and neighbor, by all of the peoples, the world around.

Epilogue I

ONE EARTH AND ONE PEOPLE

The ten great institutions of man that we have reviewed above have been the instruments by which the human race has come to be what it is today, a scientific and technological society, with an abundance in immensity. Not equally, for some have more and some have less, but the direction of effort of all the people of the world is toward a technical goal. This is so because it is technology that controls the present and will control the future of mankind.

But man does not live by tools and machines alone anymore than he lived by bread alone in ages past, for he also lives by rules and codes to guide his way of living. Without such rules his life, and especially his technology, will go astray. The use of nuclear materials is a clear example. The splitting of the atom sits at the pinnacle of man's technical achievements and there it poses the question: Shall it be used for the benefit of man or for the destruction of man and his earth along with him? And this is where a code of rules must guide the way, must set the course, both civil and moral.

The old time codes were excellent for their day and are excellent still but they are insufficient for they lack the wisdom to guide an earthman with superior knowledge. In olden years the great humanitarian philosophers and religious leaders such as Moses, Aristotle, Christ, Confucius, the Buddha and Mohammed did not know the world as we know it today. Their earth was flat, their sun circled the earth, their earth-world was their own society and nearby-locale. These great moralists could not foresee human beings leaving the earth for outer space, circling the earth in a matter of hours (even circling the earth at all), people living in buildings one-fourth of a mile in the air, a man in China in partnership with a man in France, the devastation of people and earth with a few bombs, nor the common man having the same rights as a king. This knowledge was not available to the men who made the moral codes by which we live today and so their perspective was narrow to this degree. The behavior of mankind today cannot be fully regulated by the behavior rules of the past. The moral codes of Moses' Ten

Commandments, the Golden Rule of Christ, the Eight-fold Path of Buddha, the Golden Mean of Confucius must each be amended or added to. They should not be replaced for they are still as valid as ever but must be supplemented and adjusted to the life style of mankind today, to the changes that man has undergone.

Who is to perform this mighty chore of preparing a new moral code? Not one man as in the past for the world is too diverse, too complex. Perhaps an international committee for it is not one people or group to be guided but all of the earth's people. The mentality of the committee should be that of the astronaut or cosmonaut who returns from outer space. These people have seen an earth that other humans have not and every one returns with a new idea of the earth: Before going, the earth is a great and large land of many different peoples, but when they return they see the earth as a small sphere floating in space, inhabited by one people called humans and covered with a coat of nature that is delicate and fragile and which, if much disturbed, will end the life of man on earth.

Any new code must begin from a new stance. The old codes related only Man to God and Man to Man, such a Thou shalt love God and do unto others as you would have them do unto you. These are very fine for inspiration but have not the slightest practical content, defining neither love, God, nor the reciprocal acts to be performed. Again, these were fine for another age because the need for further detail was unnecessary.

The new code must direct a relationship between Man and Man, and Man and Nature, because nature is life for mankind. To the degree that the worth of nature is reduced, to that same degree is life for man reduced. Life is not bestowed from on high, it is extracted from nature and as nature is diminished by poison and pollution, just so is there less life to extract, for man.

However the code is designed it must impinge into the mind of all men and women, of high and low estate alike, the following:

- The brotherhood of man in one world;
- Equality of rights and obligation of duties;
- Political separation is a paper barrier;
- The essentials for life must be shared with those whose native land will not yield this need;
- Pollution of land, air and water endangers all life on earth;
- War is inhuman;
- The United Nations list of Rights belong to all men and women.

Some such Code of the Earthman must surpass the present guides to behavior. And then a copy should be placed in the hands of every adult on earth. Old ways are slow in changing but a beginning must be made for as the Chinese say, the journey of a thousand miles begins with a single step. It will not bring a new heaven and a new earth, for such is contrary to nature, but it will replace much misery with much enjoyment of living.

BOOK II

THE HUMAN INDIVIDUAL

Life is a task to be done.
. . . *Arthur Schopenhauer*

In Book I, we have scanned the Society of Man, reviewing the great Civilizations, the manner in which man conducts his Social Association and then examined the Ten Life Institutions by which man manages his Social Living.

In this book we shall consider Individual Man, men and women as personal beings, the units which make-up a society. A large group such as a society is difficult to envision because it is an enormous entity, even an abstract thing that is intangible, and shadowy. But an individual person is a concrete being, visible, touchable and near at hand. Indeed, it is that very intimate and personal being that is ourselves, you and I, me and thee, friend and enemy, mother and child, king and peasant, merchant and clerk, teacher and student. It is an earthling who lives and breathes.

In Part I we shall examine the personal world of the individual person to learn what reality means to each human being. This real life has four distinct parts:

1. An experience of life in the body;
2. An experience of life in the mind;
3. An experience of life in events;
4. An experience of life as a process.

It is in, through and by these life happenings that the individual knows the reality of life and living, how each person knows the reality of his or her own being.

Part II, entitled Personal Living, examines the twelve goals of life which each individual must accomplish as their mission in life. These are the twelve arenas of living, the segments of life in which we are born, live out our term on earth and then die. They are not an artificial classification of life parts but are rather the twelve natural and human divisions of life where we each attain our well-being in life including a certain degree of happiness.

Part III reviews the enrichment of living through the common and ideal values of life.

Prologue II

THE MISSION IN LIFE

The rule of life is three-fold: You must enhance your self, protect your person, and associate with fellow humans in order to attain well-being in life, or, failing this, your condition will be one of ill-being. This is the firm and inflexible law of life for the individual and it is imposed upon each person both by nature and by society. It is not a matter of choice but one of obligation and demand, with a penalty for negligence. To obey this great rule becomes our mission in life.

The mission begins at the time of the second great life-event, of which there are a total of four:

1. The greatest event of all, of course, is to be born into the world, into a life of nature and a life of human society. Prior to birth we are each an embryo-child, after birth we are a human-child, either male or female.
2. The second great life-event occurs at or near the end of the second decade of life when the human child becomes a human adult. The dependent years of home and school are over and completed and the person is now accountable for his or her actions, who steps forth into the community of mankind as an adult, to take his or her place therein as a responsible member thereof.
3. The third great life-event occurs at about age sixty-five with a decline in abilities and actions.
4. The last great event is death.

The first two decades of life are a preparation for all that is to follow. During this early period we grow to a full maturity under the guidance and commands of our parents, nourishing the body, learning academics, and learning the proper behavior in social groups. But the decisions are largely parental. Now, upon reaching full maturity, both in body and mind, we begin to command our own lives, provide our own food and clothing, self-instruct ourselves, make our own decisions and guide our own behavior. We are now a citizen in society, have acquired the status of a self-responsible human being. We must now fulfill our three-part mission in life which has the following twelve divisions.

#1. To enhance the self.

To enhance means to heighten, to increase, and this is the first goal of life, to magnify the self. We increase or enhance our personal self through seven goal actions:

In physical health,
Mental health,
Physical ability,
Mental ability,
Life work ability,
In meaningful leisure activity, and
Religion.

#2. To protect the person.

We protect our person in two ways:

The first is with safety from accident, crime and disaster, and secondly, with enough economic wealth to sustain our life on a level of well-being.

#3. To associate with other persons.

We engage in personal association in three areas:

In marriage to a spouse,
In a family unit, and
In social groups.

These twelve components of life are reviewed in detail in Part II as the Twelve Goals of Life but here thay are to be seen in their superior role of a mission in life for each individual: To enhance the life we are given, to protect it and to live in association with fellow human beings. This distinction is made because these goals in life are not simply wants, needs or desires but are imperatives of life. They are the demands of nature and society if you are to live on earth in the environment of nature and society, as every human must. Let us note briefly how this is so, why this is so.

In the first place, if we are to live at all, to merely exist, we must have some health in the body and in the mind. If we did not we would not be alive. But to stay alive we must constantly enhance that body and mind, nourishing the one with food, nourishing the other with learning. And then, if we wish to live on a higher scale than mere existence, we must constantly enhance both body and mind to a higher degree. Not magnify to a super degree but at least to a level of well-being in health and material goods that will bring a contentment of living to the self, to the person.

Secondly, we cannot exist on earth without safety protection. Although the good exceeds the evil, the world is still filled with crime, disaster, even war, and with unsafe conditions that cause accidents. Each of us will fall victim to these unfavorable parts of life unless we take protective steps to avoid them. Similarly, we cannot exist without a sufficiency in economic resources such as shelter, clothing, and wealth (money) enough to purchase nourishing foods and health needs.

In the third place we each carry the banner of "social animal" and so we must by our very nature, and by our need to survive, associate with our fellow humans. It is impossible for one person to exist without the presence of other human beings.

It will readily be seen from the above that choice is not the reason to enhance, protect and associate, as desirable as each may be, but rather it is a requisite of life, of both nature and society. It is a mission that is imposed upon each person by two unalterable conditions. The first is time itself together with the biological process of growth to a state of adulthood. Secondly is the culture of man, with which we must comply because we, too, are a member of, a part of that culture, which takes place in a social group.

Our life then is a mission that we must accomplish each day on a small scale, each year on a larger scale, and through life on a whole scale. If the mission effort is neglected there will accrue the lesser values of life: Poverty, illness, sorrow; if the effort is pursued with energy there will accrue the greater values of life: Health, safety, enough wealth, joy and contentment. All normal adults seek these great values.

Part I

PERSONAL REALITY

Chapter 1

The Personal World

The world of reality for the individual, for you and for me, is not the same thing as reality for mankind as a whole, even though we are each a part of that mankind. A society finds its real world in a social association only, while the individual finds his or her real world in personal, intimate day-by-day contacts with other individuals, with things of nature and with man-made devices. Society is a cold and abstract thing while an individual is a biological thing with feelings of love and hate and fear, with plotting and planning and reasoning. Societies move and exist in age-long entities while an individual lives in a day-to-day unit of time, in enclaves of twenty-four hours.

A society cannot feel pain, experience pleasure, suffer loss of a loved one, achieve success in a business venture. Nor does society breathe air in order to live, eat food to nourish live tissues, perspire at work and go to bed to relieve fatigue. Only individuals do these things, have a direct engagement in the business of living, have a confrontation with life each day. A group or a society may be said to love or to hate but it is not the group as such, it is the individuals within the group because only individuals can feel emotions, have a bodily sensation, a tingling of nerves, a sense of hot and cold. If a group "takes action" it is really the persons within the group who are acting. And of course a society cannot think, cannot reason, cannot make a value judgment. These are abilities of the individual human alone, for only persons have brains.

There is no simple statement that will explain how the individual lives in his real world, how he relates to it. Poets and philosophers have likened life to a journey, to a passage, to a stream of consciousness, a long road to travel and to a flowing stream. These graphic portrayals are enlightening but not explicit. The picture of a flowing stream of water is a helpful one. Here the whole of life is the stream, with springs that flow off each embankment to join the main stream. On the one side the springs are the experiences of life such a bodily arousals, an impulse to act, a thinking, and emotional feelings. From the other embankment the streams are a flow of life events such as a birth, a marriage, a school graduation, an illness or a vacation. These springs, on the one side the experiences of life and on the other the events of life, join into a double current of behavior that never ceases.

Whether life is a stream or a journey cannot be said with certainty but what can be asserted with utmost surety is that for the individual life does take place within an environment, of which there are four: The environments of nature, of society, of technology and the self. Some divisions of reality are given as God, Nature and Man but this is a philosophical separation for God has no tangible presence in concrete such as man and nature, but is rather a conceptual realm of faith and belief.

The divisions are called an 'environment' because each individual lives the rounds of life totally immersed in these four arenas. They are not environs that are some far-off, distant abode, but are rather the immediate arena within which we live and breathe and move about each day, never free of their presence nor of their influence. We are each, in fact, a personification of the four life-environs because we, too, are part a thing of nature, a social being, a tool-material user and part a self-personality.

The scientist does not view reality in this fashion. The physicist sees the real world in atoms, particles, waves and light speeds; the chemist searches for cells and organisms in living matter; in the social area the anthropologist looks to the origin of man, adaptations and adjustments, while the psychiatrist examines the abnormal mind, the sick, the maladjusted.

For the individual the real world has a different meaning, as noted above, for he or she knows it as a conscious experience that consists in daily living, in rubbing elbows with very life itself, with pleasure and pain, misery and delight, success and failure. It is in these clusters or compositions of expressed living that the individual knows reality. The four environments are as follows.

#1. The Environment of Nature.

As all well know, this is the earth itself and all that it contains: Plants, animals, sunshine, water and air, the soil, forests, minerals and climate. It is the residential home of each individual, the locale of mankind in the universe.

One example will help to show the 'man in nature' status. The largest organ in area is the skin, our protective coating, where the sense of touch and feeling connects us to the rest of nature. Now every day of every year that we live the skin is directly affected by the weather of heat, cold, rain and snow, sun and atmosphere. It is people living in the nature environment.

#2. The Social Environment.

The social world for the individual has three parts:

a. Other individuals. This is the person-to-person meeting that we have that is intimate and private between husband and wife, parent and child, close friend and work companion.

b. The group. This is a relationship that occurs nearby, within the community in which we live such as the church, club, work group, play group and political group.

c. Institutional association. These are the contacts that we have with laws and regulations such as meeting taxing requirements, obeying national laws, complying with local laws of traffic rules and housing regulations. It is an association by influence, by rules to which we must respond.

#3. The Technical Environment.

In a broad sense, anything that is man-made, that is produced with tools and machines, creates a technical environment and so we are forever walking in this arena of life. Our homes, food and clothing are technical products, our transportation by automobile and airplane is a conveyance by technical means, and our homes have come to be a depository of technological products: Washer, dryer, radio, television, electric stove, dishwasher and typewriter.

#4. The Self Environment.

This last environment is within, a private world of our own, all aside from the worlds of nature and society. We are each a self and a personality that learns, thinks and has emotional feelings; that has beliefs, wants and needs; that has ideals to which we aspire. These belong to each self alone and cannot be shared with another. My pleasure, my pain and my dreams are mine and, although I may tell others about them, only I alone experience them.

It is within these four enclaves of life — nature, society, technology and the self — that we each live out our life here on earth. There is no scale of measurement to designate one as more important than another, one of more value than another. Each has equal worth because each is a permanent and constant environment within which we live. We must adjust our living to all of these life-arenas because they comprise our entire personal world.

Chapter 2
The Experience of Life

This chapter is to serve as an introduction to the four chapters that follow and the purpose is to clarify the meaning of the term 'life.' The four chapters review life for the individual in four areas: In the body, the mind, in events and life as a process, so it will aid in our understanding of these chapters by first defining the term 'life.'

In the broad meaning of the term, life refers to an organism that takes nourishment, has growth, has active behavior. It is the opposite of dead, of non-living. In the human being we see life as a breathing process, heart beat, growth and daily activity. The organism, the human, is alive, has life in it.

Above this basic fact of merely being alive, life has two very important meanings, namely, life is a becoming and life is an experience. A simple example is thirst. We are forever becoming thirsty, have a desire for water, and then we follow this by an experience of drinking water, or satisfying the need, the thirst.

LIFE AS A BECOMING

All life, all living things are constantly 'becoming,' are continuously changing. They come to be something they were not before. All plants and animals, insects and humans never stop this changing: They are born, they grow, are enlarged, are added to, change their ways, seek new goals, and make the final change of dying. We usually designate these activities as a process and so they are, but they are also a becoming, an acting toward an end, a goal. Thus, a tree does not just grow, it grows to bear fruit; the human being learns, not to fill his mind but that he or she might become an intelligent person, a useful citizen.

Becoming in the human being is usually an extension of an experience because of man's ability to think. When an individual undergoes a life experience it conveys a message to the mind and the person takes some action. He becomes or is becoming a different person than he was before the experience, if only by adding a minute bit to his previous life.

LIFE AS AN EXPERIENCE

To have an experience of or with something means to have a direct contact with the thing. In the example above of thirst there was a direct contact of need (thirst) and also of fulfillment (the water). Pain and pleasure in the body are additional examples of direct contact experience. We may even have 'contact' at a distance in the mental sorrow we feel upon learning of serious injury to a friend. The psychologist will call thirst, pain and sorrow motives and feelings and so they are but they are also very much an experience of life.

OTHER DEFINITIONS

The term 'experience' is sometimes taken to mean consciousness or simply awareness but there is a difference. We are always and forever conscious while an experience is a single occurrence, a temporal incident that comes to be and then passes. The happenings (experiences) of yesterday are gone forever although their influence may linger. The feel of hunger will soon be satisfied with food and the life experience is then completed.

The term is also widely used to mean the background of a person such as "my experience as a hockey player," or "my experience of an illness." These are common or loose use of the word to describe an event, not the strict use to explain a mental-physical experience of life.

The intent in this book is to explain the life of the individual, how a person comes to learn about life and how he or she then act or behave in life, and the term used to explain this person-life relationship is an experience. This experience takes place in four areas as we shall now review in the following chapters.

Chapter 3
Experience in the Body

The experience of life in the body, as distinguished from the mind, is a sensation or arousal in the cells and tissues of the body, including the sense organs. It is a biological feeling that is well known to children and adults alike and so requires a mere listing, with little explanation. What the listing does is reveal the wide extent of our bodily experience of life.

EXPERIENCE IN THE SENSES

All physical knowledge of the outside world is channeled to the brain through five sense organs. Before the brain receives this knowledge the body first receives it as an experience of life. That which the brain does is identify that which the senses have experienced.

The five senses are well known: Eyes by which we experience seeing, ears for hearing, skin for feeling, tongue for tasting and nose for smelling.

BIOLOGICAL GROWTH

We do not directly detect the experience or process of bodily growth at the time it occurs, as we do seeing and tasting, but rather have a knowledge of the event after it occurs. We can look backward at the age of twenty and recognize that great changes have taken place since the age of ten.

Age groups are given in units of six years both here an in following sections of the book. There is a life-action reason for this, namely, because life events tend to occur in multiples of six. For example, at age six the child first leaves the shelter of the home to go into the outer world of the school, biological maturity is reached at approximately age twelve, at eighteen physical maturity is attained and adult events are so grouped. The terms are as follows:

Embryo and fetus. There is rapid growth during the first nine months of life, the head being disproportionately large.

Baby and early childhood. Up to one or two years the growth is rapid, then on to the age of six the growth is slow but steady.

Late childhood, pre-adolescent. From six to twelve years the growth is gradual with occasional spurts when "that child grew three inches overnight."

Adolescence. From twelve to eighteen years of age there is very rapid growth and also maturing of the individual. In general, girls mature two years before boys of the same age.

Adulthood. There is no growth in stature between age 24 and 60. By rigorous exercise some body parts may be increased or developed but there will be no biological add-on in growth. All nourishment now is for maintenance and replacement, not growth.

Oldsters. Elderly persons not only do not grow, they tend to shrink or as some say "grow small."

BIOLOGICAL AROUSAL

Sometimes called instincts, the biological arousals are well known to all persons and require no explanation. They are a feeling within the body, a daily experience of life.

Hunger: the need for food.
Thirst: need for water.
Air hunger: need for air.
Sex urge, desire: a need to satisfy this arousal.
Pain: the need to relieve an uncomfortable feeling.
Bowel/Bladder tension: need of elimination.
Fatigue: need for sleep, to recover from fatigue.
Warm/Cold: need for shelter, protection of the body.
Feeling of motion: Sensation of moving.
Feeling of reality: of life, of living.
Feeling of pleasure: contented, pleasantness, relaxed.
Feeling of pain: as above.

BIOLOGICAL REACTION

We not only act, that is play, fight and work, we also re-act to the events of live. When we see an action or engage in one there is always an inner activity, a response that is caused by the event. It is an experience of life.

A rapid heart beat.
Stomach feeling, butterflies in the belly.
Trembling.

Adrenalin increase, feeling of more energy.
In the muscles a feeling of tightness, tenseness.
Mouth dry, saliva decrease.
Nervous perspiration, cold sweat.
Feeling of weakness, faint.

IMPULSE TO ACT, INNER URGE

Each of the following is a common experience of life which all humans know and undergo. There may be elementary thinking in the process but they are essentially an impulse to act.

Curiosity: to inquire, to find out.
Pugnacity: urge to fight.
To protect, security: one's person, one's property.
Gregariousness: to associate, to affiliate with others.
To explore: in strange, unknown places.
To construct: to build, to make.
To dominate: to assert one's self, to control.
To acquire: to hoard, accumulate.
To create: express the self, make a new thing.
Urge to imitate others: mimic.

CONCLUSION

These bodily arousals, urges and impulses are not just isolated incidents that occur and then go away but are instead a message and a warning to the mind that an action is needed or should be taken. They express a need that must or should be satisfied, are the beginning step in a process of goal fulfillment. They are part of the process of goal seeking by which the human lives his daily life: A need arises, steps are taken to satisfy that need, and when satisfied the goal has been attained. It is an experience of life in the body that is repeated over and over throughout life.

Chapter 4
Experience in the Mind

This chapter is concerned with the mind as the location or site of a life experience. In Part II we shall examine mental health and mental abilities.

We are conscious of all living through the workings of the mind. When we are hungry, have an injury, are happy or sad, it is our mind that tells us that these events are happening, tells us what kind of an event is taking place and what to do about it. The mind never stops experiencing even when we are asleep for it goes on in dreams. The mind is at work twenty-four hours each day.

Now it would seem that such an important part in the body would be easy to describe but in fact it is not. There is no problem in describing a whole person: Two arms, two legs, a head and trunk, skeletal frame, muscle and organs. There, in just one sentence, we have drawn a fair description of the human body; but the mind does not have concrete parts and cannot be so described. It cannot be taken out of the body and layed on a table for examination, cannot indeed be allocated to any one place in the body. We know that the central site of mental activity and coordinator of mind processes is the brain but it is not the mind, as such.

The mind is known by the manner in which it functions, by the actions which it performs. As we shall see in a subsequent chapter these functions are to learn, to think and remember, but here we are concerned with the mind as an instrument by which we experience life. To this end we shall review the mind as a processor of information and then as a container of information, first noting the two mind parts.

DIVISIONS OF THE MIND

Psychologists usually make a two-part division of the mind into the conscious, where normal thinking and feeling takes place, and the unconscious, a level where instinctive drives and urges take place. The greatest teacher about the functions of the unconscious mind was Sigmund Freud, the founder of psychoanalysis, who divided the mind into three categories:

1. The Id, containing the innate, primitive drives;
2. The Ego, where reasoning and intellectual thought take place;
3. The Superego, where value judgments of worth, of good and bad, are made.

These three psychic forces are not clear-cut departments of the mind but are rather recognizable functions of the mind.

The conscious mind is the most familiar aspect of mental activity for it involves the two well-known processes of thinking and emotions, the mental actions that we employ each day in the routine of our living.

1. The cognitive mind. Here the mind functions in observing, in learning and in reasoning such as making plans, making decisions and solving problems. This is where creative thinking takes place as well as value judgments. It is the thinking part of the mind.
2. The affective mind. Here we experience the emotional feelings of love, hate, fear and all of the derivative emotions that stem from these major ones. This is the feeling part of the mind.

THE MIND AS INFORMATION PROCESSOR

As all persons know, the parts of the mind noted above do not operate in separate isolation wards, entirely apart from one another. The thinking-feeling activity is combined in a single process and it is doubtful if we ever think without some feeling present or feel without some thinking involved. We will see this in the four stages of mental experience which follows. These four stages do not follow a hard and fast sequence but all are present in each mental experience.

A knowing, an awareness. The mind of course must be alerted to the presence of something: A biological arousal, a sunset, a hunger, a sexual urge, even such desires as to seek wealth or an urge to create.

An interpreting. There is always an interpretation of that of which the mind is aware: It is an automobile, it is a child, it is a flower.

Assign a meaning. We not only know and interpret but also promptly assign a meaning to that knowing, we affix a value to it. For example: The automobile is speeding and there is danger, the child is my daughter, the flower is a rose in full bloom with a rich odor.

An emotional feeling. Feeling accompanies every mental experience although sometimes it is subtle and unrecognized, at other times with high intensity. The automobile approaching at high speed induces fear; the daughter, a sense of love and affection; the rose, a feeling of pleasantness.

Most mental experiences are followed by an action of some sort but at this point our interest is solely in the experience as such.

THE MIND AS INFORMATION CONTAINER

The second experience in the mind is to store information in a memory compartment and then recall that information at will. Just how the mind or brain performs these two tasks of storage and recall is not known. Somehow, the uncountable chunks of data that we learn or experience are gathered into the brain and there stored in 100,000 pigeon holes, and then, as needed or desired, the mind will retrieve the information, run it across a scanning table in the mind for viewing and use, and then return it to its pigeon hole, there to rest until further need. Exactly how the mind accomplishes this miracle is one of the secrets that nature has not released to intelligent man.

There is no set classification for the information that is gathered into the mind but we may group it into five categories for review: Past events, facts, beliefs, attitudes and the self.

Memory of past events. This is clear in itself, consisting of well known incidents of childhood, going to school, marriage, a journey, an illness. When these events of life have come and gone their image still remains implanted somewhere within the cells of the brain, thousands upon thousands of them, there to reside until recalled for mental review many years after the event, as frequently as desired, sometimes with a pleasant feeling and sometimes in sadness.

Factual data. Clearly this would include all of the general information that we learn and retain in the mind. It would include facts of history, mathematics, geography of the earth, the great societies and civilizations, religion, scientific information, the laws of the land, even the rules of daily living such as brush the teeth, eat wholesome food, get proper rest.

Beliefs we hold. These are reviewed in detail in another chapter but they consist of the beliefs each person holds regarding God, man and nature. In addition to these beliefs which the individual shares with all mankind, we each have our own personal creed of likes and dislikes, political beliefs and values of life.

Attitudes. Attitudes are that part of the mind or self known as a mental set or a mental state. It is a fixed opinion, one that has more or less settled and solidified in the mind and as such it becomes a direction pointer in our behavior. We are not born with attitudes but rather acquire them as a result of our living of life, in thinking, in feeling and in acting toward and with other persons. Then too, our beliefs and memories are part of the attitude whole.

An attitude is an intending, a mental inclination directed toward people, toward nature and toward our own personal behavior. It is a disposition that reflects back to influence our opinions and beliefs. A well known attitude is prejudice, a fixed intention that regulates our thoughts and actions whether right or wrong, good or bad.

Attitudes are very strong forces in human behavior because every event is usually pre-judged by an attitude. There is no need to think and reason because the mind is ready-set to guide the behavior, and that set is deep rooted. Just approach condition X and all aspects of it are pre-planned: an opinion about it, the worth or value of it and what action to take regarding it. Such is the workings of an attitude.

Attitudes are not inherited but are learned in the course of living. For example:

- The attitude toward mother is one of love, a result of early care.
- Toward animals: a love, a dislike or even hate.
- Toward race: one of prejudice or not.
- Toward war: a plus or minus attitude.
- Toward religion: it is a fraud or an essential to man as a civilized being.

Words that imply an emotion are used to describe an attitude but they are not emotions. They are, as noted, a mental set, a ready-made mind that prompts and directs our thoughts and our behavior.

The self. The self is reviewed in a following chapter but here we wish to note that it is also an experience of life within the mind. The self is a concept that has two dominant aspects. The first is the self-image we each have that we are a thing apart from all of the rest of the world. It is that sense or feeling of "I," of "me," as distinguished from you, or they, or the rest of humanity. "I" am one and separate.

The second aspect is that of self-esteem. It is the manner in which we evaluate ourself and the worth we place on our behavior. For example; I live a worthy life. Self-esteem may also have its negative side: I know I am lazy, I am a wastrel with money, I neglect my civic duties, I am unkind to animals.
to animals.

Let us re-state in summary then how we experience life in the mind. The first is as a processor of information in a knowing, an interpreting and in assigning a meaning to that which we have observed, plus an accompanying emotional feeling. In the second function we have seen the mind as a storehouse of information that may be recalled for use. Whatever events or happenings occur in each life, whether slight or large, they will converge and come together in the mind as the central point for knowing, for storing, and for experiencing.

Chapter 5
Experience in Events

An experience of life in the body or in the mind is a micro part of living but an event is a macro part of life, an experience in and of the whole person. The one is a unit, the other a whole. A mental or bodily experience is isolated, is a single occurrence but an event is a composite a total happening and we know it as a marriage event, an illness in our life or a success in our employment. The thinking and bodily arousal are part of an event but are the inner, subjective elements while the event as a whole is an outward action, an overt occurrence that dominates all. Events are the minor experiences combined into an action.

An event is an encounter with life by the individual when he or she go forth into the world to struggle, to contest and to work with people and nature. It is not a battle, although these do occur, but it is an effort to achieve, to attain a goal, to succeed. It is a going forth each day to work, to play, to school, to be married, to maintain a family unit. It is in such settings that the events of life take place.

EVENTS BY TYPE

The petty events that occur each day in an individual's life are too numerous to review but we may summarize the noteworthy events in a two-part division, by age and by importance. It should be borne in mind that these incidents are not miscellaneous happenings but are rather tasks to be accomplished in the course of personal living.

Life events by age.

Baby and early childhood — Birth to six years.

1. Physical learning:
   - To walk.
   - To take solid foods.
   - To talk.
   - To control waste elimination.
   - To learn sex modesty.

To learn physical activity.

2. Mental Learning:
   To relate to family, playmates, people.
   To recognize right from wrong.
   Learning to use language.

Late childhood — 6 to 12 years.

1. Physical learning:
   Skill in games, with tools, instruments.
   Body maneuvers.
2. Mental learning:
   To cooperate with playmates.
   To understand meaning of sex.
   Skill in reading, writing and arithmetic.
   Relate to social group.
   To know values and worth in life.
   To learn moral manners.
   To share responsibility.
   How to win and lose.

Adolescence — 12 to 18 years.

A clear sense of self.
Full understanding of sex life, role of male and female.
Beginning separation from parents, from home.
Selecting and preparing for a work career.
Entrance to the social world.
Preparing for marriage.

Early adulthood — 18 to 36 years.

Selection of a mate.
The marriage.
Beginning of family living.
Raising of children.
Managing the home.
Entering the occupational career.
Engaging in civil activities, community responsibilities.
Joining in social groups.

Middle age — 36 to 60 years.

Continue the home environment.
Children leave home.
Gain financial security for latter years.
More civic responsibility.
More social participation.
More leisure time activity.

Latter years — 60 and over.

Decreasing physical ability.
Decreasing health stability.
Less activity.
Death of spouse.
Altered life style.

Life events by importance. To classify events by importance can only be done in a relative sense. The same happening will have a different meaning, a different worth, to separate individuals. For example, the birth of a child into a family will be a very important event but it will hold different values to the father and to the mother. Nevertheless, life does fall into a two-fold natural division of routine-everyday-automatic living on the one hand and on the other is a series of high points, or peak events, involving decision and planning and some that are not planned such as a serious accident. With this separation by value we may make an approximate list of events by importance.

The routine events. Our every day affairs are accomplished in a routine, habitual manner. They are repeated so often that they require little mental effort, little planning, no hard concentration of reasoning and only a soft decision. They are characterized by the remark of one friend to another, "so what is new today?" and the answer "very little." Nevertheless they are a life-event and fill our existence here on earth.

- Eating, sleeping, working, going to school, evening recreation.
- Minor illness.
- A vacation.
- Religious and civil holidays.
- Minor travel.
- An important purchase.

The Peak Events of Life. These are happenings of major importance in the life of the individual. They occur infrequently and some of them only once in a lifetime. These events require concentrated reasoning, much planning and a hard decision as to the course of action. Failure to achieve the goal that has been set is quite serious, even critical to the whole status of the individual's life. While on the other hand, success or a favorable outcome is of great benefit and may even be a turning point in life.

- Birth and death.
- New-born child in family.
- Reaching maturity.
- School graduation.
- Marriage.
- Death in family
- Religious experience.
- Divorce.
- Jail confinement.
- Personal injury.
- Art performance:
  Musical, drama.

- Work and income crises.
- Extended vacation.
- Major illness.
- Change of residence
- Financial loss or gain.
- Heavy debt.
- Retirement.
- School starts, ends.
- Extended illness.
- Pregnancy.
- Health change of permanent nature.
- Major purchase: Home, automobile.
- Child leaves home.
- Noted personal achievement, success.
- Catastrophe: Fire, storm loss, accident.
- Marital difference.

ATTRIBUTES OF AN EVENT

The following characteristics are present in every event although in varying degrees of intensity and duration. Where the rate is high then there is a high state of awareness or consciousness and where the escalation is low then the awareness of activity is low. So much of our living falls into the class of routine or habit that many small events come and go with a minimal conscious awareness of them but still the following factors are present.

A dominant motive. Humans are always "on call" to act, are constantly prompted by motivating forces within and without. To a large degree these forces lie in a dormant state until the advent of an event, of an occurrence, and then a whole motive-set will rise to the surface and dominate all other motives and become the moving force for the event now at the fore. A motivating set will include:

- A biological feeling or bodily sensation;
- A mental thinking such as desire or wish, how to solve a problem, or a decision to be made;
- A goal to achieve, an end to attain, an objective to reach;
- A belief or value judgment as to good or bad, as to worth or unworthiness.

These four elements operate as a group or set, something in the order of a train of gears. When one goes into action the other three begin to operate. They are not of course a mechanical process for man is not a machine, rather it is a unitary action, a harmony of operation. But each event is characterized by these four motive units.

Duration. Every event is performed in the immediate n-o-w. We may look forward to an event or look backward in our mind but the actual occurrence is always in connected multiples of time such as hours or weeks.

Time moves at a fixed rate but life does not, it hobbles along in spurts: Slow, fast leisurely then quickly, mildly then with intensity. And it is events that mark this alternating pace of life. The clock and calendar can measure our daily routine of uneventful living but they cannot measure our life at the time of a highlight event for suddenly we can cram into a few hours the equivalent of a year of normal, routine existence.

Direction. We can only live in one direction and that is forward, into the future. What is past is gone and cannot be re-lived. If there has been success, well and good, if failure, it is so. We will have memories of the event, may make amends or corrections of the outcome but the event itself cannot be physically recalled.

Purpose. All of life has a purpose and all of it's acting parts, including events. Purpose refers to an objective to be achieved and a reason for doing so. There is always an aim, a goal, an end. For the individual human the over-all purpose and end is the well-being of his or her person and contrarily the avoidance of ill-being such as sickness and disease. State otherwise, the end purpose in all conscious behavior is success, a non-failure.

Intensity. Both the motive and the action will naturally have a certain degree of force. Some events will require thoughts and feeling of deep intensity, others will have these qualities only in mildness. Similarly, actions before and during the occurrence of an event may involve aggressive movement and energy, or need only modest activity.

A value of enjoyment. This is sometimes called the pleasure-pain facet of an event. The feeling of pleasantness and unpleasantness accompanies all human behavior.

A value of worth. This is the value judgment we place on all human behavior, fixing upon the action a certain worth or unworth, an estimate of goodness or badness.

THE CYCLE PATTERN

Our entire life and most of the events therein are geared to a recurrent pattern of days, weeks and months. The old grouping of a day into a three-part schedule of eight hours of work, eight of play (leisure) and eight of rest is still approximately so today. Some events that follow a cycle pattern are as follows.

1. The weekly cycle for both the school years and the work years is the same: five days for school and for income production and then two week-end days for personal-leisurely pursuits.
2. The monthly cycle of living for the individual and for business firms also is an economic one. Nearly all accounting of wealth is pegged to a monthly cycle of income and outgo and the individual must conform to this pattern in his or her schedule of living. The annual statement of income and expenses is merely a summary of the monthly accounts.
3. Time cycle by the year is marked by holidays and anniversaries. For

the nation at large it is one of national or religious significance such as Christmas, Victory Day or Founding Day, or one of ethnic meaning such as St. Patrick's Day. For the individual the annual dates are birthdays and anniversaries, the latter such as weddings and reunion festivals.

Again let us note that while life is marked by a time scale it is not geared to time. Time is a straight line figure that has no substance, has no content. It is simply a measuring device for events. We do not "grow old with time," we grow old with living out a span of events. The content of life is substance, materiality and quantity, and these are what endow us with age, not time, for it has nothing to bestow. Thus time is a straight line continuum while events repeat and re-cycle.

HABIT IN EVENTS

"Habit is second nature," says the wisdom of folkways but the Duke of Wellington said that habit is not second nature, it is ten times nature. Few would disagree with this for habit is the great pendulum of life that regulates so much of our living.

Psychologists object to using the term 'nature' in connection with habit because it implies that habit is something we are born with, a thing that is inherited, is in our nature. But this is entirely untrue. Habits are acquired in the course of living, are learned behavior, not 'nature.'

Having a habit means to act in the same way over and over again, to act automatically, without forethought. It does not mean to act blindly because all habits have a history of thinking, planning and decision making in the past. But once the action has been perfected after repeatedly doing it many times over, then the thinking and planning part is discarded but the action part goes on automatically, "from habit."

All events acquire a habit character. Our daily routines of work and rest, the holiday activities and the participation in family endeavors tend towards a treadmill performance. It is good that this is so for if we had to stop and take serious though before each trivial action then life would slow down to a snail pace and we would need a day of 48 hours to accomplish what we now do in 24 hours. Little boys and girls are burdened with many bad habits but they also acquire a full stock of good ones.

SUMMARY

Events are an experience of life. They are the greater experience, exceeding those of the body and mind alone, and they mark our passage through life. Whether we look forward in life or look backward, the vision we see is a series of events for they are the great landmarks of living. Our search for well-being and contentment in life is found in life-events.

Chapter 6

Experience as a Process

The most basic, most fundamental fact of life for the human being is that all living, all existence is one of action, of never-ceasing activity. The most inclusive description of the human person is that he and she are an action creature that never stops acting from birth until death. Men and women think and feel of course but these too are life actions.

This constant activity is called human behavior because it is not done willy-nilly and haphazardly but rather with a purpose and an aim. Man thinks and therefore acts with a purpose, in a known direction. As purposeful action it is resolved into a particular manner of performance called a process, that is, a step-by-step method of conducting the business of living. There are five distinct parts to this process of behavior: Motivation, deliberation, a decision, an action and a result.

These five steps of behavior are always present in each event although not all in the same degree of presence. For example, notice that the first two steps are motive and deliberation. Now any activity often repeated becomes a habit and is performed more or less automatically so that we tend to omit the thinking part, or at least to be aware of it. For example, when the alarm rings in the morning we simply roll out of bed and go into action without any particular thought about what is to be done; we eat breakfast without any consideration of the body motivation of need of nourishment; we arrive at work concerned to perform our job well, totally unaware that the real motivation is to obtain money for the well-being of our self and our family. But despite this omission of concentrated thinking, there is always some mental direction so that the five parts of behavior listed below are always present.

A MOTIVATION

The word motive comes from the Latin and means to move, so a motivation is something that moves a person to act. We call these motives by various names such as a need, a want or a desire. For example, I am hungry because my body needs nourishment and so this is my motive for action; I desire to purchase a radio and this is the motive that sends me off to work to earn money with which to purchase a radio; I wish to have justice in the world and this moves me to support the cause of political freedom.

The motivations of man are as plentiful as the leaves on a tree, approximately 17,000 in all. These motivations take many forms but may be grouped into categories to illustrate their content. Little explanation is needed because these needs and wants are the common experience of every person.

Biological needs. The biological arousals and urges were reviewed in the chapter of Body Experiences. Prominant needs are food, water, air, sexual satisfaction, waste elimination, relief from pain, relief from fatigue.

Child care needs. This is a two-generation necessity of parent and child association, a need to perpetuate the race. Each child is born into a world a helpless creature and must have physical care to survive. We are accustomed to thinking of the mother-child relationship as a constant sharing of love but love is not necessary to survival. What is vital is food and physical care so that the child may live. If there is love then that is fine and desirable, but it is not necessary. There have been societies where the child was given away, sold or hired out as an economic tool, even killed if the child was a burden or of unwanted sex, but the children were cared for in their early years. Survival for a child is a biological need all aside from any emotional feeling.

Emotional motivation. Love, hate and fear, sometimes called the primary emotions, are all motivators in human behavior.

Personal wants and desires. In addition to our essential needs in life there is a glittering mountain to tempt our wants and wishes. Some of the things are deemed necessary to our modern style of living while others fall into the class of pleasure living. The needs of food, clothing and housing can be filled in a modest fashion and still be sufficient but man is seldom satisfied with the ordinary and so he wants and demands the superlative, wants his living trimmed with wealth, refinement, artful embellishment and sophistication. Not just potatoes and bread but shrimp and caviar, not common wood for shelter but glass and stone with indoor climate.

Personal ideals. In addition to the physical needs each individual seeks to achieve such personal ideals as honor, respect, honesty, charity and wisdom. They are values of goodness or badness, worth or unworthiness, and are strong motivators in human behavior.

Social ideals. Like the personal ideals, these are also values of life in goodness and worthiness and we know them as freedom, justice, equality, non-oppression and world peace. Although these are social in the sense that they are ideals of the group, nevertheless each individual is motivated to strive for these high goals.

These groups of motives exemplify the forces that inspire mankind in his behavior. They have no hierarchy in value for all are constant motivators and cannot be entirely removed from the human scene of behavior. However, there are some lists of motives that are given by hierarchy according to their essentiality and primacy and it is helpful in understanding motives to note one of these. The well known and widely used classification by Abraham Maslow has this escalated pattern:

1. Physical needs: Such as food, clothing, shelter and sex.
2. Safety needs: Protection of the body from harm.
3. Social needs: The relationship one has with other persons such as acceptance, love, approval and belonging.
4. Self esteem needs: Desire for worth, status and self-respect.
5. Self-actualization needs: Fulfillment of the whole person, success in life, a contentment with goals achieved.

A DELIBERATION

As man is a reasoning creature he thinks before he acts, at least where the behavior pending is of importance. After the motivation a person will consider the pros and cons, the ways and means, the feasibility of completing the action with a favorable outcome. The cost in time and money will be weighed, the availability of facilities to complete the project, even climate and weather will enter the deliberation. Such personal factors as health and skill must also be taken into account.

A DECISION

This is the sharp edge between deliberation and action, the decision To Do or Not To Do, a vote of For or Against, of Yes or No. If the decision is negative then the matter is abandoned, if favorable, then action is the next order of business.

THE ACTION, OVERT BEHAVIOR

Whatever the project — a marriage, a journey, an illness to be treated, an academic examination — then the appropriate action will be taken.

A RESULT

Man always seeks a favorable conclusion, a worthy end comparable to the original aim. But the goal attained is often negative and adverse, less than anticipated, even a total failure.

LIFE EXPERIENCE AS A SYSTEM

Many text books today explain the experiences of life in terms of a system rather than just a pattern of happenings. Here there is a sharper definition of the steps or stages and it is a most helpful insight to the occurance of an event.

Here we have a three stage division of the whole: A motivation or stimulation, the action or behavior itself, the result or effect. These stages are as follows:

The input. This is the data or information that is communicated into the system. In the case of a human being it is the information that goes into the mind, that which stimulates or motivates. As we reviewed above this would include such data as the wants and needs called biological arousals, the need for safety protection from harm, the desire for ideals such as freedom, the seeking of a goal such as a job career or achievement in art, the undertaking of a journey.

The thruput. This consists in an awareness of the input and an interpretation of it, the meaning of it, what to do about it. This is the period of thinking, planning and calculating as to means and methods. An emotional feeling will accompany the thinking.

The end of this stage will be a decision on the course of action: An attempt to complete the whole, complete only part or even modify that which already exists.

The output. This is the direct action itself including the result of the action.

IN SUMMARY

Experiencing life as a process consists in the five stages of motivation, deliberation, a decision, an action and an end accomplished. It is a process that occupies the days and years of our life in a never ending series of events. In minor happenings the whole series of steps may not be noticed but in all major events, in any important undertaking, all five are always present.

Chapter 7
Personality

In the preceding chapters we have examined the individual in his several parts of body and mind. In this chapter we shall review the whole person, the parts combined into a one, and known by the term personality.

There is no fine description for the word 'personality' but it is generally intended to include all of the mental, physical and social abilities as they are displayed in the behavior of a person. As the self is usually referred to as the inner person, so the personality is taken to mean the outer person, the visible human. It is the self in overt behavior. We see a person and we recognize his personality by such actions as aggressiveness, cheerfulness, shyness, friendliness or timidity.

Two words that are sometimes used instead of the term personality are character and temperament. These are proper but have a lesser width in describing a whole person. Character refers more to the moral make-up of an individual while temperament expresses the emotional side. Personality, on the other hand, includes these two terms within its boundaries.

It is important to recognize at the beginning that our personality is not a concrete thing that we own as a part of our being but is instead a product of our behavior. We go out into the world and act in our own peculiar way: We are ambitious or lazy in our actions, we strive mightily or lackadaisically, we succeed more often than we fail in the goals we set. It is such behavior that stamps our personality upon us. A healthy person who sat in a chair day after day, staring into space, would be described as a chair sitter and his only traits of personality would be "he sits in a slumped position and is skinny." Beyond that there would be no personality.

But few people sit in a chair throughout their life for man is an active creature, always in motion, always "on the go," for there is work to be done, a striving for success and the attainment of goals. It is in this process of behavior that we acquire our characteristics of personality and in this sense that personality is a result of behavior.

PERSONALITY AT BIRTH

The new-born child is almost totally devoid of personal traits except the physical resemblance to other humans. This is so because it has not yet begun to behave in the world of man and nature. We do inherit from our parents certain tendencies to act but we develop these in our own peculiar fashion. The total life qualities at birth may be viewed under the three topics of body, mind and social abilities.

The biological part. We arrive in the world biologically complete, fully formed, with all of the senses and organs that we will ever get including a heart, lungs, digestive system, skeletal and muscle systems. We are equipped with all that is necessary for life, including the instinct to live and stay alive. There will be no new parts added during our life time except teeth, and all that happens to the body from here on is a process of biological growth. There will be an increase in size and in abilities such as walking, running and playing the piano but these are only a deft manipulation of the biological parts we are born with such as the fingers, arms, legs, ears and eyes.

Biologically the human baby is little different than a turtle or horse and after a few early months of care will go through life in the same fashion as the turtle or horse, constantly renewing the biological parts of his or her body, protecting and caring for it. There may be a father and mother to help at the beginning but they are merely a handy provider and care taker in the biological department.

The mental part. We come into the world with a mind that is totally blank, empty and devoid of any abilities whatsoever. All that we possess is a mental capacity, a brain and nerves that can absorb information. Eventually we learn to think and reason but we cannot do these things at birth for the mind is without intelligence on day one, it has only a potential to learn and to know. In the mental department mother and father will serve a critical need in the teaching of the newly born.

The social part. Although man is described as a social animal, this term does not apply to the new-born child, for he enters the world a most un-social being. Like his mental part, the social part is a blank and must be developed from zero. His only abilities are to suck, squawk and evacuate and in polite society these things are considered anti-social, so in this respect he must start from below zero as a social creature. Despite this negative beginning he does enter the world with a full capacity to learn and to act in a social manner.

ACQUIRING A PERSONALITY

We acquire our personality, we become a whole person, during the period from birth to about eighteen years, the time when full maturity is reached. At this time our physical appearance is fixed, we have a full awareness of self, our behavior has formed into a pattern and we now exhibit our traits of personality in the manner in which we live and associate with other persons. We will further develop some parts of our person to a higher or more extended degree such as in leadership or a musical ability but the personality is largely set and fixed. We are that person known as John or Mary, Alex or Elizabeth, an entity of personality.

The years between early childhood and eighteen are known as the maturing years. It is a period of growing physically in the body, mentally in the mind and emotions and in social association with other persons. This is the normal and natural progress of all humans, but there is an unseen development taking place that is of the most extreme value and it is this: These maturing years are a preparation for all of life that is to follow. Every authority on human behavior asserts that this is the most important single period of life because that which takes place here will affect the remainder of one's life. It is here that the pattern is set, the course fixed and the ability to accomplish is developed. It is here that our personality is acquired.

Biological maturing. Physical growth in the human being is complete at about the age of eighteen years. Neither the body as a whole nor any of its parts will increase in size thereafter. The senses and organs are also complete and any nourishment taken into the body is for replacement, not growth.

Although physical growth ends at eighteen, physical development never ceases. The physical action of the body is known as motor behavior and it begins with crawling, walking, running, climbing, skipping. In time there will come the ability to maneuver the arms, legs and fingers in handling tools and instruments, in painting and carving, in throwing, hitting and catching a ball. These are coordinated by the mind but are performed by the physical body.

Psychomotor activities are sometimes given by abilities, such as: Strength to perform, speed in performance, precision of action, flexibility of the body and coordination of the body.

Mental maturing. The mind does not grow in the sense that the body does because it is not a concrete thing, not an object, although the ancient Greeks taught that it was an organ in the body. Aristotle rejected this but he thought that the mind was located in the heart. Today we know that the site of the mind is in the brain and is coupled to the nervous system.

The mind consists in such elusive things as ideas, concepts and imagination. The human does not possess these qualities in embryo and so the mind must be cultivated and developed to bring these abilities to a maturity. This development process, as all know, consists of the many years of instruction and training at home, at school, by self instruction and in the experiences of life. The objective is to acquire the abilities to think, to reason, make decisions and solve problems. These goals are attained to a reasonable degree at or about the age of eighteen at the same time that physical maturity is reached. The mind does not stop developing at this point in the same fashion that the body stops growing but instead continues to increase and extend throughout the remainder of a person's life for as long as the person attends the matter. But the mind does reach a maturity by early adulthood that will characterize the person. This mature capability of the mind will be the steersman for the person throughout the adult years.

Social maturing. To be social has one dominant meaning and that is to have a relationship, an interaction with other human beings. We do this, we relate and associate in two major ways. In the first we behave either in cooperation or in competition with another person, and in the second manner we act either aggressively or in a friendly way. It is the learning of these two types of associating that brings the child to a maturity in social relations.

We should not mistake emotions as a social relating. The emotions of love and hate are feelings within the person while a social relating is an overt action. Emotion may be present and even greatly influence the social relation because feelings accompany most actions, but these are inner springs while socializing is an outer behavior, a physical action that is either one of cooperation or one of opposition.

We acquire our social personality in four major areas of living. First is in the home, in the family environment and the early teachings of the parents. To a very large degree this first learning is also a mimic of the parents and other siblings. Next comes the school environment where the first social contacts take place outside the parental guidance. The third area of social relating is in peer groups such as the play group, neighborhood gang, and organizations such as the Scouts, youth and church units. Fourth is television, the media that has come to have a major influence on the mind of young and old alike as it presents the world of fact, fiction and opinion directly into the home environment.

THE PERSONALITY

Personality is the term used to describe the characteristics of the whole person. It is not a separate entity from the individual but is instead merely the manner in which the person lives and exhibits his or her style of living. On the one hand there is a person who behaves in his or her own particular way and on the other hand a personality of behavior. In fine, it is one and the same being, two parts of a whole.

As noted above, personal behavior takes place in two distinct ways, first within the person and is known as the self, and secondly in outward, overt actions which dispaly one's personality. These are the two aspects of the person that we shall now examine.

Self – The Inner Person. The word 'self' has two meanings in the common usage of the term. In the first case it is used to indicate the whole person as we see it in such statements as: I (my-self) am going to London, John is a very self-ish person, they all dressed them-selves in colorful clothes. It is also used in a combining form to indicate the whole person, such as: Self-care, self-study, self-disgrace and self-posed. In all of these instances we are speaking of the entire individual, not just the inner self.

The second meaning of the term is of the inner person, the inner self, the mental self. It consists in the beliefs, the attitudes and memories of past events which together make-up the major content of the mind and is thus the cause of our thinking of ourselves as a self, as a my-self. It imparts a sense or image of "I," "me," of "mine."

This inner self is the total content of our experiences in life that is stored in the mind and it is this sum that constitutes the self. It is the subjective part of the person while the outward action is the objective part.

This inner behavior of the mind or the self has no clear-cut divisions but we can distinguish several aspects that in review will help to clarify the behavior of the self.

1. *The Image of Self.* This is sometimes called the self-identity part, the knowing that "I am me, a person alone, and the rest of the world is another thing." It is the separation of our own self from all the rest of creation, an internal catalog of our separate and individual being.

   This vision of "my self" is a feeling that "I am a particular person, separate from other humans, I exist apart from you, from them, from they." Martin Buber made the distinction as "I" and "thou." William James drew the difference of the world split into two great halves, me and not-me. Others have uses such terms as Me vs. Thee, and I-self, me-self.

   We also see this self-identity in our abilities such as: I can swim, I can sing, I am able to drive an automobile. We learn at an early age and continue through life to identify the self with possessions, such as: My bicycle, my home and my books.

2. *The Esteem of Self.* Here we make an evaluation of our person, of our self-worth and of our worth as a person. It is a judgment we make as to worth in abilities, in behavior and in our status in life. We see it in such phrases as: I am a good father, I am an optimistic person, I am ill, I am never angry. And of course we also mark the negative side of the sheet as: I have failed, I slighted that person, I could have done a better job.

Esteem is also expressed in the following examples. When a person is insulting toward me he does not degrade my stooped body or my stupid mind but rather he insults "me." It is not my mind and body that goes to work each day it is "I" who report for work. My body is never sick (except to the doctor), it is "I" who am sick and in pain. When all of my wants and needs are satisfied, it is not my body and mind that is pleased, it is "I" who am contented.

3. *The Ideal Self.* When we evaluate or esteem ourselves we make a judment upon our real self as we see it. In addition to this real self we also harbor a vision of an ideal self, that which we would like to be, that to which we aspire to be. Few people are fully content with their lot in life and so desire a higher station, a loftier position, a more productive life, a greater fulfillment in the work they normally perform. These are the ideals of accomplishment and growth that we foster within our concept of self.
4. *The self as decision maker.* In the ideal self we express what we want, in the self as decision maker we express what we will. In the first case we merely aspire to a goal, in the second we firm-up the self and declare that we shall march forward and attain the end. As we have previously seen, first there is a motive but at the second level there is decision, first to take an action and then the direction to take. It is within the self that this judgment takes place as we see in such phrases as: I will, I am going to do it, my course is firmly set.

These four aspects of the self are not fixed departments in the mind nor do they remain constant throughout life. The self acts somewhat in the manner of a deposit bank within the mind. As we learn about life and experience it in our daily living, these are funds of living that become an addition to the account, not as an add-on but rather as a mix-into. That is, the whole remains a single self but a changed one, a different one. If the mix-in is good, it is an improvement, and the self becomes a better instrument to guide us in the conduct of living. If, on the other hand, the mix-in is bad or negative, to that degree then the "good self" is lessened.

We may note one further facet of the self. Many persons designate such entities as a moral self, a social self, a criminal self or a symbolic self. There is not the slightest evidence of such "selfs." A person may have a propensity to act as a criminal or in a social way but they are not wholly criminal or totally social. All humans have such qualities in some measure.

Personality — The Outer Person. This second part of personality is the visible behavior of a person, the activity that can be seen, in contrast to the inner self which cannot.

Trying to fit people into a slot by type and traits has occupied the mind of man from early times. Hippocrates, the Greek physician, was among the first to classify, dividing people into four groups by temperament: Chloric (irritable), melancholic (depressed), sanguine (optimistic), and phlegmatic (listless). But to date there is no complete and final list and probably never will be because of the great diversity in people but classifying by type and trait is an aid in understanding personality and these are the two heads that we shall use.

1. *Personality by type.* A general classification begun by Eduard Spranger and that is widely used to group people by type is as follows:

    Theoretical person, (scholars, scientists).
    Aesthetic person, (artist, musician, writer).
    Economic person, (salesman, businessman, banker).
    Social person, (teacher, social worker, clergy).
    Political person, (leaders, executives, military).
    Religious person, (those who hold high ethical values).

    There is a well-known classification by body type, given by Sheldon and also by Kritchner:

    Endomorphy, tending to stoutness, roundness.
    Mesomorphy, well proportioned in bone and muscle.
    Ectomorphy, fragile and thin in body.

    Carl Jung introduced two terms that are quite commonly used to describe a person:

    Introvert, (to work alone, to avoid large groups).
    Extrovert, (outgoing, sociable).

No person can be assigned wholly and totally to any one class shown above. About all that can be said is that these are dominant characteristics and stem largely from the manner and style of one's living. For, after all, if we pursue a political or religious life, after a time we begin to exhibit the characteristics of such a regimen of living in our person.

2. *Personality by traits.* A trait refers to only one attribute in a person such as "he is lazy." But we are all, all too human and so the trait "lazy" is spread across the whole of the person even though, in addition to being lazy, he may also be a good provider for his family, popular in the community, be wealthy and generous in his giving. But alas he exhibits laziness and to that department he is wholly relegated. The point to note is that while reviewing traits is helpful in understanding personality, it can also be deceptive if single traits are applied to the person as a whole, when in reality they are merely one aspect of a complex, behaving person.

    Some well-known trait designations are:

Trustful — suspicious	Nervous — calm
Impulsive — restrained	Cool — excitable
Timid — self-assured	Submissive — self-assertive
Sociable — anti-social	Friendly — antagonistic

Alert — inattentive	Aggressive — sensitive to others
Perserving — fickle	Emotionally Stable — easily upset
Slow — energetic	Thoughtful — frivolous
Dreamer — doer	Emotionally expressive — reserved
Cheerful — depressed	Polished — awkward

In summary we may say that the essence of personality consists in these three parts: The general appearance of the person in body type, the inner self and the outward behavior as exhibited in certain traits. After the early years of maturing, after the age of eighteen, these elements become a pattern of organization that identifies each individual as a separate and distinct one, as a particular human being.

Part II
PERSONAL LIVING

Chapter 8

Personal Well-Being

Personal living is the life that each individual lives alone, day by day and year by year, separately and to himself or herself. It does not mean to live in isolation, away from one's fellowmen, but rather it is that part of life and living in which the individual indulges, as an individual, that part of existence that belongs to each alone. For example, we live within a family group and attend school in a student group, nevertheless we are each a person apart, are separate beings within a home and school environment. The home and school are merely a social setting for our personal living.

Well-being in life is the great goal which the individual seeks in his or her personal living. This well-being, as we shall come to learn in the chapters that follow, is achieved in twelve arenas of living and designated as the Twelve Goals of Life. We know these elements of living as the family, mental ability, social association and religion, twelve in all. Before turning to these divisions of life we shall examine the meaning of the term well-being in this chapter.

WELL-BEING IN LIFE

When the French philosopher Rene Descartes began his great work of philosophy he resolved to start from one fundamental fact which he asserted to be: Cognito, ergo sum — I think, therefore I am. Let us in a similar fashion begin our inquiry into human living by stating the fundamental fact of existence: I live, and to keep on living I must forever seek a condition of well-being. This is the basic fact of life for all living things, animals and plants as well as human beings. Without a reasonable quantity of well-being organic things cannot live for they wither away and die, whereas, in a continuing state of well-being all living things prosper, increase and flourish.

For the human being the term 'well-being' has a broader meaning than it does for plants and animals which cannot think, plan or reason, construct institutions or live in a social relationship, as man does. Thus the human being must not only satisfy his organic needs but also a set of mental and social requirements as well. Man does not seek merely to survive but to do so on a high level, on a human level.

The broad meaning of the term 'well-being' is to have health, sufficient material goods and contentment. Clearly, at sight, it means a condition in our being, (our body and mind), that is well, is good, is pleasant. And clearly, it implies a condition or state of being when the body and mind are not ill, not uncomfortable, not unpleasant.

Well-being in the person refers to a condition of health in the body, free from pain, a certain mental tranquility when the mind is able to deal with the business of life, and a nominal wealth or income with which to obtain the necessities for living. When we possess these facilities in a reasonable degree they impart to our living a pleasure, a contentment, a well-being. If we have their opposite such as sickness, poverty and misery, then our existence is one of ill-being.

Such terms as joy, sensual pleasure and happiness do not necessarily express well-being in the person for they are too narrow. Our personal condition in life may be well and in good order without the emotional sensations of joy and happiness. Well-being refers to a concrete, long-term state of living while joy and happiness are transient in nature. If these emotional sensations follow upon and occur along with well-being then this is good and desirable but not a requisite to that state. Indeed, happiness is a following sensation, a by-product of having attained well-being. It is like the runner who strives mightily to win the race by crossing the line first and thus attain that state of well-being, the winner. The award of the cup is a happiness, the result of winning.

THE PEARL OF GREAT PRICE

No goal in life, no possession of life can compare with that of well-being. It is the summa bonum, the highest state of existence that we can attain here on earth. As it is the supreme good then it follows naturally that the seeking of it is the highest quest in which we can engage as we expend our time from birth until death. Every single day we must seek with some vigor to enhance our health, our skills and our friendships, and beyond this to gain freedom, equal opportunity and justice for all persons. In this quest and with these possessions we will have found the pearl of great price, a well-being in life and living.

Chapter 9
The Goals of Life

All human living is conducted according to a plan, by a method that is inherent in the process of life itself. In general terms this is the plan: There is a goal or an end to attain, there is a striving or effort by the person to reach that goal, there is a satisfaction in the mind and body upon attainment of the goal. This is not an artificial design of the philosopher, is not a formula of science, is not a doctrine of faith. It is simply the way of nature and the way of mankind, the manner by which the individual alone and the human race itself proceeds along a continuum of living.

This process of life and living is called goal seeking. It is the way of man because it is imbedded in his basic being, is the system by which life is renewed and revived. Dr. Harold G. Wolff and others state that the very function of the brain confirms the nature of man as a goal seeker. When we have a need or a desire the brain both perceives the need and indicates the direction of action that is to be taken. For example, when a danger appears and is noted by the brain it immediately sets a goal to be achieved, namely, an action to protect from the danger. It is a process of goal directed activity, is the way of life, is the way of living.

We should note that the terms 'task' and 'goal' are often used interchangeably here. The goal of course is the end to attain while the task is the work to perform to achieve the goal. For example, if the goal is to form a sports team then the task is to do so; if the object is to marry and establish a family then the task is to do so. While the goal is merely an end, an aim, and the task involves all the work and labor, nevertheless, the two terms do designate the same activity of effort.

THE PATTERN OF GOAL SEEKING

The goals of well-being that we seek in life such as health, safety and a family unit must be striven for. They are not a product to be purchased at the store but are a condition of life that requires effort and behavior to attain. This seeking follows a pattern that applies to all of the goals.

Of course the details and actions will differ according to whether the end is love, war, health or sex but the pattern will be the same. Even the child, who knows nothing about goals, copes with the business of living through the goal seeking pattern. His needs of food and diaper change are goals that he achieves through loud howling and his "baby ways" gains him the love and friendship he desires.

The pattern as here outlined is something of a logical order but we must remember that the several steps may be taken in a different sequence for life does not proceed in a strict order. Human behavior is not a chemical formula or a mechanical process into which one can feed raw materials and have pop out a finished product. We are each differently motivated from within and we perform our tasks with a different fire of effort but the pattern, the steps and stages, are similar for all.

Motivation. We have reviewed the basic motives in the chapter titled Experience as a Process and only need to state here that all of the twelve goals are of course the great motives for our behavior. We are motivated toward these ends for two reasons. First, they are the source for all of our well-being, for our enjoyment and contentment in life. Secondly, it is just plain common sense to do so. No human seeks ill-being such as pain and misery as a way of life for it is simply un-human to do so, is anti-human. It is even anti-animal for no living thing seeks pain and discomfort. A person ill in the mind might do so but not a normal human. The whole urge of nature and the reasoning of man is to seek high and beneficial ends, to struggle to win, not struggle to lose.

Cause in motivation. The word 'goal' is not a vacant term but is instead a cause of behavior, the reason for an action. This is so because goals are a teleological cause, a condition in which the cause is in the future, before the event, not in the past.

There are two principal types of causes. In the first, called the efficient cause, the reason for the action or force is in the past. For example, if you chop at the base of a tree, the tree will eventually topple over. Here the cause (chopping) came before the effect (tree falling). Again, when you have an illness in the body (cause), you will suffer pain (result). In both cases there was efficient cause for the effect.

In human behavior the cause is not in the past but is in the future, it is teleological. For example, the thing in the future that causes me to act is a goal I wish to attain such as wealth, health, leisure activity, social association. I see these goals as desirable ends and so I act to obtain them. The cause in in the future, not the past, or as Aristotle put it, a final cause, that on account of which the action is taken.

Accordingly then, we shall constantly remark on the goal of health, the goal of safety and the goal of religion, bearing in mind that these are also the cause of our behavior.

Set a goal level. The life goals themselves are set, are fixed because they are necessary to life and there is no question of selecting one or another. What does involve choice, however, is the level to which we each may aim and attain in each of the goals. This is quite clear at a moment's notice. For example, shall education end at middle school or should I go on to college, or even select a trade school; shall I have a family of five children or perhaps none; shall I forego much leisure for high success in my chosen work career; shall I live in the country or the city. These are levels or degrees of goal selection that each must make alone or decide with the help of counseling.

Planning. Clearly this involves the devising of a method to attain a goal, a mental formulating of the ways and means. The usual procedure is to use the problem solving scheme outlined in the Mental Abilities chapter. The extent of planning will depend on the project but will include such elements as the facilities needed, the means of obtaining them, the cost, the means to execute and the manner of executing, of procedure.

Assemble the means. All plans must be implemented with the tools to do the job, usually classified in two lists.

1. The physical resources. This will extend into money, tools, equipment, land needed, housing, machines, goods and perhaps labor. Few jobs can be accomplished without some physical facilities, if only a pencil and paper to compile a list of the things needed.
2. Ability resource. This means the intelligence and skill to perform the task which might range all the way from the professional ingenuity to perform a heart transplant to the skill in tying a shoe lace.

Action toward the goal. Here we shall alter the old adage of nothing ventured, nothing won to nothing attempted, nothing done. We will not say "nothing won" for even to try and fail is something done even though it is nothing more than a lesson learned. This step of the process is the actual engagement in the work, the overt effort toward attainment of the goal, the physical behavior of the individual.

THE NATURE OF LIFE-GOALS

Life-goals do not have the same meaning, do not dignify the same attainment as do the ordinary objectives of living such as the runner who dashes across the finish line and achieves his goal as a final end, or the carpenter whose goal is the construction of a table that, when completed, has attained his objective, his end. Life-goals are never accomplished in this fashion, that is, as a final end, a single completion. They do not have an absolute end. They are, in fact, a temporary attainment that is reached and held for a time period and then must be re-attained again, over and over again.

This need for repeated goal attainment is caused by the nature of our wants and needs which are only satisfied for a short time and then must be re-satisfied. The goals that we achieve are "life thing," are living goals much like an organism that must be constantly nourished. Our thirst is an example. When thirsty we reach for a glass of water. Now the water is not the goal but simply the means of reaching the goal, namely to satisfy thirst. Soon, within a few hours we are thirsty again and so the cycle is repeated once more.

Like thirst, the great goals of life have this same need for re-achievement. Health, family needs, mental ability and social association must forever be renewed, the goal re-attained on a time basis of daily, weekly, annually. For example we strive to acquire money to purchase the necessities of life which are soon consumed and then there is a re-seeking of money to repeat the process; a family never reaches a state of completion for it is a life-time project of sub-goals to be reached such as food, clothing, shelter, family affiliation, joint ventures.

We see then that these goals of living have no ultimate attainment, the individual never arrives at a terminal point. They are like mile posts where one arrives and then pauses for a brief time in temporary satisfaction, but soon the urge to move forward appears and the journey begins anew toward the next mile post. It does not mean a new beginning but rather a continuation of the life journey toward a new achievement.

THE MANY ROLES OF GOALS

All goal seeking, whether the twelve life goals or one of the many sub-goals have values beyond the mere process of seek and find satisfaction. We shall review these extra qualities briefly.

The dual-action in goal seeking. In all striving to attain a goal or an end there is a two-way action, an outward flow of energy and an inward flow. In formal logic this reciprocity of action is expressed as "the end which" and "the end for whom," and it means the goal that is sought and the person for whom the goal is sought. The outward action is a striving *at*, an effort to *attain.* The inward action is the benefit that is received, the positive result, the gaining of a possession (the goal). Or, in the case of a failure, the inward flow of an un-benefit.

As direction finders. When the sailor puts to sea in the northern hemisphere he has an unfailing direction finder in the North Star. When the individual human pursues the journey of living, he too must have a direction finder, a guide toward the distant harbor. The great harbor is of course personal well-being and the way to it is found in the twelve life goals to be examined in the following chapters. We constantly steer our course by these goals, traveling toward each of their harbors.

Goals stabilize and orient. Goals not only serve as direction finders but they also stabilize our life along the journey enroute. They impart a fixation to our living that gives order, unity and coherence. They allow us to move forward with a certain precision and confidence that we are doing so according to the dictates of man and nature, and perhaps even God.

The absence of goals in life is a sign of abnormal living, is one of frustration, stress and despair. This is one great problem with mentally retarded and demented persons. These people have lost the vision of goals or else never developed any and so they have nothing by which to orient their life, no project to undertake, no task to be accomplished. What ever minor task they can perform must be of short duration and under close supervision because they cannot set long-term goals, cannot foresee a distant achievement. While there may be organic deficiency, these persons are also ill from a lack of goal seeking.

Goals belong to the individual alone. Goals, as goals, cannot be shared with other persons, they belong to the individual alone. Other persons may be involved such as family, friends and work partners, but these, too, are individuals seeking goals and well-being. A group of people may band together in pursuit of a project but the goal accrues to the individual as a personal accomplishment, the value of well-being is known only to the individual person, not the group as such.

As man is a social animal, most seeking of goals is conducted in a social setting or in accompaniment with other persons. It is a sharing of goal seeking. But, although the process takes place in a social environment, the seeking and attaining is performed by the individual alone.

One at a time. While it is possible to kill two birds with one stone throw, it is a very rare success. Solving goal problems have something of this nature. While all of the life goals always require attention, only one is usually dominant in presence, the one that is in process of being sought, the one upon which action is being taken. Even the human brain which can solve a thousand problems a day handles them one at a time.

Life goals cannot be set aside. Small projects may be pushed aside, delayed or even abandoned but the life goals cannot be so treated. They are a life process and life may not be tampered with. In addition, there are two prompters to goal seeking that further preclude neglect. First, it is inbred in human nature to seek goals for it is the basic process for survival. Secondly, every social culture has standards and norms to which the society requires the individual to conform and so these norms are goals which the individual must attain. Seeking goals is the treadmill to which both man and nature have committed the individual person.

THE TWELVE DEMANDS OF LIFE

Man's love of freedom is such that the term 'demand' seems to be a restraint but it is not so in the twelve goals of life for they are not demands to restrict but rather to increase, to make better, to improve. Attainment of a goal is not a constriction but an expansion of the self and the personality and as such is an avenue to well-being, the ultimate attainment. So if man and nature together demand that we each achieve within the twelve goals of life, it is a demand that is good, not evil.

These life goals, the twelve demands will be reviewed in the chapters immediately following.

Chapter 10
Physical Health

The ancient symbol of health was the serpent because it could shed its skin and thereby renew itself, appear young again. And of course this is the aim of all humans who become ill, to restore the body to a condition of health and well-being after a time of sickness, to shed the affliction from the body and thereby regain health.

Although the ancient symbol still appears in modern literature, modern man, through medical science, has learned to prevent ill-health as well as to restore to health after an illness. Man knows that disease and sickness does not come from bile, vapor and miasma but rather from tiny bugs called germs, living organisms that invade the body, and from harmful chemicals and rays. Armed with this knowledge men of science and medicine now work as hard to prevent sickness as they do to cure it.

The miracles that medical science can perform in both prevention and cure of disease must still be viewed in perspective for it is largely corrective, not curative. The doctor and his medicine can kill the disease germ, or remove the injured part by surgery but it is the body itself that does the healing. And that body belongs to the individual, to you and I, who must perform the action, first to prevent and then to nurse the healing process after the doctor has done his part of halting the forward progress of the illness.

Health care of the body is the domain of the individual alone, the one on whom the full responsibility falls. The physician or surgeon can advise but only the person can perform the chore of personal care. As we shall note below, this care is a technique of action to maintain the body in a state of good or reasonable health.

HEALTH DEFINED

Health is a condition in the body in which the tissues are free from disease, are nourished with energy building food and there is a feeling of vigor, of well-being. Given this condition then the body can perform its normal functions of work, play and thinking and is resilient enough to endure the usual shocks and disturbances of life. Health is the opposite of sickness, disease and continued exhaustion.

We must take note however that health does not mean the total absence of illness or disease. The human body is never totally free of all disorder. There are always aches and pains, worry and strain, perhaps injury or deformities in the body. There is always some "bad" along with the good. But the presence of these negative qualities does not mean "not healthy," for the body still has a sufficient reserve of "good health" as to offset these lesser deficiencies or to fight off their invasion. Even when these afflictions become established in the body, if they are not excessive, the human can adjust to them and still live a normal, a healthy life.

BODY DIVISIONS

The several body parts shown here are also given in the chapter Man on Earth, where they were given as the biological structure of man. They are re-listed here as the several parts of the body that must be cared for in order to attain a state of physical well-being, a condition of health.

The sense organs. These are the gateways to the brain and nervous system. It is through these organs or orifices that we receive and learn to understand the physical environment in which we live. As such, they are also the entrance way to the body for disease germs.

- The eyes, for sight, for seeing.
- The ears, through which we hear the sounds of life.
- The nose, with which we smell the odors of life.
- The tongue, for tasting the bitter and the sweet.
- The skin, by which we feel the cold, the heat, and pain.

The body systems. Each of these body systems operates as a separate and distinct unit because each has its own separate activity or process for maintaining the body in good health. But they also operate conjointly as s super-system within the whole biological structure of the human body. Accordingly, disease or deficiency in one system may have a mild or serious effect on another one.

1. *The skeletal system.* This consists in the muscles and bones by which we achieve our locomotion of walking and running, dexterity and skill of movement such as dancing, drawing, and instrument handling.
2. *The nervous system.* This includes the brain, spinal cord and the strings of nerves that extend from the brain to every part of the body. This is the center of the mind, the site of our thinking and feeling abilities.
3. *Digestive or gastro-intestinal system.* This includes the mouth, stomach, intestines, liver, bowels, colon and rectum. Here we absorb the food we eat, convert it to energy use and then eliminate the waste.

4. *Circulatory system.* This is the heart, veins and arteries for circulation of blood through the body.
5. *Respiratory system.* This is the nose, mouth and lungs by which we breath in and expel air.

Circulation and respiration are usually combined into one unit and referred to as the cardiovascular system.

6. *Urinary system.* The kidneys and bladder.
7. *Reproductive system.* The sex organs of the male and female by which and through the birth of a child is accomplished, the method by which the human race is reproduced.

These body parts, the organs and systems, comprise the whole of the human body. It is incumbent on each individual to study and learn about these body parts for their care is the road to good health while their neglect or abuse is the sure road to illness. When these organs and systems are free of disease and in proper function, then the whole body is in good health. When any one of these parts is ill, the effect is usually felt in the other parts of the body.

HEALTH CARE

Disease cure is the province of the doctor, health care is the domain of the individual. If you wish to acquire a state of good health in the body then no one, neither in heaven nor on earth, not the doctor or his medicine, can do this for you, only the person, only you yourself, can perform the acts for health maintenance. The physician can help with advice but only you can diet, exercise and take preventative measures.

All health care begins with a schedule which the individual must prepare and adhere to because of the many factors that enter into health care such as age, general state of health, disabilities, even the facilities of the environment which vary so greatly. For example, there will be no snow skiing or mountains to climb in Florida but water skiing and swimming are readily available. Thus there is no set of rules that applies to all persons alike but there is a catalog of requirements that all must follow closely and this is listed as follows.

Nutrition. The body must have six types of chemicals for good health and must have all six on a continuing basis. If any one is omitted from the diet then the body cannot attain a condition of good health and may even be damaged by the lack. These chemicals are: Proteins, carbohydrates, minerals, fats, vitamins and water. These chemicals are obtained from four major food groups which, if eaten in amounts according to individual requirements will supply the body with the necessary nutrients for good health. The foods are:

- Meats, including fish, poultry, eggs and legumes.
- Vegetables and fruits. All fruits and all vegetables, part of which

should be green and part yellow.
- Bread — cereal. The foods made from grain.
- Milk — cheese. Source of calcium.

Hygiene.
- Personal cleanliness of the body.
- Sanitation. A clean house, garbage disposal, sewage disposal.

Clothing and shelter. For protection from the elements: Sun, rain and snow, excessive cold and heat.

Body function care. Exercise, rest, play, relaxation, elimination.

Avoid the harmful. In drugs, foods, tobacco, alcohol.

A clean environment. In air, water and soil, absence of pollution.

Preventative action. Such as: Immunization, preventative drugs, first aid for small injuries.

Stress reduction. Stress is an affliction of modern man, the result of the life-style of pressure living. The cause of stress is intensive activity and high-strung behavior, a condition that has come to be a permanent fixture. Most people can and do learn to control the affliction but some cannot cope with it and fall ill.

Stress is a two-pronged affliction, affecting both the body and the mind. The need is to reduce the stress pressure and this is accomplished for the mind by adopting a mental set or attitude which limits the mind activity to the job at hand, that is to the present circumstances of living, without working at a project and worrying about it plus other aspects of life. When the current circumstance is completed then the mind should abruptly turn to other thinking. As for the body, it finds relief from stress in relaxation and activities of a leisure nature.

The above elements of good health are learned early in life, in the home and at school, and require only the careful attention of the individual during the following course of life. But they must be practiced and attended to on a daily - weekly basis for the body wears out in the same fashion, day by day, and so it must be replenished and rejuvinated on the same basis, day by day.

Many writers look upon the business of living, including physical and mental health, as a process of adjustment. For example, we must adjust the body with the proper foods, adjust to the environment with proper clothing and shelter, adjust to the frustrations of life by coping and relaxing. This, too, is a helpful way to view life, but it seems to imply a negative attitude at least so far as the total way of life is concerned. While there is of course always a continuous process of adjustment going on, man does not wait for a condition to occur and then adjust to it. On the contrary, he acts as a goal seeker, one who strives to overcome rather than merely adjust to. In the case of health we cannot wait until disaster strikes and then adjust to it for in many cases it may be too late. If we are to attain health we must set the objective, the end to reach, and then pitch in and work toward that goal, through health care.

THE GOOD OF HEALTH

Although we designate health as a state of being it is not a static condition, not something acquired and then consumed. Its value reaches into all of life and living as we may note in the following points.

- Let us first note the wisdom of our forebears in the old adage that 'early to bed and early to rise makes a person healthy, wealthy and wise.' Observe that health comes first in priority, and that wealth and wisdom follow.
- Health for itself alone is most desirable for it is the infusion of zest and good feeling into life. Though were we to sit in a chair all of our life, (highly unlikely), yet even such neutral living would be the better if the sitter were in good health. But to go out and contend with the world and have health as a companion is the maximum in human living.
- With health as a base, all living is performed with efficiency. The mental processes, emotional feeling, motor skills, working, playing, leisure activity and social association are all accomplished with facility and proficiency.
- Health endows the body with a capacity to enjoy life, to take pleasure in the necessary activities, to experience the feeling of well-being in the self and even to embrace that most desirable state, happiness.
- And health is the great prolonger of life. Although illness is part of living, if the balance is tilted toward health then the possibility and the probability favors longevity.

Health, we may say with utmost certainty, is our most precious possession, exceeding all other aspects of life. And, although we must strive to attain a health condition, there is still something of the gift of the gods in the result.

Chapter 11

Mental Health

The human mind is considered to have two parts because of the manner in which it functions. The first part is called the cognitive mind, where our thinking processes take place and secondly, the affective mind, where our emotions are centered and controlled. In this chapter we shall review the affective mind, the emotional aspect. In a later chapter we shall consider the cognitive mind.

The word 'affective' comes from the Latin 'affectus' meaning to influence and that is precisely what the emotions do, they have an affect upon our behavior. The cognitive part of the mind performs the thinking while the affective has an influence upon that thinking and consequently upon our actions.

Mental health and physical health go hand in hand for they are after all only separate parts of the whole body. Indeed, professional persons combine the two into one word to define the whole human organism using the term psychosomatic, psyche (mind) and soma (body). But each has its realm of health and each its realm of illness, the one a physical condition of good or bad and the other a mental state of good or bad.

Mental health is acquired and maintained in the same fashion as physical health, namely, by satisfying a need. In the latter we have the need for food, exercise and rest while in the case of mental health the emotional needs are feeling needs. Following are some examples of the emotional needs that must be satisfied for good mental health.

- Need for love, including kindness, sympathy, helpfulness.
- Need for security. Not physical security and safety but rather a feeling within the self of assurance, of contentment, of firm control of one's behavior.
- For independence. Although we have a strong sense of belonging we also have a need for freedom, for liberty of action.
- For achievement. The need to win, to succeed in goal seeking is an ever-present need in the human.
- For approval by others. Approval imparts a sense of satisfaction that our behavior is appreciated, that it conforms to the group standard.

- For companionship. This is a strong need in humans and we see the ill effect of its absence in elderly persons who lose a life partner and then go on living alone.
- For expression of the self. This need is satisfied in a hobby, a leisure activity or an art project.

In addition to the complex emotions listed above, the single emotions such as love, fear, anxiety, pity and shame also play a large role in mental health. Like the complex feeling, these are also closely allied with the biological and nervous parts of the body. For example, when an emotion such as fear arises there is a response in the body of skin tingling, rapid heart beat, even a message to the motor system to take flight and run. This psychosomatic link is often expressed as: He had a look of hatred, he screamed in anger, she fled in shyness. And most humans have had occasion to express their emotions in this fashion: Crying at a time of sorrow, shouts of laughter at a time of joy and expressing determination by pounding on the table.

Satisfying the complex emotional needs or expressing the single ones strongly affects the mental health of a person. Good health requires a control of the feelings within a certain tolerance, in which they should not be exhibited in excess but then they must not be suppressed either, for all emotions are normal and natural in the human.

THE PROCESS OF EMOTIONS

Our mind, which is close to a blank page when we come into the world, is filled or develops in two ways: The thinking part grows by learning and practice while the feeling part develops largely by our living, from our behavior. That is why emotions are designated as being learned behavior, they come into being and are cultured as a result of our daily living, as we go about seeking goals of education, material well-being, a family and social association. As we pursue these quests in life we experience success here and failure there, goodness and badness, frustration and triumph. It is these activities that cause our emotional arousals and it is from these life actions that we experience our love, hate, fear, exceeding joy and dismal distress.

When an emotion is aroused it does not follow a particular path or channel but feelings do include the following four steps:

1. An arousal within the body, an inner motivating force.
2. An experience of feeling, a sensation, an excitement in the nervous system.
3. A biological action of tensing muscles, heart beat, butterflies in the stomach.
4. A physiological expression, a facial look, voice raised, an aggressive posture.

It is not correct to distinguish between emotions as being of a good or bad character, except perhaps as they apply to social manners. Conduct resulting from an emotion may be labeled good or bad but the emotion itself is not so. Love, hate and fear are simply an arousal within the body that acts as a motivating force and each has its beneficial side, even the "bad" ones. For example, without a sense of fear we might step off a cliff expecting a happy landing; persons go into war and into a new job experience with a healthy fear that alerts them to their new or dangerous environment; anxiety over a failure is proper for it prompts the person to examine the case and correct the cause of failure; love in excess can cause persons to swoon and in moments of high joy to fall down.

EMOTIONS BY NAME

There is no definitive classification of the emotions. The classical division has always been pleasure — pain, or pleasant — unpleasant. Some claim that there are only three true emotions, love, fear and anger, and that all others are derived from these. The following is a list of the common emotions, with a possible grouping into love, fear and hate.

LOVE	FEAR	OTHERS
Joy	Anxiety	Pride
Hope	Wonder	Elation
Friendship	Surprise	Shame
Sympathy	Suspicion	Forgive
Admiration	Despair	Remorse
Generosity	Bashful	Piety, reverence
Respect		Conceit
Humility	HATE	Inferior
Gratitude	Anger	Repulsion
Grief, sorrow	Jealousy, envy	Disappointment
Pity	Resentment	Boredom
Contentment	Reproach	Irritable
Affection	Hatred	Elation
Sex	Disgust	Contempt
Faith		

MENTAL ILLNESS

Every person carries within himself or herself the "germs" of mental illness in the form of anxiety, stress and frustration. These are normal in all human living and must be endured in our daily life and so long as we adjust our living and our emotions to them they come and are dispelled in the usual course of things. But if these feelings become powerful and excessive or uncontrollable, then we have stepped over the borderline into mental illness. For example, if our fear ascends to abject cowardice, if we become a recluse, if we disassociate from the normal events of a day or from our fellowmen, then we have reached a condition of mental illness. Again, if our anger ascends to an extreme height and we turn aggressive or maniacal, destroying property and injuring persons, or even inflicting injury on one's self and in far out cases even committing suicide, then this too is a state of mental illness.

In psychiatric language the terms for the cause of mental illness, as noted above, is anxiety, frustration and stress. Thus, under the stress and strain of living we become anxious and frustrated and as a result mentally ill. We become ill because the stress and tension of life is excessive, is too much for our affective mind, it is stretched too far, and so it breaks down in mental illness. Here are some typical causes of stress:

- Pain and discomfort in excess will induce a stressful condition.
- Frustration from restricted action, an inability to accomplish, more losing than winning, constant failure, high losses.
- Conflict, to be torn between two options, two goals, or with friends, spouse, job choice.
- Pressure, such as competition in work, sustained effort, difficult problems to solve or a series of rapid changes in life style.

In physical illness the body becomes disabled but in mental illness the mind becomes distorted, anti-normal, and functions in such states as moods, fantasies, phobias, withdrawal, suppression and regression. These various mind actions are grouped into two main types, the one called neurosis, meaning nervous disorders and the other called phychosis, meaning mind disorders. But the mind and nerves function as one and the common term is simply mental disorders.

The following list of disorders is representative but is not complete. It is based on the American Psychiatric Association list. A reading will acquaint one with the extent of mental disorders.

Alcohol and drug disorders. The term that is widely used is alcohol abuse and drug abuse.

Affective disorders. A depressive, mania condition, with feelings of hopelessness, loss of appetite, tendency to cry.

Anxiety disorders. These are phobia disorders, panic, obsessive tendency, nervousness, fear, uncertainty and tension.

Coversion disorder. In this disturbance the person converts his psychological stress to a physical condition, such as "not my fault because of what happened."

Child-like disorder. Mental retardation, bed-wetting at a late age, conduct disobedience, abnormal behavior.

Disassociative disorders. This is exhibited in amnesia, loss of memory, refusal to accept blame.

Personality disorders. These include some of the disorders in this list but when they become deeply ingrained in the person they appear as a trait of the person, a personality characteristic. For example, there is the person who is seclusive, shy and avoids; the emotional person who is dramatic, vain, demanding, overly forceful; and the anti-social person who ignores the social rules, is deviant in morals, has no sense of guilt, is undependable, irresponsible.

Psychosexual disorder. Here there is fetishism, sexual sadism, exhibitionism.

Paranoid disorders. This is characterized by delusions of grandeur, of persecution.

Schizophrenic disorders. Schizophrenic means split personality, that is, a psychotic condition in which the person retreats from reality, has delusions and conflicting emotions. In simple cases the person is dull, withdrawn, inactive, while in severe cases the emotional disturbance may lead to aggressive action against people, extreme display, destruction of property.

Sleep disorders. Insomnia, nightmares.

MENTAL HEALTH CARE

Physical health care can be achieved by complying with a list of Do's and Don'ts such as, "Do eat nutritious foods," and "Don't abuse the body with drugs." But mental health is not so easily controlled for the mind cannot abstain from having feelings which are the main cause of mental illness. Emotional stress is an integral part of living and it is therefore always present in the mind to some degree.

The general rule in mental health care is to know your limit and then recognize when you have reached that limit in stress and tension of life and there call a halt. Or, if not a total stopping, then to take another course of action, one in the opposite direction at least for a time, to relieve the stress. It need not be a major vacation but simply a new environment of work, of activity. Thus, it might be an evening of enjoyment with the family, a week-end of relaxation in the outdoors, engagement in an art or hobby. Many persons turn to volunteer work in the community where there is a giving of self, not work for remuneration. Others may retire to the quiet of the study for reading and a renewal of self.

The following suggestions are vague in content but help point the direction to mental health and emotional maturity.

- Have trust in the self and confidence in your abilities.
- Worry is the high road to illness.
- Abolish the sense of guilt, the sense of failure.

- Recognize your shortcomings and make allowance for them. No person is perfect.
- Share your problems with others.
- Look upon a day's work as useful employment.
- Try always to see the betterment in life, not the worst.
- Free yourself of the heavy burden of prejudice.
- Accept friendship, give friendship.
- Be dependable, be truthful.
- Conflict is part of life and all must engage.
- Alternate work with play and recreation.
- Plan for the future but live by the day.

THE GOOD OF MENTAL HEALTH

A healthy mind means more than freedom from illness for the benefits extend to all of life, all of living. A mind in health will bestow the lavish gifts of well-being, peace of mind, satisfaction in living, enjoyment of life, contentment with the world. The goal is health but the end is happiness.

Chapter 12
Physical Ability

In the language of psychology physical abilities are called motor skills, meaning the skill with which the body movements are made, such as running, dancing or using tools with the hands. Inasmuch as the mind is also involved in all body actions the exact term is psychomotor skills.

Motor activities are well known to everyone, consisting in the bodily movements such as walking, swimming, eating, talking, handwriting, car driving, drawing, piano playing. It is a combining of the body and the mind, working together in a coordinated behavior. It also includes the body and mind working in un-coordinated behavior when the brain is dulled with alcohol or drugs and the person staggers as he walks.

Motor skills have two essential parts, the learning of them and the performing of them, which we shall review in that order.

LEARNING MOTOR SKILLS

As in any type of learning there must be a goal to work toward, a mark to shoot at, an end to attain. In motor skills this will range from crawling across the floor to pet the family cat, up through running to school and then running to win a race, learning to use a scalpel to operate, performing a violin solo on an opera stage. These are goals of attainment that each must set according to his or her wish and want.

After setting the goal there must be a willingness to achieve, to succeed. And the doer must have an interest in the goal, a reason to struggle, in addition to the attitude of do or die, or else the project will come to naught.

A physical application to the task follows next. This is something of a trial run, a first effort to determine if the person is suited to the task, has the potential to succeed. The person might lack the stamina to run the marathon but is well suited to the 100 yard dash; lack of the proper dexterity with the fingers might prohibit piano playing; some physical deficiency of the eyes or ears might restrict the type of goal to which one might aspire. These are the factors that must be considered early in the learning of physical skills.

The last phase in motor learning is practice, practice, practice. For the simpler goals the practice might culminate into routine habit and require little practice and little concentration after the first learnings have been achieved. But for high and worthy goals this is not so. For the great sportsman, the violinist, the soprano, the surgeon, the athlete, practice never ceases, even after reaching the heights of the profession. In many occupations such as typing, driving a vehicle or operating a machine, practice is inherent in the daily work but learning this work did require practice in the beginning.

In the matter of practice both the physical instructor (coach or trainer), and the mental instructor (the psychologist), have a common word of advice to one and all and it is this: When you practice to acquire any type of motor skill it is best accomplished by a short period of work followed by a period of rest. Hard, sustained effort is self-defeating. This is true whether the skill you seek is in sports, music, dancing, mental activity, instrument manipulation or golf playing. The rest period allows the body to relax and the mind to assimilate new information. This method, of alternating short periods of effort with short periods of rest will produce better results, better skills, than a long practice period and then a long rest.

PERFORMING MOTOR SKILLS

This is the action itself, the "doing" of what was learned. It is body movement and motion performed with dexterity, precision, coordination, and rhythm, in short, performed with skill.

There is probably no real division of motor skill into classes but we may observe it at two levels, as follows:

Normal actions. This is random action, even habitual activity, requiring little or no concentration of thought. It would include such behavior as household chores, walking, idle talking, using simple tools, handwriting. These require little skill to perform in daily living but in the beginning had to be learned and practiced.

Skill activity. This is physical ability developed to a high degree, requiring regimen, discipline and hard practice to acquire. And then, once learned it becomes an organized pattern in performing, requiring both thinking and dexterity of movement. We see this behavior, this motor skill in the artist, musician, singer, skier and runner, the craftsman in using delicate tools, the scientist in research and experiment. It is physical ability developed to a high and precise station.

THE WHOLE BODY

There is a common saying that humans do not wear out, they rust out. The meaning is that without physical activity the body parts, especially the motor parts, will become crusted over and then be unable to move except with difficulty and in pain. With disuse the bones and muscles stiffen and harden, they solidify. Even so simple an activity as walking is an exercise of high benefit that prevents the joints from tightening.

Well-being in motor skills is achieved by learning and then by frequent practice, and there is no other way, no other road to competence in physical ability.

Chapter 13
Mental Ability

In a previous chapter we reviewed that part of the mind known as the affective mind where the emotions and feelings are centered. In this chapter we shall examine that part of the mind called the cognitive mind, where the ability to think and reason is centered. It is this ability that sets man apart from all other creatures in the world. He is Homo sapiens, the one who thinks. In all of nature only man possesses this quality, making him the supreme one on earth, the one who commands and controls the destiny of himself, all animals, even the course of nature itself.

Other creatures have a mind but they cannot think or reason. The horse may have some vague notion that he is not like a dog and therefore he lives with and according to his kind, not with and like dogs, but it is an instinctive sense at work, not a reasoned thought. Even if the horse could talk he could not explain why this is so because he cannot think.

There are no words to sing the praises of man's ability to think, it simply ranks with the giants of the universe in a list such as: Plants, sun, nature, think. It is customary to rank all of creation in the order of God, Nature and Man. In one sense this is inaccurate because man is a thing of nature just as other animals and plants are, except for one ability and this is to think, so a strict classification would be: God, Nature, Think. Man, like other creatures of nature breathes, sees, has sexual urges and waste elimination but unlike other creatures he also makes governments, airplanes, pyramids, skyscrapers, wars and goes to the moon, because he can think.

THE COGNITIVE MIND

The word 'cognitive' comes from the Latin word cognito, 'to know,' and so the cognitive mind is where we do our knowing such as learning, understanding, reasoning and judging. This knowing is not a pure and undefiled process for, as we learned in the chapter on the affective mind, emotions and feelings are also present at the time of thinking and reasoning and these have an influence upon the cognitive mind.

Strangely enough, this gigantic ability of man is entirely lacking at birth and the so-called "man the intelligent" is far from it when he enters the world. The human mind is totally blank at the beginning, without fact, without information, without knowledge of any sort. All that the newcomer has, be it male or female, is a capacity or potential to learn, to think and eventually become intelligent. Man becomes Homo sapiens, the wise one, only after a long process of gathering information, learning, being taught, and then experiencing life, a process called education.

We usually think of the brain as the place where thinking occurs but this is not totally true. Thinking is something of a chain reaction in which we see, feel and hear the outside world, and these sensations are then conducted through a chain of nerves to the brain. The brain then "thinks" about the matter, following which it sends back an impulse through the nervous system to the arms and legs, which then respond with a motor action. As someone has said, the big toe is also a part of the mind even though it is a very small part.

Just what happens in the brain, in the mind, when we are thinking is not known to man despite the mountain of books that has been written about the subject, from the time of the ancient Greeks down to the present day. It is well known that the brain and nervous system make up the structure of the mind and the manner of learning to think and how to produce reasoned thought is well known, but the exact process within the system is not clear. Information gets into and out of the brain by a channel of nerves but the brain has its own mysterious way of making this information intelligible. Information that is generated within the brain, such as ideas and concepts, is an equal mystery buried somewhere within the 10 billion nerve cells of the brain.

The two types of thinking that take place may be termed concrete and abstract, briefly described as follows.

Concrete thinking. This is most common and is performed constantly during the course of the day's living. For example, you look out the window of your home and see a tree and very quickly "know" that it is tall, has large limbs and the leaves are green. Then you also notice that a large branch of the tree has come loose and is hanging over the house and immediately begin to reason that unless the branch is quickly removed it will fall off and damage the roof. All of this knowing, observing, gathering information, reasoning, planning and decision making is a process of thinking which occurred within a time span of a few seconds. We can depict these steps quite clearly but do not know the mechanism within the brain that made all of this data a cluster of reasoned intelligence.

Abstract thinking. This is the brightest star in the firmament of the human being for while animals can learn and perform simple thinking, only man can think and reason in abstract terms, with symbols. The grist for this mill is not tangible objects and events but rather ideas, concepts and symbols. A symbol, as we all know, is that which stands for or represents another thing. For example, the oak tree is the symbol for strength and endurance, wings are the symbol of flight and swiftness, and a flag with its markings is the symbol of a nation. One glance at a flag which displays the maple leaf and the great nation of Canada is envisioned in the mind.

But true symbolic thinking resides in the province of mathematics and logic. Thus, $2 + 2 = 4$ is utter nonsense unless one can reason that when two is added to two the total sum will be four. But the symbols are even more "symbolic" because they do not specify what the two's and four's represent. They might be cows, men, buildings or mountains. They are even more symbolic for they might represent two potatoes and two onions for a total of four vegetables. Other well known symbols are H_2O for water, X is the unknown quantity, the cross is the mark of Christianity, and the great symbol for energy, $E=MC_2$. Just the mere presentation of these symbols conveys to the mind an enormous quantity of information.

Thinking in terms of concepts is also symbolic thinking. A concept is a mental image, a generalization of many things grouped by the use of one term. For example, the word 'round' is a concept for it may apply to a ball, a coin or the earth. The word 'animal' includes ants, rabbits, dogs, bears, cows, even man. The concept 'time' refers to seconds, minutes, hours, weeks, years and enternity. 'Green' applies to trees, clothes, the sea or paint. These examples illustrate man's ability to think with symbols.

THE MENTAL FUNCTION

The human mind performs two major operations, namely, to learn and to reason. The first is to acquire knowledge and the second is to make decisions and judgments. The total process is called thinking and reasoning which we shall now consider.

LEARNING

To learn means to absorb, to take in facts and information and then to retain it in the memory. Learning comes before reasoning because there must be facts, information and experience in the mind in order to have something to reason with and about. The learning includes not only informational knowledge but also physical skills, the knowledge of which is also stored in the mind.

Learning begins in the cradle, continues through the A, B, C's, the 1, 2, 3's, and then on through life, never ceasing until we die. Learning never stops for in addition to the formal education our every life experience is a source of learning. When we succeed or fail, experience joy or disappointment, these also enlighten and instruct, telling us to continue as before or to turn in another direction.

The learning process has three parts, as follows.

Observing. We observe with the five senses of seeing, hearing, touching, tasting and smelling. This is the method by which we communicate with the world outside our self, the avenues through which we gather information.

Comprehending. After we receive information from the outside world we must understand it, recognize what meaning it has. We observe the snow falling, we comprehend that it means a protecting of the body from cold which is uncomfortable and might even result in sickness.

Memory. This is the storehouse of the things which we have learned and comprehended. Just how this information is stored in the brain and then recalled is not known even though the chore is performed a thousand times a day. We look at the calendar and recall that it is mother's birthday or we see an airplane crossing the sky and remember our own plane trip of a year ago. The detail of this process of storage and recall by the brain is still to be uncovered.

Two types of learning are usually distinguished. First is the simple acquisition of knowledge such as learning a language or a motor skill like running and dancing, or gathering general information from newspapers, radio, television or government reports.

The second level of learning is of that knowledge which changes behavior. This consists in serious study, creative thinking, scientific investigation or technical applications. This type of learning will enlighten a person with new ideas and visions that lead to a change in action, in behavior. Even the child who burns his finger on a hot stove and decides it is unwise to touch hot things is learning at this level because what he has learned by experience will change his behavior toward hot objects and their relation to his sense of feel.

REASONING

Reasoning is the quality par excellence in the human being, the great asset that man alone possesses. Every human thinks, even the imbecile and the madman although their level of thinking is poor. The usual classification of thinking by degrees is: Feebleminded, retarded, normal, bright and genius. Most humans grade out at normal or bright, in that great common domain of the average.

Reasoning entails a conscious awareness of what one is doing, a willful effort to achieve an end, a solution. Day-dreaming and reverie are not reasoning because they are not directed toward an end, although elements of thinking are present. If there is any direct thinking it is toward a fanciful ideal while reasoning is a process of knowing, of weighing facts, of contrast and comparison.

In our everyday speech we use the words 'thinking' and 'reasoning' interchangeably but a distinguishment must be made for clear understanding. Thinking refers to any use of the mind, any mental activity. Reasoning, however, is a mental process in which ideas are formed, plans for action devised, problems are solved and value judgments are made. We shall consider this process first by the two types of reasoning and secondly by the objective methods of reasoning.

TYPES OF REASONING

All reasoned thinking consists in the two well-known types of inductive and deductive reasoning. Before reviewing these two types let us recall that all reasoning is performed in the form of an argument, that is, to make a statement and then offer a conclusion. Here are several examples:

The sky is darkening, it will rain;
Tomatoes planted early will be killed by late frost;
Most men wear blue shirts, their favorite color is blue.

Each of these sentences is an argument, first a statement and then a conclusion about that statement. Both types of reasoning work toward a conclusion but their approach is different, hence the terms inductive and deductive.

Deductive reasoning. The term deduction is from the Latin *de* and *duco*, meaning to lead down from. Thus you must state one or two particulars, called premises, and then the mind will deduce a conclusion. Recalling the example of the sky above, we shall re-state it this way: When the sky darkens it rains, the sky is darkening, therefore it will rain. Again: Humans must eat or die, I do not wish to die, therefore I must eat some food. The first two statements are the premises (humans must eat or die, I do not wish to die), and the last statement is the conclusion (I will eat some food).

The great Greek logician, Aristotle, developed the most formal type of deduction called the syllogism in which the conclusion is inferred from two premises. In this method of reasoning the two premises are called major and minor premise, and from these the conclusion is drawn. Three examples follow:

1. All humans are mortal (major premise), I am a human (minor premise), therefore I am mortal (conclusion).
2. Either that person is John or he is Mike, it is not Mike, then it is John.
3. All Frenchmen are Europeans, this man is a Frenchman, therefore he is an European.

Most of our common thinking does not include the use of the two premises but rather a modified form of deduction with one premise and a conclusion. This is so because usually one of the premises is so common or so familiar that is unnecessary, even redundant, to use it. For example, we say "that man is a Frenchman" and know immediately that he is also an European. Again, we say "that cat has claws" without bothering to mention that all cats have claws and since that is a cat, it too will have claws.

Inductive reasoning. Induction means to lead into and so in this form of reasoning we induce the mind, we lead it into a conclusion, in contrast to deduction where the mind is "lead down from," to form a conclusion.

In order to lead the mind into a conclusion it must be presented with a number of facts from which to draw the conclusion. The well known example of this type of reasoning is that of T.H. Huxley in which a man bites into one green apple that is hard and sour and then another, another and another and is lead to the conclusion that all green apples are hard and sour. Now this is proper inductive reasoning so far as it goes although we know that a more extended investigation will show that some apples that are green are not hard and sour. But the reasoning is correct as another example will show. Suppose one believes that water will run uphill on some surfaces and so fifty trials are made on glass, wood, plastic, earth, macadam, metal, etc. One must finally be induced to believe that water will not run uphill on any surface.

Much of our everyday reasoning follows the inductive method. Thus, it is time to buy a new pair of shoes and so I reason like this: The old brand that I wear fits well, feels comfortable, has given long wear, the price is reasonable as compared with other makes of shoes and so I conclude that I will purchase new shoes of the same manufacture as the old.

The detective when he investigates a crime, works by the inductive method. He will search out one clue, then another and another until he has accumulated sufficient evidence to reach a conclusion that the crime was committed in such and such a manner and by such and such a person.

The scientific method reviewed earlier is largely inductive although deduction is also used. The scientist conducts a large number of investigations, constructs a tentative model, makes further tests and finally comes to a conclusion called theory.

OBJECTIVE THINKING

The two types of reasoning, deductive and inductive, are employed in many ways in what we may call objective or practical thinking. It is the kind of reasoning we apply to the daily tasks of life and which we shall now review under the four headings of simple reasoning, problem solving, decision making and value judgments.

Simple reasoning. This is the daily activity of children and adults alike as each goes about the routine activities of life. All of the daily chores of eating, dressing, going to school and to work involve some thought, some planning but the brain is taxed only lightly with these chores because of the repeated, habitual nature of the behavior. At one time, in the beginning, there was reasoning and analysis to set up the action but from continued performance they become automatic. An illustration is children playing in the school yard. When the school bell rings the children stop playing immediately, turn toward the school building and begin to walk. They do not need to reason thus: I must return to the building, I must resume my studies, I must study with diligence, I wish to obtain good grades in my learning, there are penalities for failure. All such thinking is present but submerged.

Although we designate this as simple reasoning we should bear in mind that it carries the highest of values because it relieves the mind of having to stop and fully consider each and every action we take. To do so would over-tax the mind, would burden it with such a mass of trivia that it could never ascend to the three heights of thinking that we shall consider next.

Problem solving. This is the method by which we overcome the problems of life, the manner my which we solve a task of life or a difficult condition, one that is above the mere routine. This is the major tool that is used to crack the nut of complexity in a life situation. Many writers in psychology feel that all of life is a matter of problem solving and so address their entire subject as a problem.

Everybody uses the method of problem solving, scientists, the carpenter, businessman, housewife and the school child, for this is the means of "getting things done," of overcoming obstacles to attain an end. The step or stage method applies to every problem whether it is one of illness, the need for house repairs, conducting an orchestra, sailing a ship or selecting the food for the daily dinner.

The original pattern for solving problems was layed down by John Dewey. Since that time many books on "how to think" have addressed the subject of problem solving but they all conform to the step-by-step method and vary only slightly from the Dewey strategy.

Step 1. First recognize that there is a problem. Very often the matter is a routine action, an effort to reach a known goal. Instead of a problem it is merely a need for energetic effort to accomplish the deed, to get the job done. But if the condition or the project is complex and the end is not immediately clear, then a true problem exists.

Step 2. Here the nature of the problem is examined carefully and is written down on paper so that the difficulty is clearly understood. If the problem is one of illness then the cause must be found and the cure devised; if it is a plan to do a project, reach a goal, accomplish an enterprise, the obstacles to be overcome must be reviewed so that the nature of the problem is clear and vivid.

Step 3. Here you search for the possible solution to the problem. This would include the means of solving and the method. As in all goal seeking you will assemble the information on your resources such as money, time, material things needed, plus your ability to perform the job yourself or managing the employment of others. Often the final decision cannot be reached at this stage but the capability of solution should now be known.

Step 4. This stage is an extension of the previous one. Here will come an examination of alternate methods of solving the problem. The considerations in step 3 will almost certainly present new ideas, new visions, causing a number of changes. The objective is, of course, to discover the best way, the better method. This will include much comparison of costs and materials plus outside influences, the interest of other persons, the environment, even legal considerations.

Step 5. This is the testing of the most promising solutions considered. This means to select the course that appears most feasible, that suggests the best answer to the problem. With this decision made the action follows.

Problem solving is a mental process and is not, as the term is sometimes taken to mean, an end, an attainment of a goal. The one is a mental activity and the other a physical action. Problem solving is a mental manipulation of the environment, doing in the mind that which we think is possible to do in the physical world. The action may be likened to the game of chess. The first effort is problem solving in which the figures are moved back and forth in a mental exercise, trying to solve the problem of besting the opponent. Then, when the solution is seen or discovered the physical action is taken of moving the figures on the board.

Decision making. Decision making is more than an addendum to problem solving which is an inquiry into the possibility of a solution. Decision making involves two further steps beyond inquiry.

1. Desirability of the goal. When the full facts are revealed as a result of the inquiry, then the goal must be re-assessed as to its desirability. The original proposal may now appear impossible and therefore should be abandoned, or perhaps the end may appear not worth the effort. Or if desirable, perhaps altered, postponed to another time, or even employ a substitute plan. It is a decision that is possible after the problem solving details are known.

2. Probability of achievement. Before the ultimate decision is made to go, to proceed, the possibility of success or failure must be finally weighed, including the penalty in case of failure. This would include the reliability of source material and funding, government controls, code requirements and suitable environment. Even such considerations as economic stability, world unrest, war and business ethics may affect the probability of success and would therefore enter into the final decision.

Value judgments. This is sometimes called evaluation thinking and is the process by which we reach a conclusion or a judgment about the worth of an object, event or a person.

Value judgments function two ways. In the first, it is a result of prior thinking, a conclusion reached after considering the worth of an object or an event. For example, before purchasing an automobile one would naturally make a judgment of value as to cost as compared to features, the economy of operation, availability of repairs, comfort of the vehicle. Again, if a neighbor is kind, generous, supports his family well, is a dutiful citizen, we then characterize him to be, judge him to be a good and worthy person. And when we are impressed by a colorful sunset we pronounce the value judgment of beautiful.

In their second function value judgments act as guidelines to behavior, they are the direction pointers to worthy goals. When we plot a course of action we do so along paths that are known to be good, that are judged to be worthy and avoid the ways that are unworthy. Values inspire action as we strive to emulate the worthy works of artists, musicians, architects, teachers and statesmen.

Values are separately defined in two categories of knowledge, that of ethics and aesthetics.

Ethical value. Ethics is the study of right and wrong in human conduct and behavior, of that which is good and that which is bad. There are two forms in ethical values.

1. A judgment of value, of goodness in itself. This might be the appraisal of a city or of its slums, an environmental hazard or a legislative action.
2. A judgment of obligation or duty. This is the appraisal of rightness or wrongness in conduct, a judgment as to whether the behavior is worthy or unworthy, is foolish or wise. It is a judgment of morality.

Aesthetic value. This is a judgment of good or bad made with respect to form, color, shape and ingredients of an object, of a structure, or a painting. It is a judgment of beauty as the object expresses a feeling of awe, inspiration or tranquility and the viewer responds with a sense of these qualities within himself or herself.

All aesthetic judgments espouse a double criteria, one of equivalence: Is this blue vase better or less worthy than that blue vase; and, one of ranking: Is this blue vase higher on the scale, more prestigious, than that red vase. The first is a judgment of quality, the second a judgment of comparison, of marking one as superior and another as inferior.

Value judgments have a very high value to the individual for they impart a meaning to life, to behavior and to the institutions under which we all live. There is no yardstick by which to measure human living but value judgments do provide a substitute for measurement with such evaluating terms as good or bad, worthy or unworthy, right or wrong. These carry to our mind a relative estimate, an approximate scale of life, and in so doing they provide the light of guidance, a standard for conduct and expression.

HEALTH AND MENTAL ABILITY

It is not proper to rank the twelve goals of life in an hierarchy because all are essential to human living. It is correct, however, to rank them by priority of effort to be expended, and in such a rating it is surely health and mental ability that stand in first place. When these qualities of life are possessed in sufficient or adequate quantity, then all other tasks will be performed better, more accurately and with more surety of achievement. Education, the effort to acquire a high skill in mental ability, must always occupy a front position in the business of personal living, in the seeking of goals.

Chapter 14
Lifework Ability

When the young boy or young girl come to the age of maturity they are faced with that great question: What shall be my lifework? In what employment shall I spend my life for the earning of income and for enjoyment of my work activity? Shall it be as a craftsman, artist, farmer, business person, housewife, doctor, lawyer, factory employee, sailor? We call this work employment a career after the person has become established in it for a reasonable length of time, but in the beginning it is a lifework condition for which the individual must prepare. It is lifework because it is the means of livelihood, the source of economic well-being.

In the days of yesteryear the selection of a lifework was not too difficult to make, the major choices being farming or a craft. To a large extent the son followed the father's occupation and the daughter became a housewife. In nearly half of the world today this is still the pattern because agriculture and natural resources work is still the dominant industries. But in the industrialized nations the choice of work is extremely wide. An example is the United States where the Dictionary of Occupational Titles lists 20,000 separate occupations.

THE WORK EXCHANGE

One of the prime lessons in life is that one must give something to get something in return, a process of exchange. In the matter of lifetime work the exchange is thus: The individual gives the two valuable possessions of part of his life time and all of his work ability and receives in exchange an income or more properly a livelihood. This rule is true whether one is going to work for a wage or operate a business for profit. In both cases it is a giving of personal time and ability in exchange for an economic benefit.

The time exchange. The child exchanges all of his or her time for play and learning. The prisoner in jail exchanges his free time for a confined time because of his crime. In the matter of employment the adult exchanges approximately one-third of his adult life time for the earning of a livelihood. This is calculated on the old rule of thumb of eight hours of work, eight of leisure and eight of rest.

The ability exchange. Ability is the skill one brings to his employment where it is exchanged for a monetary benefit, where application of the skill is converted into wealth. Depending on one's learning and training plus the energetic effort that is made toward the job, ability might be classed as skilled or unskilled, brilliant or dull, dexterous or clumsy, professional or craftsman, leader or led, artistic or shabby, educated or ignorant.

These are the two elements, then that we each bring to our own particular world of employment, namely, a certain amount of time devoted to productive work and a certain ability of cleverness according to our education, training and aggressive spirit.

PREPARATION AND TRAINING

All preparation may be summed up in one word — education. The learning of the early years in home and school is solely a preparation for entering mature life as a responsible adult. While education is designed to enlighten in all aspects of life the core part is or should be learning aimed at a life employment. This is quite clear to one and all because our very lives depend on the ability to earn food, clothing and shelter, so each must acquire some degree of skill, and the higher the better, in order to earn these necessities of life. And the tool for acquiring is education.

In addition to the general education in academic subjects, every field of employment requires some special training. In the case of lesser skilled work such training may be minimal but in highly skilled, technical and professional work, much specialized instruction and self-training is needed. Even in such high careers as the medical doctor, airline pilot, prose writer or computer technician, even these persons, must still begin as trainees in their respective fields.

MOTIVE FOR WORK

The easy answer to the question "Why do people work?" is that they do so in order to earn the necessities for living. Clearly, this is true but it is a narrow answer. For example, persons who inherit or gain great wealth need not work but all engage in a daily employment of hard work is such fields as legislators, business executive, political leaders or research workers. The missionary and social worker who goes in a hazardous area is prompted by more than a monetary reward for the returns for comparable work would be greater in their home nation.

There are millions of volunteer workers who receive no reward for their time and expenses except the personal satisfaction for the work they perform.

The underlying cause and reason of why people work is because they cannot do otherwise. It is the nature of man to be active, to engage in a work performance. In essence, what each must do is point this work-impulse in the direction of his or her choice. A brief classification might yield the following three fields.

1. *Work for economic reward alone.* The incentive is simply to obtain the necessities of life, of food, clothing and shelter for self and family plus some excess for pleasant living. Common types of such employment are found in factory, farm, natural resources, service jobs and unskilled work.
2. *Work for economic reward and personal satisfaction.* Persons in this category are sometimes called people with a mission and include such as teachers, writers, scientists, nurses, ministers, political leaders and industry chiefs.
3. *Work without economic reward as a goal.* Such persons are necessarily wealthy and engage in social work, public administration, are legislators, statesmen, philanthropists.

CAREER FIELDS

The U.S. Office of Education has grouped occupations into fifteen categories that offer an across the board view of the employment areas and are helpful in choosing a career. The categories and a brief sampling are given here. Although this is an American list, every nation will have a similar listing although perhaps not identical to this one.

- Agriculture and Natural Resources: Farmer, game warden, miner, forester, animal breeder, botanist.
- Business and Office Worker: Accountant, bookkeeper, clerk, secretary, computer operator, office manager, typist.
- Communication and Media: Author, writer, photographer, editor, reporter, printer, radio/television/telephone work.
- Consumer and Homemaker: Dietician, fashions, food specialists, economist, seamstress, nursery school.
- Environmental Work: Fish and game, hydrologist, industrial health, landscaping, sanitation, urban planner, wildlife manager.
- Fine Arts and Humanities: Actor, actress, composer, conductor, writer, musician, philosopher, photographer, vocalist, sculptor.
- Health Career: Dentist, medical technician, laboratory technician, nursing, physician, X-ray technologist.
- Hospitality and Recreation: Athlete, flight attendant, host/hostess, hotel/motel clerk, recreation supervisor, travel agent, waiter/waitress.

- Manufacturing Work: Assembler, drafting, machine operator, tool and die maker, welder.
- Marine Science Career: Diver, ichthyologist, marine biologist, marine scientist, oceanographer.
- Marketing and Distribution: Buyer, delivery, model, clerk, stock keeper.
- Personal Services: Barber, chauffeur, cosmotologist, escort, travel guide, masseur, mortician, valet.
- Public Service: Fire fighter, customs officer, mail carrier, police, politician, public health, social worker, teacher.
- Transporation: Aircraft mechanic, pilot, automobile mechanic, bus driver, locomotive engineer, ship work, taxi driver, truck driver, ticket agent.

  There are standard departments in all of these industries such as:
  - Managerial.
  - Research and development.
  - Production, manufacturing.
  - Selling, delivery, service of product sold.

SUMMARY

The importance of one's lifework resides in the fact that after reaching adulthood it will be the central activity of life in addition to being the means of livelihood. This work will extend across a period of forty to fifty years of the most active period of life, not occasionally but every day of that period except for rest and relaxation. All of life's relationships such as family, leisure time, health, social association, one's possessions, even religion, center upon and depend upon this lifework. And, not to be forgotten, is old age — which must be provided for during the active work years. Lifework is the source of all economic well-being for the individual, the application of skill and ability to produce wealth.

Chapter 15

Leisure Ability

Leisure is that part of human living that may be defined as the opposite of necessary work and it has two distinct meanings. The first is that of leisure time, that part of the day, week or month in which the person is free from imposed duties, is unhindered, not obligated to work, not compelled by the necessities of life to labor and not under a time pressure to accomplish a work goal. Here one ignores the clock and the calendar, if the desire is such, for they have no control of one's comings and goings. Leisure time is un-obligated time.

The second meaning is that of leisure activity, the manner in which one spends his or her leisure time. This would be such activities as playing, fishing, games, art enjoyment, voluntary service, strolling through the countryside, vacationing or a family picnic. It is activity that is the opposite of obligated work action.

Leisure time activity does not mean thumb twiddling or just staring up at a beautiful blue sky through the course of a day. Far from it. Active people will often exert more strenuous effort at a leisure action than a routine work activity. Witness the runner who drops exhausted at the end of the race, the bird watcher who rises at 3:00 A.M. to tramp through swamp and jungle, the worker who hurries home from work to paint through most of the night on his canvas, and the endless hours of practice of the dancer and musician. If every school athlete would study and learn as stenuously as he or she play in sports, the schools would surely graduate more geniuses. We see that leisure, then, is not the absence of activity. Perhaps we might say that leisure is work by choice while career work is a labor of necessity.

LEISURE IN HISTORY

There is no period in history when man did not engage in play and recreation, even when he lived by fang and club. Early weapons were used not only for war and hunting but also for sports contests in archery, weapon throwing, playing at warfare. The primitive Indians of Central

America played a game with opposing teams on a field about 200 feet long and used a rubber ball.

Music, drama and the dance were all part of the Egyptian civilization. Babylonia is known for its boxing and wrestling and the Olympic Games of the Greeks are common knowledge. But there was more leisure activity that just the great games, for the children enjoyed dolls, hobby horses, toy carts, horseback riding, and gymnastics. The Romans engaged in most of these activities and are known also for their famous chariot races.

Recreation was enjoyed in many forms in the Middle Ages with games and jousting, hunting and hawking, dance and music, weight throwing and cock fighting. Gambling was widespread with much drinking and brawling.

The Colonial Period experienced all of the games of old and added such pastimes as boating, horse racing, dueling, cricket, and ball games between town teams.

Today's world has seen the rise of giant parks and recreation areas for the enjoyment of the outdoors away from the busy cities, stadium fields for sports contests, theaters and amphitheaters for music and drama viewing, tracks for automobile racing and sky shows where airplanes are demonstrated.

TYPES OF LEISURE ACTIVITY

The separate behavior in leisure time activities has no sharp division but it will aid in our understanding to make a three part separation into recreation, play and art, with some representative activities in each.

Recreation. This is the broad term that might cover the whole of leisure activity. The word comes from the Latin, 'recreatio,' meaning to create again, to restore, to refresh. The following may be classed as recreational activity of the individual.

Reading — Hunting, Fishing — Swimming, Skiing, Golf
Traveling — Archery, Tennis — Skating, Bowling
Dancing — Walking, Running — Camping, Picnicing, Hiking
Viewing sports, watching television or motion picture.
Attending operas, concerts, circus, amusement parks.
Any hobby activity, most social activities.

Play. This word comes from the Old English and means to frolic, to engage in a game or sport. It seems to imply a competition or a challenge. No fine line separates play and recreation when engaged in by the individual but the following activities tend toward the play side.

Games of children. Skip rope, swinging, see-saw, hide and seek, racing. There is much imitation, mimicry and make believe in child's play as the boy pretends to be a soldier, policeman or cowboy and the girl sets up housekeeping as cook, house cleaner and mother.

Games of Adults. Any sporting game where there is competition such as golf, bowling, pitching horse shoes, running, gymnasium work, track, ball playing.

Non-strenuous games. Such as card playing, dice, lotteries, checkers, chess, manipulative games.

Art. We have examined art as an institution in Book I, here we shall review it as an activity of leisure time for the individual.

The term 'art' spreads itself across the whole world and all that is therein because nature, man, even heavenly things, are all a work of art. It is for this reason that the term has no accurate definition. We know that it deals with the beautiful, the province of aesthetics, but not necessarily with truth, the domain of logic. We know that beauty resides in the sight, the sound and the touch and also in the emotions of man. And we know that art refers to things superior, that it is the opposite of ugliness, clumsiness and inferior effort. And lastly that it is that which lends excellence and enrichment to human life.

In former times art consisted in the several fine arts of painting, music, sculpture, architecture, drama and poetry. These are still regarded as the finer arts but the modern view of art extends to every area of life. The fabrics we wear, the products that are manufactured, the persuasion of millions by radio and tellevision, all these are matters of art. Even the vehicle we drive for pleasure and work must have beauty of line, interior and exterior finish.

Is this modern view good or bad? It is very good because it means that art need not and should not have any restrictions beyond the fact that the object bears the ingredient of beauty. It also means that art is not the property of any select group but is an aspect of life, for the enjoyment of all and to be participated in by all. Art is as much a part of life as existence. If a thing is, it has art within it, and each man and woman may enjoy the sweet reward of its beauty.

Art Activity. If you are viewing art work in a museum, theatre or auditorium, you stand in the position of a 'receiver' of art. That is, another person has produced or created the work and you are merely an observer. The art will convey a meaning to you, an aesthetic feeling, of hope, suffering, reward, of place, evil, war or perhaps only a sense of beauty of line, shape and color.

On the other hand, if you are a 'doer' of art, a maker of art, you then stand in the capacity of artist, of producer of an art work, a maker of those meanings and feelings noted above.

Our interest here is with the individual as he or she engages in a leisure activity and so we shall view art from the standpoint of doer. Viewing art induces a pleasure in the view but generating art is a source of well-being for the doer. When you engage in artistic activity, when you are 'at art,' there is a three-part inclusion, as follows.

1. The skill part. This is the motor action, the physical doing. If the work is music, sculpture, pottery or dancing it will require a bodily movement of hands, feet, lips and eyes. The performance will be distinguished as between fine and course, crude and excellent. In whatever field one participates, the high objective is a skill of manipulation for otherwise the result will not be an artistic production, because art is a fine honing of delicate parts.
2. The creative part. This is the thing created, the completed product, the whole compounded work. It is a new thing in the world, something that did not exist before. And what has come into being is your own interpretation, your own idea about some part of nature, of man, of God. It many not be a masterpiece but it will have lines and color or sounds in a form never before produced.
3. The expressive part. One of the most general descriptions of art is that it is an expression of the person who produced it. That is, you show in a concrete object or performance your inner emotions and feelings, your concept of beauty in a thing, your idea of how an object is or should be. You are not concerned with how others will see this thing or how they will feel about it, it is *your* feeling and idea that is being expressed. If it is a picture it will express your joy or sense of beauty; if music it will express your sadness or elation; if a poem, your love of nature; if a dance, your sense of beauty in motion.

In today's world much art is produced solely with the viewer in mind. All commercial art is such, must political literature is such, as the work is intended to arouse the spectator to an action. But these activities are more a matter of business than of art. If artistic expression is present, fine and dandy, but the first intention of the producer is not art but popular appeal, whereas the aim of the individual who engages in artistic work is to express one's self, one's emotions in the work.

There is no limit to art forms ranging from fine art through useful art to practical art but there is a limit or distinction in art skill. The ballet is not to be compared to the mountain folk dance although both are art dance forms and a Michelangelo is not the same as a newspaper cartoon. Art as a serious endeavour would include the major arts such as painting, music, poetry, the dance and theatre. Art as a leisure activity would tend to the lesser skilled fields of crafts and hobbies such as flower arrangement, interior decorating or landscaping.

LEISURE VALUES

There are many theories about leisure activities and their values. Some have held that it is pure instinct to play, others such as Herbert Spencer that leisure and play are needed to burn up excess energy. One view contends that leisure is a safety valve for the emotions, another that leisure action offsets the work action in the balance of life.

All of these suggestions have truth in them but as our interest is the goal of well-being in living we may sum-up the values in leisure from the following two aspects.

The physical good in leisure activity. The human body functions best with a frequent alternating between work and rest. It is a stop-and-go process that elevates the body to its maximum efficiency. The rest does not mean a complete stoppage of motion but rather a change of action, and this is what leisure activity provides. In times past the natural cycle of living provided this change of pace and direction of action but in today's world, especially in the industrial areas, too much of life is a sedentary routine, lacking in energetic action. And the consequence is ill-being, even outright illness. Aristotle said that leisure is an activity performed for its own sake but for sedentary man it bestows a well-being to the body.

The emotional good in leisure. Aside from consultation with a doctor, there seems to be no other means by which a person can escape the mental stress and frustrations of life, so prevalent today, except by engaging in a leisure activity. The theory of leisure as a safety valve for pent-up emotions is true also for the stress and strain of life. The person who hurries home from the pressure of daily life to engage in golf, fishing, volunteer work or chess is opening the valve of stress, lessening the change of emotional or mental illness.

Thus we see that leisure time is not a period of idleness but rather a relaxation from stressful time. Life demands this free-choice activity to achieve well-being in daily living. Leisure ability is competence in using free time for relaxful behavior, for the enjoyment of life as well as a release from stress.

Chapter 16
Religion

When we speak of religion our thoughts turn immediately to such matters as God, prayer and worship. This is proper because religion is that relationship that one bears to a supreme being, to his or her God. But this is just one half of the total for in addition to being a man-to-God relationship, religion also decrees a man-to-man association to humans. From primitive time man has not only related himself to a God or gods, but he has also built his moral codes of conduct as he believed his God would want them to be. The Ten Commandments are a well-known example.

It is this dual relationship of man-to-God and man-to-man that has been the cause of religion to occupy such a major place in the personal life of each individual. Even the person who denies religious belief still accepts and lives by the moral and legal codes that are a direct product of religion. For the individual who accords with religious belief, the progress of daily living is filled with a deeper meaning, a greater expansiveness, a fuller satisfaction. We will see why this is so as we examine the source of religion and how religion relates man to God and man to man.

SOURCE OF RELIGION

All religion begins in the mind of the individual. Although we see the great church building, the priest-leader, and the ritual and ceremony, these are merely the outer aspects of religion. It is within our personal being, within our self, that religion begins and ends because it is a relationship between one person and his God. The church official may assist in the matter but it is the individual himself or herself who is saved or condemned, who wins or is the loser, overall and in the end, throughout the journey of life, and in whatever hereafter there may be.

Man is born with a sense of religion or as some say born with a religious consciousness. It may be cultivated and cultured by a church organization but the feeling or awareness is there from the beginning. It is probably inbred by our early baby and childhood sense of helplessness in such a mighty and gigantic world. It may be likened to the prayer of the Brittany fishermen who entreat, "Help me, oh God, my boat is so small and thy ocean so great." It is even so with the human being who finds himself in a world that is so great that his little craft of a mind cannot cope with the forces and wonderment of it, nor solve the many problems. The only recourse then is to turn to a supreme being and this mankind has always done.

As we have reviewed in a previous chapter, even before the rise of the great religions of today, early man felt this need for religion in his life and practiced it as magic, witchcraft and sorcery. We do not call these practices 'religion' but they were such in every sense of the word for they related man to a supreme spirit and also provided the rules of conduct. The priest or witch doctor held his intercourse with spirits and demons rather than one supreme being. He did not worship the spirits as modern man does a God but he held them in great respect and affirmed their power to influence and change both nature and man. It is even so with modern religious practice.

There are three major life occurences that inspire a sense of religion in all human beings, namely, the beginning, change in, and the end of life. These events were the concern of the old time spirit religions and they are still the focus of the modern spiritual religions.

The beginning of life. This is birth, the springing into life of a new being, the astounding wonder of such an event, the act of creation by man and nature.

Change in life. Three great changes mark the journey of life for all human beings, changes that no power on earth can alter.

Puberty. This is the change from child to adult, the infusion of sex into the body, acquiring the ability to make new life. And more, it is the time to accept the responsibilities of life itself, to accept the burden of adulthood, and discard the dependence on a parent.

Illness. Illness is a hindrance to life, to living. If a thing is born to live it is meant to live life, not suffer life. And illness is a suffering of life, a negative living.

Disaster. This, too, is a life hindrance, imposed from outside the body. When the bounties of nature are denied or restricted by storm or flood, drought or catastrophe, a life change also takes place.

End of life. Man has always accepted the fact of death but never the mystery of it. Surely it is only a transition to another state, for a certainty there is "something" beyond the grave, our life on earth is only a testing ground, surely such great minds as Aristotle, Newton and Einstein must continue to live in more than books.

These momentous happenings of birth, change in life and finally death are still the secrets of nature and God. Science can tell us how they happen and what occurs but cannot tell us why. They are still today, as in the past, awe-filled events. They are not dreadful things of a strange and mysterious portent but they do inspire a religious sentiment in man.

RELATING TO GOD THROUGH RELIGION

Each human has a relationship with his or her God in two ways, through belief and through worship, which we shall now review.

Belief in God. Belief in God and in His power is the core of religion. This belief is an innate feeling that there is a Supreme Being, some superior force that regulates the courses of nature and of man. If it is not a 'being,' at least there is a power in the world that is greater than man and nature and this power emanates from a God.

This belief is not a one-way track for it provides an answer, an insight, into both the known and the unknown aspects of life. First, it explains the process of nature and the behavior of man, and secondly, it provides an answer to the universe as a whole, the origin of creation and of creatures, the destiny of the human race and of the individual, especially one's own person. In sum, the belief supplies a meaning to life on earth plus a hope of reward and a better life in a hereafter.

Religious belief has never been pure and uncontaminated for man was and still is ever the skeptic. Indeed, some even claim that there was a faltering in Christ when on the cross He cried, "My God, My God, why has thou forsaken me?" The inquiries of science over the past several centuries have caused many of the strictist beliefs of the past to be modified. The shades of Western belief may be examined under four categories.

1. *Strict belief — There is a God.*
   - God created the world, nature and man.
   - God controls the affairs of man and nature.
   - God responds to prayers.
   - Some (Christians) believe that man has a soul and will live in the hereafter.
2. *The Naturalist — Perhaps there is a God.*
   - Man is a thing of nature, is born, lives and dies by the laws of nature.
   - Man evolved from lower forms of life.
   - The universe has an ordered method according to the physical laws of motion, waves, particles and rays, perhaps even super strings.
   - There is no factual evidence of a supreme being.
   - If there is a supreme being, He does not interfere with the processes of nature.
   - Belief is founded on faith alone, not evidence.

3. *The Neutralist — I don't know.*
   - This is the undecided, one who oscillates between pillars. In times of plenty and well-being he has no need of God; in time of want and distress he turns to an Almighty Being for help and protection.
   - A second person of this type will concede there may have been a God who made the laws of nature but who then retired outside of the universe and no longer exercises any control.
4. *The Atheist — There is no God.* There are few outright atheists in the world and fewer still the number who remain so. The atheist offers no valid reason for his view, has no data to support the position. The statement that "there is no God" is an idle opinion, lacking conviction in the sayer and lacking evidence in proof. Where believers give reason, the atheist gives none, saying simply "it can't be so."

Worship of God. This is the second method by which the individual relates to God. Worship is the immediate process of communion with God, the direct communication with a Supreme Being, and it is conducted through prayer and ritual, as we shall here note.

1. *Prayer.* The believer in God prays to his God, for it is the manner of direct communication between the person and the Being. It is a solemn time when the individual lays bare the depth of his thoughts and feelings. Nothing is hidden, nothing can be concealed, for one now stands before his very God. Here man recites his humility, gives thanks for affluency, asks for help for himself and all humanity, expresses praise for the majesty of one who is Supreme.

   The exact nature of prayer is that of a meditation, expressed aloud or silently, upon the enormity of life, of man, of nature. It is a soliloquy, a mental recitation, from out of the depths of the person. If man has a soul then it is here layed bare before God at the time of prayer. There is more to a man or woman than mere mind and mere body for there resides within also a spirit, combining the mind and body, an energy of life. Prayer helps to uncover this spirit, this energy.
2. *Ritual.* While prayer is a matter between the individual and his or her God, ritual is conducted by the church organization. The special concern of ritual consists in the following: Public worship; marking the great events in the life of an individual such as birth, puberty, marriage and death; observing certain Holy Days set aside for fasting or celebration such as Easter and Christmas in the Christian church; and the receiving of instruction from religious elders.

RELATING TO FELLOWMAN THROUGH RELIGION

The great moral concepts of religion have always regulated the conduct of mankind. A concept of God instills a high moral sense in the individual and all religions teach such good behavior as part of the religious philosphy. We have previously noted the Ten Commandments as a moral code for Catholics, Jews and Protestants. Confucianism is only slightly a religion and very much a structure of rules of conduct. The Mohammedan follows a strict code of behavior in eating, fasting, and social relations, even the number of times to pray each day. Buddhism teaches these rules of conduct: Do not destroy life, abstain from unchastity, take nothing that is not given, do not lie or deceive, abstain from intoxicants.

Man adapts religion into many of his life undertakings. The help of god is invoked on coins, at the dedication of buildings, launching of a ship, in winning a war, in educational instruction, to guide the deliberations of legislative bodies and courts. It is a belief that God not only cares for the soul but also for the physical and material well-being of man.

For the individual, religion is very much a behavior code of "you shall" and "you shall not," that affects his daily living. Here one is warned of the evils of stealing, killing another, deceit and non-permissible marriage. Here, too, one is instructed in the good of charity, the brotherhood of man, the good of wisdom, to love one another and to help in time of need.

The laws that relate to social conduct are largely derived from the rules for moral guidance. Legal codes first prohibit the act such as theft, murder, fraud, physical assault upon another and secondly spells out the punishment for those who commit the act, who violate the law. In a sense, all that the law does is specify the punishment for offending good moral conduct. Early church codes included the punishment part but today this is the province of government.

RELIGION IN WELL-BEING

The human mind is imbued with a religious sense, a feeling of relatedness to powers and forces that are superior to common man. It is a latent mental state that is always present in the person, sometimes faint and sometimes strong, but never totally absent. It is a part of the human mentality and should not be neglected in the seeking of well-being.

Adherence to the teachings of one's church should be followed for they are part of the early training that is imbedded in the whole person. Even if some doctrines are questioned, are doubted, are not observed, as many thoughtful persons might, this is still no reason to discard the whole. There is no need to remove the entire eye because of a mote, as one great teacher has declared. The ritual, the ceremony and the code of behavior that stems from the basic teachings of the church can lend an enriching quality to life that can be found in no other way. The furstrations that living creates, both physically and mentally, can be leveled out in communion with the Great Supreme.

Chapter 17
Personal Safety

Health in the body is a biological matter of sickness and disease. Safety of the body means protection from physical forces, from hazards and perils. To maintain our health we protect the body from disease germs, to maintain a condition of safety of the body we protect it from danger, from the hazards of an accident, a criminal attack or a disaster, both natural and man-made.

Just as one is never free from the presence of disease germs, just so one is never free from the presence of hazards and perils. In our homes, on the street, at work, while traveling, while vacationing, the three dangers of accident, crime and disaster are always near, always present. This is simply a fact of life and it carries a very clear message: We must always be on our guard with never-ceasing care, caution and protection from the many perils. Of course the presence of these dangers does not mean that they are a fiery monster constantly breathing catastrophe, but it does mean that each individual must always maintain a constant awareness of the possibility of accident and disaster. These three negative elements are part of our life environment, they are conditions with which we must ever concern ourselves. Fortunately, since they have been a presence of danger from the earliest times, man has accumulated a large knowledge about them, including how they occur and the preventive measures to take.

PREVENTION ABOVE ALL

In the matter of accidents, crime and disaster there is no second chance, no opportunity to reverse the occurence. Once these events take place they are over and done with, they have happened and there is no reversal of the incident. All that one can do now is salvage that which remains, that is, repair the damage and salvage the broken parts.

It is this total finality to the matter that distinguishes the physical reversal from health reversal. When sickness strikes the body there is usually time to cure, a method to stop the intensity of the illness, a medicine to arrest the disease when it is in progress. But in the physical sphere it is not so, for once the incident occurs the condition is final. There is no second chance to stop the onward progress of the occurence, no possibility of reversing the course of the event.

The only option in accidents, crime and disaster is prevention, that is, take concrete steps to avoid the occurence, to avert an involvement with them. This is a hard lesson that one must learn, and then follow through with the necessary action to implement the prevention. The old adage, "an ounce of prevention is worth a pound of cure," rings out with solid truth in the matter of avoiding the physical dangers of life.

THE ROOT CAUSE

Every particular accident, crime or disaster has its own particular cause and circumstance of occurence, and each must be analyzed to ascertain that cause, but there are two core conditions, two root causes that underlie all accidents, crimes and disaster. These two basic causes are an unsafe condition and/or an unsafe action by the person. We shall now take note of these.

Unsafe condition. Unsafe conditions are known as hazards and dangers. They are found in the presence of other persons and the environmental surrounding. The surrounding might be in the home, at school or in the factory workplace. The hazard might be a machine, an electric tool, a home appliance or a weak and wobbly ladder. The weather can be an environmental hazard with its lightening and storms of rain and snow. A wet surface is the source of persons slipping and vehicles skidding. A vehicle that moves with high speed and strikes with a mighty impact is part of today's environment. And chemicals and explosives also create an unsafe environment.

These unsafe conditions in our surroundings are not permanently and irrevocably unsafe but are so only if we take no action to remove their hazardous nature, to contain and control them. Where such steps are taken the result is one of prevention but where there is laxity and neglect the result is an accident, a crime or a disaster.

Unsafe action. This is the human element in physical protection, the action the person takes or fails to take to prevent the happening of an accident, crime or disaster. This cause may be a lack of knowledge, poor attitude, bad habits or a body-motor lack of skill. In essence it is a lack in safety education on the part of the person, a lack of knowledge about preventive measures or a negligence in the application of known safety methods.

Although we call this cause of accidents and crime an "unsafe action," the culprit is more a mental condition than a bodily action. Most persons have the motor skill to react rapidly at a time of impending danger but do not pre-see the need for caution or apprehend that an accident or crime is probable. It is a lack of mental awareness that a hazard exists, that a danger is present. For example, one drives a vehicle at fast speed on a wet highway surface, allowing no possibility for an emergency stop; matches are left at places in the home that are convenient for children to obtain, strike and then result in the burning of the child and the home; persons drown while enjoying the pleasure of swimming when they forget that tide tow or stream flow are ever-present dangers; and falling down, one of the most frequent types of accident, results from ignoring a slippery surface, an object on the ground or failure to grasp the handrail on a flight of stairs. These are all unsafe actions but their real cause is a lack of awareness, a failure to act in a known safe manner.

To be aware of these two basic causes for all personal injury and property damage, an unsafe condition and an unsafe action, is the foremost lesson in safety, in accident prevention. The watchword must be: Make the personal surroundings safe from hazards and perils, and secondly, maintain a sharp awareness of the environment and one's actions in that environment. To that end we shall now review the three categories for safety protection, accidents, disaster and crime.

ACCIDENT SAFETY

The importance of accident prevention in an industrial nation is exemplified by the statistics of the United States, a nation that takes extensive steps to prevent accidents. Each year 100,000 persons die in accidents. Of these, 50,000 die on the highways, 25,000 in the home, 15,000 at their place of employment and the remainder in public places. Quite remarkable is the fact that in the age group of one year to forty years, the leading cause of death is accidents. Between one and forty years of age, one is more apt to die by accident than by disease.

We see in these figures the great need for personal caution because even with the safety regulatory laws and intensive education in safety measures, still the loss by injury and in property damage is tremendous.

Public highway safety. Man conducts most of his public intercourse in two places, either the market, factory or office or the public highway, where the flow of traffic in humans and goods is carried on. While there is much traffic in the sky and on the seas, the immense bulk of persons and goods flows across the highways and bi-ways of the land, partly by rail, largely by vehicle. To move this mass of persons and goods safely requires a blending of five conditions, as follows.

1. The vehicle, which includes motor vehicles, motorcycles, bicycles, even horse drawn carriages.
2. The highway surface, paved and dirt, crooked and straight.
3. The laws and regulations to control the traffic such as privilege of

way, instructional guides, driver licensing.
4. The weather condition at the time of driving such as wet or dry surface, clear or dark day.
5. Skill of the driver in operating the vehicle.

These five ingredients must meet and mix in a matrix of harmony, wherein there is a safe condition of the vehicle, the highway and the weather, and a safe behavior of the person in operating the vehicle with a fixed attention, with a keen awareness. The details of these conditions are wide and extensive, nevertheless they must be complied with to a high standard if safety on the highway is to be achieved and loss of life and property reduced.

Home safety. The great haven for peace and comfort and for retreat from the dangers of the world has always been the home but this is hardly so today with that same home so well equipped with the marvels of technology: Electricity that shocks, drugs that kill as well as cure, strong poisons, toys that jag and cut the child and then trip the adult who falls, flammable liquids and appliance defects that set the home afire. Hazards in the home are not a new condition of course, for the olden days had their share in the form of open flame cooking, lack of ventilation and poor lighting, but today's hazards are more extensive and more intensive. They have more power to inflict greater injury and damage property, more rapidly and more deeply.

Safety in the home requires continued attention to these most prevalent dangers: Fire hazards, prevention of falls, care against suffocation of children and the elderly, guarding against the poisons of gasses, liquids and solids, and electric shock from home appliances.

Safety in the home must be pursued in the same fashion as in an industrial plant, namely, a periodic inspection for hazards and then a removal of them. It should be a routine, as follows.

1. Once each month, make a list of each room in the house plus a space for the outside yard. Place the list in the left hand column of a sheet of paper.
2. Make an inspection of these rooms and the yard, listing any hazards noted such as electricity, poison, poor lighting, tripping hazards, loaded guns, broken steps.
3. Immediately correct any unsafe conditions.

Work safety. The common rule throughout the world is that the employer must provide a safe place in which to work. But this regulation does not absolve the individual, in whom we are interested in this book, from all responsibility. Proper working procedure such as, don't spill oil on the floor or don't throw matches into a pile of wood, must be observed by the workman. And most importantly, it is the workman who moves about in the place of employment and must exercise the necessary awareness of environment and care in handling materials and operating a machine.

The workplace today is not only in a factory or a mill but includes also the mines, the office and the highway. Millions of persons now engage themselves as craftsmen, businessmen, professionals and technicians who work independently and must therefore provide for their total safety from work injury. Here each must analyze the work hazards, place physical guards around dangerous machines and exercise the necessary care in performance of the work.

Farm safety. Safety in agriculture is not greatly different from any other protective need except that animals are involved and the machinery used is large moving pieces. Farm safety may be considered in three principal areas, as follows.

Farm machinery. Planting and harvesting machines are necessarily large and clumsy because of the type of work they perform but the lesser number of farm accidents occur with these machines. It is the farm tractor that is the black sheep of farm safety. The cause is well known for this is the power unit of the farm, the most used machine, and its use is not across a smooth-paved highway but on ground that ranges from mushy to rocky, up and down hill sides, across ditches, in semi-swamp and pure desert. More, the tractor is not operating as a single machine but has in tow heavy and awkward machines. And still more, these towed machines are not free-wheeling but are dug into the ground with tongs and tines. It is under these multi-hazardous conditions and operations that the tractor becomes the source of most farm machinery accidents.

Livestock. The old adage of "contented as a cow" does not apply in the barn where old bossy must be milked, fed and cared for, because this so-called contented creature causes most farm animal accidents. Some reports state that the cow is the source of one-half of all farm animal accidents. Part of this high frequency is because cows are the most numerous of large farm animals.

Most animal related accidents are caused by kicking, biting, crushing, butting and trampling. A lesser cause is infection from animals such as anthrax and brucellosis which can cause sterility in both men and women.

Farm chemicals. Most farming is done today with the use of chemicals such as pesticides and vermicides. These are used largely to protect foods and fibers from destruction from insects, bacteria and fungi, and some are used on livestock. Long exposure to these chemicals, either by inhalation or contact on the skin, can result in serious injury to the body unless protective measures are taken.

Recreation safety. Recreation is an engagement of rest and relaxation in moderate play and sports, in the city and countryside, in the mountains and at the seashore. But it is not a time to relax from the vigilance of safety precaution. Each vacation environment contains its own list of hazards and dangers, its own potential for an accident. The principal areas for caution are:

- Fishing: Care in casting, caution against boat overturn, drowning.
- Swimming: The greatest single cause of all water fatalities is inability to swim or swimming in hazardous waters.
- Hunting: Skill in handling and using the gun is paramount in the prevention of hunting accidents.
- Boating: The rules for small craft operation must be obeyed and life saving equipment carried aboard, such as life preservers, fire extinguishers, first aid kit. Most fatalities associated with boating occur from drownings.
- All outdoors: Whether camping, hunting or fishing, the outdoors person must contend with natures tiny creatures such as insects, bugs and snakes, and also with nature's poisonous plants. The bites and stings and contact with harsh plants cause rash and poison of the skin and the bite of a snake injects a poison into the blood stream.

Fire safety. That great friend of man, fire, is also a most vicious enemy unless it is controlled, uless man handles it carefully. The enormous toll in lives and property that is taken each year has set fire safety apart for its own special attention, in all the nations of the world. In most accidents and disasters there is usually some part to be saved, to be retrieved, but not with fire for it does not merely damage, it consumes. The only residue is smoke and charred ruins.

There are many causes for the starting of a fire but three may be mentioned as dominant ones in personal living.

1. An open flame or spark such as matches, wood and coal fires, and cigarettes.
2. Heating and cooking equipment such as stoves, heaters and fireplaces.
3. Electrical fires, in wiring, in tools, in machinery.

Although commonly known it is also frequently forgotten that fire is a chemical process called combustion. It consists of the three ingredients of fuel, heat and oxygen, known as the fire triangle. All three must be present for a fire to occur and present in the right proportion. If any one is absent, combustion will not take place.

Fires are divided into four classes, as follows.

- Class A fires. The combustion of such materials as wood, paper and textiles.
- Class B fires. Such materials as grease, oil and paint.
- Class C fires. Caused by electrical equipment or the burning of such.
- Class D fires. Fire in such metals as magnesium and titanium.

In this day and age of high exposure to fire, all homes, vehicles and boats should be provided with a fire extinguisher. One extinguisher, the A-B-C type, is effective on any fire of the A, B, or C Class.

DISASTER

Disasters, like accidents, have been the lot of man from the beginning of man-time and we know them by such names as flood, volcano eruption, tornado and earthquake. But from the beginning of the Industrial Revolution a second category of disasters has confronted man, called man-made disasters and we know these by such names as fires, marine disaster, chemical disaster and finally nuclear disaster. Some authorities now list riot and civil disturbance as part of the man-made class.

Natural disaster. When a disaster occurs it is usually of a massive character, with extreme violence, extending over a wide area, affecting the lives of many people, with loss of life and destruction of property. The major types of natural disaster are as follows.

- Hurricane: Has strong winds, torrential rains and a sea surge (tidal wave) that inundates coastal areas. Destruction is over a wide area.
- Tornado: Extremely strong winds, a funnel-shaped cloud. Highly destructive in a narrow zone.
- Winter storms: Heavy fall of snow, ice, deep drifts of snow. Usually covers a wide area.
- Earthquake: A shaking and tilting of the earth's surface causing great destruction in a close area.
- Volcano eruption: an eruption of fire and lava from the earth. The volcano opening is small but the molten lava spreads in the immediate area, destroying man-made property and all vegetation.
- Flood: When water escapes its natural course or a dam breaks, it spreads destruction over a wide area.
- Landslide: Also known as mudslide. The loosening of a large piece of earth on a hillside and then sliding down and causing destruction to persons and property.
- Drought: An extended period without rain, causing loss of food supplies and resulting in starvation of people.

Man-made disaster. Man-made disasters are not new as witness the burning of the great library at Alexandria and the burning of Rome while Nero played his fiddle, as legend has it. But the disasters of today are more extensive than in olden times and much more intense in destructive power. Three general types are dominant.

1. Fire. We have reviewed this category above and need only add that no burnable substance is exempt, being: the forest, ships, buildings, the home and the human body.
2. Hazardous materials. These include chemicals that burn, corrode and explode; radiological materials and machines that emit hazardous rays, explosions that result from gasses and liquids.
3. War. The objective part of war is to conquer or defend. The subjective part of war is disaster, both for the conqueror and defender.

Whatever the high aim may be, the process of war is one of destruction, both of lives and of property. To embark on war is to embark on disaster, even for the victor.

Disaster safety. When a disaster occurs or is approaching it is known as an emergency condition, meaning that danger is present or eminent. As disasters are massive in character the basic protection from their violent action must come from the national or state government which has the facilities to aid and the power to enforce compliance. The organizations that perform this work are Civil Defense, army personnel on civic duty or the Red Cross. The protection takes the form of a warning of emergency conditions, providing strong shelters in which to seclude the public from the violent dangers, providing food, medicine and clothing, and in many cases evacuation from the area.

But individuals also must act for their personal safety, must take protective steps of their own. For example, if one lives in an area that is subject to hurricanes, earthquakes, flood or tornadoes, then long range plans must be made and ready for the type of disaster that is likely to occur. To delay is like locking the barn after the horse has been stolen. Steps for protection should supplement those mentioned above for the mass of people, such as: Have ready a plan of evacuation or else a safe shelter nearby, a stock of such basic materials as food, clothing, means of cooking, means of waste disposal, necessary medicines, a radio to hear instructions from authorities. Only basic needs should be provided, no luxuries.

CRIME

The third type of safety protection is against crime, known to all by such names as murder, burglary, robbery, theft, rape, and forgery. Like other forms of danger and peril it has been a part of life throughout the history of man but unlike accidents and disaster which might happen by chance, crime is perpetrated by deliberate intent. Although man abhors crime in its every aspect, it is celebrated in tales of fiction around the world, exceeded only by the subject of love.

Crime is a violent attack upon a person's body or upon another's property. It has many definitions such as negative behavior, social injury, anti-social behavior. We may note the types of criminal attack under two headings, as follows.

Crime upon the person.

- Murder: The willful killing of another.
- Manslaughter: Killing another due to negligence.
- Aggravated assault: Physical injury by force or violence.
- Sexual assault: Rape.
- Enslaving another, cruelty to children.

Crime upon property.

- Robbery: Taking the property of another by force or threat.
- Theft: The stealthy abstraction of property.
- Burglary: Forcible entry into a building to commit larceny.
- Motor vehicle theft: Larceny of an automobile.
- Arson: Willful and malicious burning.
- Forgery and counterfeit: Anything that is false but made to appear true, such as money, checks, passports.
- Embezzlement: The taking of money or property entrusted to one's care, custody or control.
- Fraud: To convert another's money or property to one's own possession.

Prevention of crime. The first protection for the citizen against crime must come from that branch of government known as the police force. Although every city and community has this police protection it does not prevent or stop crime but it does control crime and keep the number of occurences to a minimum, according to the facilities of the police force.

The second line of defense is the individual himself or herself. Self protection in public places consists in caution and awareness, such as: Where police may be reached, avoidance of known or likely criminal areas, travel with a companion, keep to lighted areas and avoid the dark, even carry a non-lethal weapon to resist assault upon the person. Within the home, locks are needed and a burglar alarm may be necessary.

Protection of property is a matter of erecting a physical barrier around the property. Such a barrier consists in locks, window bars, steel or concrete enclosures. In the case of property of high value such as money, art objects or jewelry, then a burglar alarm system connected to a central station or police department is needed, to supplement the physical protection.

THE WORTH OF SAFETY

The good or worth in safety, in protection from injury and loss, is self-evident, for it means freedom from personal injury and the preservation of property. And to this is added the resultant economic benefit. But beyond these good results is a higher worth for any injury or loss detracts from the general well being of life and daily living. To attain these good ends, these multi-benefits, is worth the effort to prevent and protect from accidents, crime and disaster.

Chapter 18
Economic Security

The critical need for the means of survival and well-being in life is quite apparent to all persons. This need is filled when a person has sufficient property such as money to purchase his or her many needs and wants. Some contend that this need for an economic security takes front rank before health and safety because food, clothing, shelter and safety cannot be obtained unless there are means to do so.

An economic resource consists in material property and for the individual this means everything that one owns: Money, home, land, furniture, animals, vehicles, tools, pencils and clothing. It is the sum total of personal economic wealth, of the financial standing, of the individual person. This property is divided into two categories, as follows:

Real property. This is land or real estate. Any building on the land is not considered real property but rather personal property. This is so because buildings depreciate and lose value but land does not.

Personal property. This type of property has three forms.

1. Cash. This is the money in one's pocket, money in the bank, savings bonds, drafts, even warehouse receipts.
2. Intangible property. This property consists in accounts and loans receivable, stocks and bonds, notes receivable, patents, copyrights, annuities such as a pension, retirement or trust funds and social security.
3. Tangible property. This includes such things as the home one owns or is buying, all household furniture, automobiles and boats, machinery, buildings, livestock and natural resources such as coal, gas and oil.

It is well to note that the term 'wealthy' is not a measurement of value but merely a descriptive term. Some persons are immensely rich merely by having good health and contentment in life with a small monthly income while others are poor even though they own enormous sums of money, land and buildings. Wealth merely states that a person has a quantity of something in a large or small amount. The true measure of wealth is found in the term Property for this defines the concrete possessions which constitute wealth.

ACQUIRING PROPERTY

One of the first steps in our Lifework Ability is to acquire an education as noted in that chapter. In the process of acquiring economic security this learning is put to work in a very real sense and it is an activity that will occupy the major portion of one's lifetime. So we may lay it down as a life rule that to acquire wealth in property it is first necessary to obtain a lifework ability to do so and this ability is embedded in education and training.

An individual acquires property by all of the three methods listed here.

Work. Any employment where the person engages in a personal action and receives remuneration for that action is work. This might range from the prime minister of a nation to the head waiter of a restaurant, from a doctor to a coal miner, from a fisherman to a farm employee. The term that is usually applied to an employed person is that of a wage earner, one who works for and receives a wage for his or her employment.

Profit. This is income from the sale of a product, either a manufactured product or the re-sale of goods such as in retail and wholesale firms. Profit is the amount earned over and above all costs to manufacture or sell the product. For the individual so engaged it is an income of money property.

Investment. This is a profit transaction but the profit or income is called an interest or a dividend. Instead of placing money in goods to be sold, money is placed in stocks, bonds, savings accounts, and insurance policies. From such invested monies one receives an interest or a dividend payments.

MANAGEMENT OF PROPERTY

"A penny saved is a penny earned" has always been good advice and the way to do this is by proper management of the pennies, of the property one has acquired. It does not mean to be miserly but rather to exercise good judgment in the income and outgo of property, to keep judicious control of receipts and expenses. It is impossible to keep good control without the use of books and records. For one's personal life it is not necessary to keep a complete bookkeeping department such as a business firm must do but it is necessary to keep a modified record. In fact, in this day and age of taxes and transactions there is a legal need and a legal requirement that such records be kept. Thus records are not only a convenience for saving pennies, they are a must for legal purposes.

All record keeping, both for the giant corporation and for the individual, consists in two types of records, one for transactions and one for the assets that are owned. The transaction records consist of two parts. First is the record of the income of property and second is the record of the outgo of property, or as it is usually called, expenses. These records are called books of which there are three: Income Journal, Expense Journal and Asset Record Book. All bookkeeping, all accounting, is recorded in these three books which we shall now review.

The Income Journal. In this book one records every type of income that takes place: Wages, salary, interest, dividends, profit, gifts, and so on. One page is used for each type of income, that is, write WAGES at the head of one page, write INTEREST at the head of another, etc. Each time there is income of wages, interest, etc. the date received and the amount received is entered on one line. At the end of each month these sums are added up, (you total the column), and this shows the total amount received for each item, for the month.

The Expense Journal. In this book one records the outgo of property and the column headings will be such as these: Food, Clothing, Utilities, Medicine, Insurance, Taxes, Contributions, Debts and so on. When you pay out such expenses, enter the date and amount on one line, then at the end of the month the columns are totaled to show the total amount of outgo for the month, for each item.

End of the year action. At the end of the year you take two sheets of paper, one for Income and one for Expenses, and list the total of each month from these two journals. These monthly totals are then added to give the year's total. Next a subtraction is made of the lesser from the greater. If income is greater than expenses then the result is gain; if expenses are greater than income, then the result is loss. This is exactly how a business firm or a bank keeps their records and the annual summing up is called a Profit and Loss Statement. An individual usually terms it Gain or Loss Statement (for the year).

The Asset Record Book. In bookkeeping terms, all property is referred to by two names: Assets, which are all of the things which one owns such as house, land, furniture, automobile, boat, tools, cash in the bank, bonds and money that is owed to you; and Liabilities, also called debts, and these consist of the money that you owe to other persons.

Sometimes you may have both assets and liabilities in one piece of property. For example, if your house cost $20,000.00 and after a few years you have paid off one-half of that amount, then you have an asset of $10,000.00 in the house and a liability of $10,000.00.

These assets and liabilities should be kept in the Asset Record Book and the value of each should also be entered.

Net Worth. As in the Income and Expense Journals, a summing is made at the end of each year in the Asset Book and it is from this source that the total (property) worth is known. The process is as follows:

- Add-up all of the assets to obtain a total sum.
- Add up all of the liabilities to obtain a total sum.

- Next you refer to the two sheets that hold the Gain or Loss Statement for the year. If there was a gain or profit, it is added to the assets total. If a loss, then it is subtracted from the assets total.
- In the last step you now subtract the liabilities from the assets to obtain your net worth.

For the individual or small family the records need not be extensive and may consist of one ruled sheet of paper for income and one ruled sheet for expenses, and a small book in which to record the assets or possessions.

THE GREAT ASSET

Property or wealth is the great asset in life, the material contributor to our well-being and in many ways the fundamental one. It is by, with and through property that the individual finds the means to life and living. A modest amount of property such as food, clothing and shelter is necessary merely to exist at all, but few persons are content with mere survival and so one constantly strives to enlarge their wealth and consequently enhance their living and well-being. Wealth in sufficient amount for economic security brings to life a pleasantness and contentment, an enriching quality, even a sense of happiness.

Chapter 19
Married Association

When a man and a woman enter into a state of marriage they automatically enter into a double condition in life, that of a spouse at the moment of marriage and eventually that of a parent. These roles in life are entirely different and distinct and must be examined separately. Accordingly, we shall review the status of spousehood in this chapter and that of parent and head of a family in the following chapter.

In the course of normal living the great tendency is to treat the state of marriage and the condition of a family as a single enterprise in which two persons marry and then disappear into the limbo of the family as parents. This is a serious error and the cause of much disruption in marriage and family life. A man and a woman, a male and a female, in a united state of partners in marriage is one thing, and these same two persons as head of a household and family of children is quite another thing. The importance of these two separate roles is further emphasized when it is recalled that the separate entities continue throughout life.

THE MARRIAGE AGREEMENT

Every marriage in every land of the world is consumated by two separate contracts or agreements at the time of marrying. It was so in ancient times and remains the same today. The first agreement is a legal contract and the second is a moral uniting called pledging. These we shall briefly review.

The Legal Contract. Widely known as the license to marry, this is a registration with state authorities and is a legal agreement in every sense of the word. And it is here that we most clearly see the distinction between spouse and parent, as mentioned in the beginning. There are four principal aspects to this legal contract.

1. A property agreement. Whatever property each person brings to the marriage, the laws of the land will be quite specific about the ownership of that property after the marriage ceremony, whether it is to be mutually owned or separately owned. The laws will also specify

ownership of property acquired after the marriage ceremony. By mutual consent the persons may draw up an agreement in writing and make an assignment of property, if this is so desired.
2. The inheritance. Death always requires a disposition of one's property and this is done by a last will and testament. This disposition is made as a spouse, not as a parent. Each individual must assign his or her property interests from the standpoint of a legal owner of that property, not because he or she happen to be a parent of children.
3. For violation of the law there is always a penalty and this is a burden layed on a spouse, not a parent, even though it may be a parental offense such as a father abusing a child. The penalty is assigned to Citizen Spouse, not Family Parent. Or, in case the marriage should come to blows it is a matter of two spouses, not two parents, even though both are parents at the time.
4. In case of divorce the law can only separate that which it bound and in this case it united two spouses so this is now what it will separate, not two parents, although parental considerations may enter into the proceedings.

The Moral Uniting. This is the pledging of love and devotion, the agreement aside from the legal contract. There are two general forms of this uniting, being religious and by custom or folkways.

1. Religious ceremony. In this uniting the couple stand before a leader of their religious faith, or as it is sometimes expressed "stand before God and man," and make a solemn pledge of love, faith and devotion. At the same time each now acquire a new title to their status in life, that of husband and that of wife. They are still not parents until the arrival of children.
2. Custom ceremony. In lands where religion is not a factor and in cases where a civil ceremony is preferred, the pledging ceremony is performed according to the custom of the people, according to the folkways of the land. It is always a solemn occasion, usually with a leader in attendance to conduct the ceremony, which is invariably impressive and profound, signifying to the society that the two persons have made a public vow and have now become husband and wife.

THE MARRIED PARTNERS

After the marriage ceremony the husband and wife now begin a social association exactly like any two human beings with three great exceptions, namely, that of a love relationship, a sexual association and the raising of a family. We shall review the love and sexual relationship below and the family raising in the next chapter.

As all persons know, the act of marrying is consumated in an hour but the state of being married continues for the remainder of life. Thus the choosing of a mate and preparing to establish a family calls for the wisest of decisions. The couple themselves will of course finalize all but good preparation for marriage calls for the seeking of advise from counselors, parent, and clergy, always remembering that these persons speak from past experience and thus have some foresight of the future. Such advice reduces the way of trial-and-error, a most hazardous and sometimes disasterous course in marriage.

Love relationship. This thing called 'love' is so common, so widespread and so deeply felt that it should be easy to describe, but it is no so. We love children, love dogs, love music and love food, all widely scattered loves. If we may believe the works of drama and fiction, love makes the world go round, causes empires to rise and fall, is the reason for much murder, and is the cause of great sacrifice for love of country and love of man. A thing so prevalent should be easily defined but there is no ready answer.

The reason is of course because love is not a commodity despite the old profession of the prostitute. Love cannot be bought and sold because it is a concept, an idea in the mind, and also because it is an emotional feeling. It can only be known by the actions of a person. With respect to love of a person, as it exists between the persons of husband and wife, we know it by such visible and tangible acts as:

- The arousal of an emotional feeling;
- An affection and liking for the person;
- A feeling of care and concern for the welfare of the person;
- A sense of respect for the person;
- A feeling of responsibility for the person;
- A willingness to sacrifice one's self for the person.

These feelings and emotions are the internal or subjective parts of love. When we look upon the person for whom we hold these strong affections, we then see the traits that inspire the feelings, such as:

- A physical attractiveness;
- A set of personality manners that are pleasing;
- An esteem for the person because of his or her ideals;
- An admiration of the person for his or her objectives and goals in life.

It is this combination of psychological feeling and physical observing that make-up the ingredients and elements of that mystical thing called love. But the love is expressed in the overt actions of helping, sharing, doing, even suffering and sacrificing.

Sexual Association. Love and sex are so utterly different that they should not be used in a combined phrase, all of the fiction, drama and romantic tales notwithstanding. Love, as noted above, is an emotional feeling with help-related actions. Sex on the other hand is a biological urging, a physical force. There may be and usually is, between husband

and wife, an emotional feeling present at the time of sexual intercourse, but largely and overall it is a biological force and sensation. Animals indulge in sexual intercourse and it is doubtful if love enters into the matter. Where sex is purchased or forced upon a person, there is no love involved. If love is present between a man and woman at the time of sexual intercourse it will heighten the experience but each is a separate entity.

The fact and act of sexual intercourse is well known to every adult both as an intimate association and as the process for giving birth to children. What is important to recognize is that it is a biological action all aside from any love attraction that may be present.

SPOUSE AND PARENT

Let us restate the distinction of spouse and parent in a family. As a spouse, the two persons will relate to one another, as parents they jointly relate to a family unit. As to a spouse they are husband and wife, male and female. As to the family unit they are father and mother. It begins with a romantic courtship, then a uniting in marriage, then a partnership for life. If love is present then this is fine and excellent but if love is not present the course of life remains the same, both as to spouse and to parent. Well-being is attained when the partnership is one of nearness, affection and harmony of acts.

Chapter 20
Family Association

The crowning gem of society and all social living is the family unit for it is here that the whole process of nature and humanity is consumated: The sexes are united, a new human is born and introduced to life, is cared for and trained in the way of living, and then sent forth as an adult human, to begin the process all over again. The family is not just important to humankind, it *is* humankind personified. As matrimony, the origin of the family is sacred before God, just so is the family sacred before man and nature.

The family has existed since the beginning of the human race, so much so that one wonders which came first, the family or the individual. Since man came down from the trees, (if that was his original habitat), there has always been a home unit of father, mother, children and a shelter for this biological group. And this is true for all of the world, without exception. Here life was and still is lived by the rules of love and affection, not the commands of political or religious law. Here life is lived not by stark demands but by a labor of enjoyment for the well-being of all members of the family.

THE TWO FAMILIES OF ONE LIFE

In the course of one's lifetime each human being lives in the environ of two separate families. The first is as a child in the home of our parents and secondly as a parent in the home of our own establishment. In the first we live under the guidance and care of a father and a mother and then in the second home we in turn perform the duties of father and mother in the care and guidance of our own children.

It is in and through this double family living that one generation is linked with the next. By this means the knowledge and customs of a people are transmitted down through the generations, down through time. It is a two-fold process in the first of which the race is propagated and renewed, and in the second the culture of man is passed on.

TYPES OF FAMILIES

Sociologists today distinguish between two types of families, the nuclear and the extended. The first consists in the well-known group of father, mother and children. The extended family consists of this nuclear group plus other relatives such as grandparents, grandchildren, aunts, uncles and in-laws. These relatives may or may not live in the same building as the nuclear group but usually live near-by. In times past the extended family was the usual, the normal, and it still is in agrarian countries and isolated lands such as jungles, deserts and mountains. The trend in industrial nations is toward the smaller nuclear family.

FAMILY ROLES AND RELATIONSHIPS

Everyone has a part to play, a job to do in the home. These roles are not spelled out as they might be in factory work but traditionally they follow a pattern similar to this outline:

Father. The father is generally considered to be the head of the household. Until modern times this was so by law as well as by acts for he was the breadwinner and disciplinarian of the family. But this is no longer true for the wife and mother now plays as prominent a part in managing the family as the father. Even the children, when they have attained a few years, help make the household rules, if not by declaration at least by behavior. But in common usage the father is usually recognized as head of the home.

Mother. It is mother who bears the children, guides the household routine, performs much of the house work and spreads a warm and intimate love through the home. The literature of the world depicts this love and sacrifice of the mother for her husband, her home and her children. Men may be the heroes of the world but mothers are the heroes of humanity. But few mothers as such see themselves as heroes. Being a good mother is their sufficiency, the only reward they want. Perhaps that is why a mother is a mother.

Children. Children cause the greatest number of problems in the home and bring the greatest of family joys. A home without children is a barren place indeed. It is as Dr. Samuel Johnson said, marriage has many pains but celibacy has no pleasures.

The new born child is a new creature in a strange world, utterly helpless to begin with, both in mentality and in the ability to help itself. If it were not for parental care it would not survive at all, much less pass through the first three normal stages of life, all of which take place in the family environment.

1. *Early childhood.* This is the pre-school period when the child is fully dependent on the parents for nourishment, bodily care, the first

learnings and the first trainings in how to cope with life. It is the first orientation the child receives in a great and unknown world. This is the job that falls fully upon the parents within the home environment. In a very vital way this first training and instruction will set the stage for all of life that is to come, for at the age of six years the pattern of living has begun to set and will soon harden into a fixation.

2. *First school period.* The early school period extends from age six to twelve years. This is the child's first separation from parent and home, the first entrance into the social world alone, and the first tasting of formal education. But even though the outside world is now beginning to shape the life of the child, he or she are still under the complete control of the home, of the family. The rules of life are still layed down by the parents and the child must conform to this parental direction.
3. *Adolescence.* These are the 'teen years' when the person is no longer a child but rather a young human maturing into full adulthood. The lower grades of school are completed and these years will see the advancement through middle and high school. The higher studies are now learned in language, mathematics and science plus the social relations of humans. For many this will be the end of formal education while for others the next phase is advanced learning in college.

But more is gained than an education during this residency in the family because the child of the family is such no longer even though he or she may reside there. During adolescence the change has been made to adulthood and the acceptance of one's own responsibilities. The interest of the person is now directed toward the self rather than being centered in the family and the separation from the family will soon take place. There will be fond memories and close friendship but a physical separation will occur for each must set about the making of his or her own family.

Post-parental period. There is still a family of two after the children depart but the role of parent, of mother and father, has ended. The style of life will change with many years of active and energetic living but the direction will be less family directed, more social and personal interests directed. Finally come the senior years of advancing age, retirement and eventually death, which completes the cycle of the family unit.

FAMILY FUNCTIONS

We have reviewed the family as an institution in the section on Institutions. Here we shall consider the major functions of the family in personal living, with some slight redundancy. These functions are six in number.

1. *Reproduction.* Only the family environment can reproduce the race which is done by sexual intercourse of male and female. Some children are born outside of wedlock, some by artificial insemination, but these are incidental to the norm of a family environment. In many ways these accidental methods of birth are a burden on society.
2. *Early physical care.* The helpless new-born must have nurture and nursing through the first years and this is provided in the family environment. There are two aspects to this care. First is the actual cleaning, feeding, clothing and shelter of the body of the helpless one, and secondly, protection from the outside dangers that may penetrate such as disease, accidents, and physical hurt from others.
3. *First education.* During the first several years of life the entire world so far as the child is concerned is the home and the family. To the child there is no other existence even when the family leaves the home campus for he or she is closely sheltered within the family group while traveling, with little or no freedom to act alone. All knowledge, all skills, emotion control and social association that is acquired is the result of education in the home. The child will gain a personality and self in time but until the end of this period he or she will bear the label "family made."
4. *Material means.* There must be a material base for a family to operate and this consists in three parts, as follows:
   (a) A shelter of home and furnishings. Family housing may range from a tee-pee or hovel to a penthouse apartment or a single dwelling, according to the desires and abilities of the family, but it will provide a shelter from the elements and a privacy from the world where members of the family may live in intimate association.

   There must be furnishings for the home and these will consist in such basic needs as tables and chairs, beds and rugs, a stove for cooking, knives and forks for eating, facilities for cleaning clothes. Beyond these basics the gadgets for the home are limitless, such as: Refrigerator, radio, television, stereo sound, dishwasher, and so on. There is no rule for well-being in the home or its furnishings for some need little and some desire much but the rule of thumb for judging is this: It should not be a hovel but need not be a palace. The objective is well-ordered and pleasant living, not a dwelling over-stuffed with superfluous goods.

   (b) Food and clothing. These are basic needs of the body, for nourishment and protection from the climate.

   (c) Other needs. Beyond the three basics of food, clothing and shelter there are no other needs of life for biological man. Just obtain these three and there the matter should end. But man is a thinker and so he has wants and desires that exceed these minimal needs, wants and desires that are kept aflame by the great flow of products for pleasure. for leisure and life-enjoyments. These products include gourmet foods, fancy clothes, vehicles, boats, games, exotic travel and creature comforts.

5. *Economic means.* There must be monetary income to purchase the needs of the family. In times past the income was expressed in terms of goods, so much meat, vegetables, clothing and wood for the fire. In modern times income is stated in terms of money, so many dollars, francs, pounds, yens, pesos and rubles.

This change over from goods to money income has imposed upon the family a very important economic fact, namely, that inasmuch as the home is now operated with business values of money, it must therefore be operated on a business basis. And "business basis" means the management of money, the control of income and outgo.

In the chapter on Economic Security the use of the income and expense journals was explained. For the home, income would be shown as wages, interest, dividends, pensions and such like. Home expenses would include food, clothing, rent, mortgage payments, utilities, recreation, debt payments, and so on.

The outgo of money requires special care and wisdom in dispensing. The watchword is: Do not spend more than you receive, expenses must not be greater than income. This does not mean earn a dollar, spend a dollar. You may spend "on credit," making purchases that are greater than your income for a month or a year but only on condition that your normal income will allow regular payments over a reasonable period to pay-off or retire the debt. But the use of credit must be done judiciously. Credit is not an asset, it is a debt condition, a liability the moment you use it. After the purchase is made you must then spend your income to pay off this credit-debt.

6. *Affection.* Feelings of love and affection are as much a part of the family operating system as are material goods. It is impossible to visualize what sort of child creature would emerge from the home if only his or her physical needs were administered to and loving affection was not included. Or, conversely, if the child itself did not express affection to father, mother, sisters and brothers. It would certainly not be a human creature as we know humans because love is essential to human beings. When a person cannot or does not express affection for another or does not receive care-attention from others, his life becomes a sterile existence, an alien state. Such a person cannot engage in true human living and the end is a mental illness, a withdrawal from normal life.

This reciprocity of love-feeling is an innate part of human nature and nowhere in the world does this tenderness exist with such force, such intimacy, such depth and expression, as in the family. This emotional feeling will bind a family together through every conceivable trial of sickness, disaster and catastrophe. The government, the church and friends may show a sympathy and lend a physical hand but only the family can ooze a love potion that infects all of the members, gluing them together as a family, with a giving of self and a sacrificing of person for one another, that is unknown otherwise on earth.

MORE THAN A SOCIAL RELATIONSHIP

Although we classify the family as a social institution, it is more than that because there exists in the family more than a social relationship. There is an extension of the person, a condition where each member becomes a family-self, losing the identity of a personal-self. The phrase so often applied to the family is "the cradle of mankind," and it is certainly this in every respect. But beyond the cradle it is also the haven of mankind, a shelter and refuge from the harsh realities of the world. Just as nature renews itself each year and dresses itself in new garments, so must the individual make a constant renewal of the self, adorning the heart and the mind with new inspiration, with renewed faith and hope. The haven for doing this is not secluded isolation but rather the family environment.

THE DECISIVE PERIOD

The life period that the young person spends in the family, culminating at about the age of eighteen, is of such high importance what we shall gather here in one list the major events that take place at this time. These events are such that they are irreversible. Their content may be be changed, for it is a ritual of nature, of society and of culture combined. It is that moment in time of which St. Paul spoke when he said, "When I was a child I spoke as a child, I understood as a child, I thought as a child, but when I became a man, I put away childish things." It is that moment when we put away childish living, leave the parental environment, and set forth into the world of adult living.
ment, and set forth into the world of adult living.

- Biological growth is complete.
- Mental development is complete, although learning and reasoning will continue through life.
- Attitudes and beliefs are largely fixed.
- That second nature of man, habit, is in full force.
- Career choice is determined, or will now be determined.

- Social relationship living is fully developed.
- The age for marriage has been attained.
- A life partner has been or will now be selected.
- First plannings for a family unit are made.
- The age of full citizenship has been attained, with its attendant rights and duties.
- Armed forces eligibility is reached.
- The Self is set, how you view y-o-u, how actions are seen.
- The Personality is set, how actions are performed and the traits exhibited that distinguish character.

These are the major events that occur in the first one-quarter of life which is lived in the parental environment, the decisive period for every individual.

Chapter 21
Small Group Association

The word 'social' comes from the Latin and means ally, to associate, So, to be social you must ally yourself with another person or persons. If you stand alone on the top of a mountain there will be no association, no contact with fellow humans. When you come down from the mountain to the family, the job, to friends, then you begin to have a social relationship, an interaction with other persons. You are in a group association where your social well-being takes place.

In the section of the book titled Culture of Man we considered social association in the large group, in the institutions of Government, Science, Economics and so forth. In this chapter we shall examine the social association in the small group, in the arenas where the individual has a personal contact with other individuals.

THE MEANING OF SOCIAL RELATIONS

To pass a person on the street and remark "hello," perhaps chat briefly and then pass on in a casual fashion is not social interaction, not a role of behavior. In social relations there must be reciprocity of action between two or more persons. There must be a certain give and take, a commonality of action, a unity of purpose. Stated otherwise, there must be a working together or in opposition. There is a goal, an aim, and each of the parties press for the objective, jointly for the same or conversely each for his own. This is the manner of social interaction in which all persons indulge every day, within the family, with friends and in the work environment. It is small group association.

All human relations take place within a group environment. A group may consist of two or more persons such as a husband and wife or two friends; it may consist of ten persons such as a work group or a sports team; and it may also contain the two hundred students in a school class. Or, as we noted in another chapter, it may comprise a whole nation.

A group is not a mere cluster of human beings. For example, here are twenty boys standing on the playing field and staring at the sky. Their adjacency does not constitute a group, they are merely a number of boys standing on the field.

In a field nearby is another group of boys engaged in a game of soccer. They are organized into two teams, each player has his place, there are rules on how to play, how to score, how to contest with the opponent. These teams are each a social group for they are bound in joint action, under certain rules, with values such as no fighting, no cheating, must play hard to win, must be in good health to play.

Despite the great variety in the number of persons in a group, all groups act and behave in a similar manner because each acts by a set of rules and regulations that spell out the conduct of the members. This is so because groups serve a directed purpose: They are organized, have a set of norms, have rules of operation and seek some goal or end. Sometimes the rules are not clearly stated and complying with the regulations is lax but the controls exist nevertheless. For example, the family has very precise objectives such as propagating the race and raising children but no family draws up these objectives in the form of a formal agreement. Most social clubs and sports groups operate in this fashion, having very definite objectives, but "everybody knows them," and so they are not specifically stated.

It is well to note one aspect of the group that is often overlooked and that is that the group as such does not act, behave and have social relations, only the individuals within the group perform the action. It may be a concerted action, a group behavior, but it is still the individuals who do the acting. This is quite apparent because a group is a concept, an idea, not a concrete object. For example, a group can be three persons in a business partnership although one is in London, another in New York and the third in Tokyo. Again, when the 'family' goes on a picnic, in reality it is father, mother, the children and dog who go. It is people who have social relations, not abstract ideas or concepts.

TYPES OF GROUPS

In the course of our personal life in daily living we have a social relationship with two types of groups, as follows:

The close group. These are the persons we know intimately and associate with daily. These groups include the family, a few close friends, immediate neighbors, perhaps a small work group. Here the relations are informal, loose, without strict rules, and is often called plain-folk living. In such groups the atmosphere is warm, there is trust, and there is assurance of reciprocal help and assistance in time of need.

The community group. These groups are found in the community environment and are the very groups that make-up a community. We may say that they are the essence of a community for if they were to be taken away there would be no such thing as a town or a community condition. The following are representative groups:

A club	Volunteer group
Play group	Fraternal society
Committee	Neighborhood association
Church group	Recreational club
Military Unit	Ethnic, folkways group
Job — work group	Political unit
Chamber of Commerce	Rotary club
Business association	Volunteer Fire Department

Unlike the close group which functions informally, community groups have organization with rules of operation, norms of conduct and goals to be achieved. There will be elected officials to manage affairs such as president and secretary and committees to carry out duties such as recruiting new members, conducting meetings, and acquiring finances with which to operate.

SMALL GROUP ASSOCIATING

The three methods by which humans associate was reviewed in the chapter Man in Association, which are: Cooperation, competition and conflict. These actions take place in all social relationships but in the close and community groups the associating is not strict in character, more in the order of a joint striving to reach a common goal. They are actions that accrue in a mutually beneficial result and so the behavior is one of cooperating or countering, as follows:

Cooperating actions.

- Agreement on a mutual task or goal, an end that the group is to strive for.
- Agreement on positions and roles of the members.
- An attitude of trusting others and a willingness to collaborate.
- Accepting the view of others, seeking and giving a constructive help.
- Open communication with truthful exchanges of ideas and plans.
- An effort to minimize differences, to find a common ground to achieve a common goal.

Countering actions.

- Disagreement over goals, over methods of achievement.
- Non-agreement over who shall serve and in what positions.
- An attitude of doubt, of suspicion, of altercation. Habitual difference.
- Rejection of group proposals, dismissed with little or no consideration of their merits.
- Communication is guarded or withheld.
- An enlargement of small differences.
- Obstructionist tactics.

Well-being in small group relationships must conform very largely to that of cooperation. This is only normal because such groups are organized to attain a common end, an objective that has mutual benefits. Any serious opposition will defeat the original intent. But there will be differences as we have seen between such close persons as husband and wife, parent and child, neighbors and friends. There is no magic to prevent disagreements for such is the nature of life. What is important is that they do not get out of hand, out of control. Indeed, many would not have it otherwise for differences can also be beneficial, opening the mind to new vistas and pointing the way to a better goal. In this sense and use, differences are constructive.

No cut and dried formula for resolving a difference has yet been discovered by man, but counselors in human relations list a four-step process to follow in trying to solve a disagreement. This is quite similar to the problem solving method previously reviewed.

1. State the facts. The facts, both pro and con, must be set forth in clear language so that they are well understood by all parties.
2. State the goal. This is the objective sought, the end in view. If it is a common goal then the problem is simplified by that much but if each has a different goal in mind, then this is the stage where this obstacle is removed.
3. State the method and means. These are the facilities that will be needed to attain the goal, usually consisting of money, supplies and the workers to do the job. As in the case of facts and goals above, these must be clear and known to all persons on both sides of the difference, if there is one.
4. In the end, if resolution of the disagreement should prove impossible, then outside counsel and advice should be obtained. In general, the advice sought should be for new insights and new vistas, not direct resolution of the problem for this can only be accomplished within the group itself.

THE NORMS OF CONDUCT

Norms are the rules that guide and regulate the behavior of groups and also the individuals who are members of the group. These norms exist in three forms, as Folkways, Mores and Laws. The Laws were reviewed in the chapter on Government and here we shall consider Folkways and Mores.

Folkways. These are the norms and rules of everyday behavior. Other common words for these folkways are customs, manners and etiquette. These regulations tell the proper way to act in associating with other persons and the behavior that is improper. If you violate any of the folkways it is not an offense of great importance but more in the order of an embarassment, an act of bad manners and poor etiquette. You may be frowned upon but will suffer no great penalty.

Folkways are the old and familiar ways of acting, the "you should" and "you should not" rules of common social intercourse in the presence of other persons. You should take meals at a certain time of the day, use the knife and fork in the proper manner, wear dress that is the fashion of the time, decorate the home in good taste.

After the personal manners comes the conduct in public places. One should give proper greeting to persons, use proper manners at school and in church, give proper respect to persons and places of importance. Then there are the "customs of the people," such as the ceremony of marriage, the holidays that are to be celebrated, graduation exercises, puberty rites, birth and death rituals. All these are folkways of the people.

Mores. Mores refer to the rightness and wrongness of an action and are quite similar to what are usually called morals. Mores deal with matters of life that are more serious than folkways and so a mores offense is of greater significance than a violation of a folkways custom.

Mores are midway between formal codes of behavior and the laws of the land. These are rules of conduct in which all of the people believe, that which they think is correct and necessary for the well-being of society without stating the rules in a formal code of laws. The use of alcohol is an example. Some believe that drinking whiskey or gin is improper, is wrong, while others think that alcohol in modest quantities is proper. However, when a person becomes stupidly drunk, then all parties oppose this use of alcohol.

One of the widest known set of mores is the Ten Commandments of the Bible, with its prohibitions: Thou shalt not kill, shalt not steal, shalt not bear false witness. The great moral rule of Confucius was: Do not do to others that which you would not have others do to you. Where the custom is to have one wife then the taking of a second one is breaking the moral code. To love children is proper while the cruel treatment of a child invokes a moral condemnation. Freedom from oppression, a proper wage for labor and to worship as one pleases are all social mores.

In most of the ancient and primitive societies the folkways and mores were the only guides to the conduct of life. It was a straight ritual of thou shall and thou shall not. That which was forbidden was taboo. As societies grew larger and more highly organized, many of the folk-rules were stated in specific terms as laws, but these laws have not replaced the folkways and mores of the people for these still flourish in every land.

STATUS – POSITION

In each and every group to which an individual belongs, he or she will occupy a certain position or status in that group. This is so whether it is in the home, the factory, the ball team, the church or the army. The status or station that every person occupies in a group consists in two parts, that of a position and that of a role.

Position in a group. Position refers to the division of labor, the place that each person occupies in a group. These positions are known by their titles such as secretary, truck driver, clerk, factory foreman, photographer, mother (in the family group), prime minister of government, nurse, army corporal. These are the titles for the duties to be performed and there is no consideration of age, sex or race, not even the ability to do the work that is required. A lazy clod might very well occupy the position of ruler of a nation. Position is merely a station, a fixed place within an organization, within a group.

Persons may and do occupy more than one position at a time. For example, Mr. Smith is a father, a husband and child teacher, all positions within the home. Outside the home he is a church member, truck driver, baseball player on weekends, lodge president and volunteer fireman. These are his positions in these work and leisure activities.

But position does carry three very important conditions, as follows:

Duties. Every position and job category exists for a purpose, it is intended to accomplish some end, to complete some job process. The truck driver is obligated to drive his truck and deliver goods.

Responsibilities. All positions impose an obligation over and above normal duties. The truck driver must drive his vehicle in a safe manner.

Rights. Rights vary by position. Thus the father may punish the child for misconduct, the school may not. The truck driver has the right to decide the safest method of operating the vehicle while on the highway.

These duties, responsibilities and rights set the boundaries to a position. They are the rules, regulations and procedures that direct people in their tasks, in their jobs. They describe the operation, specify the competence necessary to fill the position, state the qualifications of the person, relate the promotion rules and designate the remuneration.

Positions usually fit into a heirarchy of authority, a sort of ladder of power or influence, and they are fixed in one of several ways:

- By custom. Some positions are inherited such as from father to son, some come by long established experience such as in factories and institutions.
- By competition. Here the position is assigned on the basis of ability, of superior skill.
- Fixed by authority. These positions are fixed by a legal body or government such as prime minister (even though it is an elected position), army general, policeman, research team.

Role in the group. Role is the behavior of the person in the position(s) he or she occupies. It is simply the duties that are to be performed according to the position or status. Thus, the postman in his position of route carrier will carry out the role of sorting the mail and delivering it to the persons to whom it is addressed. A manager's role is to guide and direct, a doctor's role is to attend the sick.

The term 'class' is not part of position or role in human behavior although it is very commonly applied. The class terms are usually high, middle or low and what they refer to is not status but rather power, influence or prestige which the position affords. Thus a president would occupy a high position of power and influence but from the behavior standpoint it is merely a position and the person filling it must execute the proper role, must carry out the duties required of the position. The person in the position is not necessarily high class.

Class is usually a division by wealth or property, by birth or ascribed status, by political rank, religion, profession or intelligence. Class is neither good nor bad so far as the individual is concerned for it is merely a division by culture, not a grading of people.

THE SMALL GROUP

The real social living of man the social animal takes place in the small group environment. Institutions are too big and cold, a nation of millions of people is too large for social relating between persons. And sociality requires a person-to-person relationship which is only found in the intimacy of the family, a few close friends and perhaps a work group. Here there is a warmth, a closeness and a personal feeling that gives true meaning to sociability. Here one gives and receives such giving in return. It stands out bold and clear that the small group is the great matrix of man as a social being. It is here that social well-being of the individual is both cultivated and achieved.

Part III

ENRICHMENT OF LIFE

To enrich means to increase by adding in-to. It does not mean to enlarge by adding on-to for such is a matter of increasing size and this cannot be done with human life. An illustration may be seen in a loaf of bread. The loaf may be enlarged by adding more flour and water but it is enriched by adding salt for taste and vitamins for nourishment. Again, a house is enlarged by adding another room but is enriched by adding into the old house more comforts for living such as improved cooking, bedding and toilet facilities. Thus we see that enriching is an act of infusion rather than an attaching to. The adage that "bigger is better" is not true where the enrichment of life is concerned.

The same holds true in personal behavior, namely, that to enrich our living we must add in-to our life those worthy ingredients which will increase the enjoyment of living. Or, conversely, subtract that which is not good, that which is unworthy. Clearly we cannot add more hours to the day, cannot eat ten more pounds of food to increase health, cannot take the pleasures of living in excess for these actions would merely enlarge, not enrich. The only quality that we can add in-to our life is a value, that is, a good or a worth. And a value is a goal of choice, not necessity.

When the human being has reached the state of adulthood, at about the eighteenth year, he or she will have attained the condition of a whole human being. One is 'whole' in the sense that bodily growth is complete, thinking and feeling abilities are fully developed, the general course of life is set with a spouse, a family and life career. For the remainder of the person's life the process of living will be a daily-weekly repeat of work, play, rest and social association. Hereafter there will be no more to add-on to the personal life, only an add-in to that which now exists.

To strive for more and bigger is an action in a horizontal direction. To strive for enrichment of living is a vertical effort, an action in height and a feeling in depth. And the qualities one seeks for this enrichment are values, that which is good, that which has worth. These are the attributes of value that we shall examine in this part of the book.

Chapter 22

Values in Life

The word 'value' is a cloak of many colors for it includes such terms as Good, Worth, Right, Useful and Desirable. We must put these colorful terms into their proper setting in order to gain a more accurate understanding of values in life.

Value. This is the general term that includes all of the others such as worth, good and right. It refers to anything and everything that is beneficial, useful for good ends, is helpful to a person, has worth, has merit.

Worth. Very similar to value in meaning and use and the two words may be used interchangeably.

The Good. This term has two meanings. In the first it refers to the value or worth in material objects and in the second it has reference to the value or worth in human conduct. In behavior it means the opposite of bad, of evil. The twelve goals of life have the value or quality of Good because they are goals of well-being that all persons seek and therefore have worth in human living.

The Right. The Good is a judgment that is made upon the conduct of a person or a group whereas the Right refers to a privilege of conduct. "I have the right to do this, it is my privilege to do that." While there is no precise classification of rights we may divide them into four groups for added clarity.

1. Legal rights. These are the privileges that a person is granted by the laws of the state in which he or she may reside. Such laws would of course include non-rights, those acts which the citizen is forbidden to do.
2. Political rights. These are such entitlements as the right to vote, the right to dissent, the right to seek office, the right to protest, right to free speech, right to trial by jury.
3. Human rights. These include the right to live, to work, to liberty, to own property, right to privacy. (This list is extended below).
4. Moral rights. We know these rights by such phrases as: "He had no right to strike his wife; I have a right to live in poverty if I choose;

It is wrong (not right) to steal; It is proper (right) to work hard for one's welfare."

We see from the above that the term 'value' has many components and we shall attempt now to extract a clear meaning of their content.

THE VALUE JUDGMENT

The value judgment was reviewed as a method of thinking in the chapter on Mental Ability, here we shall relate this judgment to human behavior.

A value judgment is a conclusion about the worth of an object, an idea or an action. It is a judgment that each individual forms about the worth of life, of living, of experiences. A thing is not value itself, it merely has value according to a mental judgment. Let us review a few examples of how this is so.

Here is an apple that is ripe and wholesome and so we say that its value is good. Here is an apple that is rotted and so its value is judged to be not-good, to be bad. Again, an act of justice has the value of worth while an act of murder is unfair, is not right. A charitable gift has a worthy value, an act of theft has a negative value, is unworthy. Here is a violin worth a king's ransom in London but a tribal indian in the jungles of Brazil would consider it an insufficient amount of wood to cook a fish for his dinner and throw it away. Mr. Smith believes that war is normal for humans, Mr. Jones thinks it is an act of savage behavior. Here is an artist who captures the beauty value of a sunset on his canvas while another beholder considers it a waste of time when a camera will capture the same scene. Here is a family set for a vacation: Father prefers fishing in the mountains, mother thinks the city, theatre and zoo is best, the children vote for the sea shore — all value judgments on the type of vacation that would be best, would be of most value to the family.

We see in these examples that value is a mental conclusion, is a judgment of worth, not a tangible, concrete thing. It is a personal evaluation, a considered opinion. In some matter everyone's judgment will be the same: Thou shalt not kill another human being. In other matters there may be opposite poles of opinion, such as: One man holds that all dogs are a nuisance and should be destroyed while another is certain that dogs are beneficial to mankind and necessary for his pleasure.

BASIS OF JUDGMENT

A judgment of value is usually made of and from the following three components.

The thing in itself. There must of course be something about which to make a judgment such as a person, an object, an event or some action of human behavior.

Beliefs and attitudes. The teachings at home, in the school and from religious instruction, plus our own behavior in life, become in time a fixed attitude toward life. We have at hand a whole crystal ball, ready to pronounce judgment on the goodness or the wrongness of persons, things and human behavior. Psychologists call this 'crystal ball' a frame of reference, meaning that we refer to our attitudes and beliefs as the basis for making value judgments. It is the way we look at life and all of its numerous activities.

Standards. Standards refer to laws and social customs which are more clear cut and better defined than an attitude. They say in effect: You may do thus and so, you may not do thus and so. Then, if your actions are contrary to these rules, these values, a judgment is made as to rightness or wrongness, according to how you obeyed or disobeyed the rules. If a rule, either law or custom, states that you may not break into another man's house and steal his goods, then you are un-good, un-right if you do so.

It is from out of the vortex of one's beliefs, attitudes and the standards of life that each one forms his or her judgments of worth, of value.

ETHICAL JUDGMENTS

Human conflict and behavior when considered in general is a subject of psychology and sociology. These same actions and behavior when examined for their value, for their good or worth, belong to the realm of Ethics. This value-behavior is best known as morals, a subject and study of Moral Philosophy.

Human conduct does not have a material value such as a tool or a house but rather a moral value and so when we come to judging the behavior of a person we are making a moral judgment. That is, we come to a conclusion as to whether an action is good or bad, is right or wrong, both for the person who has acted and for the influence or result of the action. It is a verdict of approval or disapproval. If the action is one of virtue then it is judged to be good and therefore approved, if of vice then it is not good and therefore disapproved.

Moral judgments are familiar to all for we go about our daily business pronouncing them without end. But we should take note that these same moral judgments are not only formed about other persons, they also act as a guide for our own behavior. Here are several examples:

- This is the right action to take in the matter (or wrong action).
- His reputation is good (or bad).
- Honesty is the best policy.
- The statement he just made is true (or false).
- They are riddled with corruption (or are incorruptable).

- This is a just law (or unjust).
- Her reputation is good (or poor).
- His middle name is vice and he has no virtues.

Two classes of judgment are considered in ethics. The one of value and the other of obligation.

A judgment of value. Value judgments were reviewed above. They are a conclusion as to the moral worth of an action when directed toward a goal, toward an end. Such things as pleasure, virtue and knowledge have the status of goodness while pain, vice and ignorance are judged to have badness.

A judgment of obligation. Obligation, or duty, has the status of rightness, or right action, as opposed to wrong action. Obligation also has the quality of necessity rather than choice. We are obliged to obey the law because it is right and necessary that we do so; it is not only good that you care for your children, it is an obligation and a necessity.

But obligation extends beyond mere law and necessity for it has a higher value in such realms as justice, welfare, equality and freedom, even the right to life itself. All of these, too, are moral obligations, the duty of one person and one people to themselves and to their fellowmen. A judgment of obligation is made upon these great parts of human behavior according to their attainment or failure.

TWO PROPERTIES OF VALUES

Values have a dual worth in that they are good in themselves and are then a means to an extended good, a good beyond the value itself. The twelve goals of life reviewed in Part II are an example. Each goal such as health, safety and economic security are a value and good in themselves and it is quite apparent. But they also shed good at a secondary level in our daily living, our contentment with life, our experience of happiness. These two aspects or properties of values are called intrinsic and extrinsic.

Intrinsic value. This is the good or worth that a thing has as an end in itself, a good that resides within the thing. It is a good without equivocation and depends on nothing else for its goodness. Thus health, mental ability, shelter, safety from injury, and friendship are all good in themselves, are worthy possessions.

Extrinsic value. Here the value is not in the thing itself but rather outside of the thing, outside of that which has created the value. The value created is usually that of a means, an instrument to a further value. For example an automobile has worth itself but it is also the means of transporting people and goods. Gold coins have two values, the intrinsic one of a valuable metal and the extrinsic one of exchange value in the purchase of goods. Paper money has only one value, extrinsic, as a means to purchase. The intrinsic value of food is that it contains nourishing elements, the extrinsic value is to energize the body and bring health.

These two attributes of worth within and worth without are characteristic of values.

TYPES OF VALUES

There is no proper classification of the limitless values in life but a grouping of the better known ones will aid in further understanding. For this purpose we may divide the values into five classes: Material objects, personal values, social values, the environment and time. Of these, the last four are values that relate to human behavior.

Value in material objects. Material objects are generally considered to have three types of value, as follows:

Market place value. This is the monetary value of an object, having a worth equal to so many dollars, yen, rubles, francs, pesos or pounds. The world and all that is therein may carry a "for sale" sign, including virtue, integrity and honor. Even the human being had a market value when bought and sold as a slave.

Material value. Here the base is one of quality of the object. Are the ingredients sound, durable, of 'good' quality. Or are they of poor quality? Has the finished product been constructed in a craftsman-like manner, is there good utility in it, including perhaps some aesthetic value of beauty.

As the human body is also made up of material things, it too has been considered for its material value. This has been calculated to be, when rendered down to the basic parts, approximately as follows: Two and one-half gallons of water, a thimble full of sugar, a dozen pinches of salt, enough iron to make a nail, a bit of iodine, traces of other minerals with the whole amounting to about $1.00.

Utility value. All things of nature such as trees, cows, and oceans; all things man-made such as shoes, automobiles and eye glasses have a use or utility value. This value may be good and worthy or it may be poor, even bad. A gun has a good value as a hunting or survival instrument, it has an unworthy value as an instrument to kill and murder.

Personal values. Everything in the world has personal value to some individual. Thus, world peace is a great social value but the benefits still accrue to the individual. Use of the term 'personal' here refers to the values that are directly associated with the person of the individual. These are the values ones strives for, the goals of well-being that one seeks. We have reviewed the twelve goals of life and here need only list them as values instead of goals.

The value of health. A healthy condition in the body and the mind is the basic value to all of life's living.

The value of abilities. Skill and abilities are the working tools with which one engages in the business and in the pleasure of living.

The value of resources. The conditions of safety and of economic security are the main ingredients of this value.

The social values. These are well known as the family group, the immediate friends and the community associations.

The religious value. Blaise Pascal has said that man finds his lasting happiness only in God, and if this is so then that is value enough.

Other values. Some other well known personal values are: Prestige, leadership, independence, service to others, self-respect, social recognition, determination, perseverance.

The doctrine of Epicurus, who taught c. 300 B.C., is probably the great water shed in any discussion of personal values. This is known as the Pleasure-Pain principle which states that the ultimate course in all human living is to seek pleasure and avoid pain. The pleasure vs. pain argument has occupied philosophical and religious teachers through history and it is still alive today. It is also sometimes misinterpreted. Epicurus thought in ethical terms and did not sponsor a life of uncontrolled pleasures. His argument was that by avoiding pain, its opposite, pleasure, would result. Pleasure is to be thought of as a summary value in life, a major good resulting from the accumulation of many smaller goods.

Social values. These values are clearly set forth by the United Nations and the following list follows the U.N. assertions, which opens with the general statement that all human beings are born free and equal in dignity of person and in rights to the needs of life.

Human Rights Values — Civil and Political.

- The right to life, liberty and security.
- The right to equal protection under the law.
- The right to fair trial by jury.
- The right to freedom of movement and residence within a country.
- The right to leave and return to your own country.
- The right to nationality.
- The right to own property.
- The right to freedom of thought, conscience and religion.
- The right to freedom of opinion and expression.
- The right to freedom of peaceful assembly and association.
- The right to participate in government of your own country.

Human Rights Values — Social and Economic.

- The right to social security.
- The right to work under just and favorable conditions.
- The right to a standard of living adequate for health and well-being.
- The right to education.

- The right to participate in cultural life of the community.

Duties.

- Respect for these same rights in others.

Environmental values. Nature as the source of mans' life and sustenance has always been of the highest value to man but in recent years this value has come to be endangered to a high degree as a result of population increase and the waste material from people and industry. It is not yet on the 'endangered species' list but is on the 'endamaged' one. This value has a two-part aspect.

Space value. With the great increase in world population there has been a resulting decrease in nature-land, in leisure-land and in dwelling-land. Although the earth is far from being full of people, the availability of space-to-live has greatly diminished. This does not mean space for new buildings and work areas but rather the open space of land and water needed to support farm land, forest land, water sources and land resources.

Clean environment. Here the value is one of cleanliness, a living space free from pollution such as people wastes, chemical wastes, factory/smoke wastes, automobile exhaust fumes, and radioactive materials.

Time value. The platitudes about time fill much of the vocabulary: Time is short (referring to life time), it is precious, it is a thing in which to waste away life, it drags, it flies, it stands still, it is the only thing that is eternal. There is much wisdom here but not the kind with which we are concerned at this point. Our interest is the worth of time in the life of an individual person.

The time span in conscious awareness is of course only instantaneous, plus perhaps a few moments. But the duration of time as a life value is a twenty-four hour period. We can make plans for the morrow and for the year ahead but cannot project our awareness there, and any remains of yesterday or yesteryear are merely memories, pleasant or unpleasant. We can only experience pleasure or pain on a per day basis.

Both the body as a biological thing and the mind as a thinking instrument are geared irrevocably to a 24-hour cycle. As a thing of nature the body must alternate between activity and rest in a one day span and the brain as a thinking-feeling 'thing' must pause on a daily basis for restoration. A new start, a new beginning, is then made the next day. Except for the memories it is a ritual of life beginning anew each day.

The real value of time, then, lies in one's day-to-day living. As one seeks the goals of well-being and completes the tasks of living, these can only be accomplished by the day, and of course neglected by the day. Pleasure, satisfaction and contentment are a one-in-twenty-four hours experience, just as is the absence of illness, insecurity and pain. So we may plan for tomorrow but may only live in today. As the quotation from the Sanskrit says: In this day lie all of the verities of life, therefore, look well to this day.

THE DOUBLE REWARD

The human values that we seek are obtained by an outward effort in the world of concrete things but each of these values bring with them a second value, and inward flow from the outward action. It is something like the chemical process of osmosis, as one good is sought another is absorbed or assimilated. We seek safety and security but also receive peace and contentment; we seek health and group association but receive also satisfaction and enjoyment. Our life receives a double enrichment of betterment, it acquires a multiple value.

Chapter 23
Ideal Values

The common definition for the term 'ideal' is that it signifies something that is supreme, far above the ordinary, of great worth. It implies perfection or an archetype. In this sense an ideal value is something to desire and aim for that is precious above the ordinary.

Ideal values exist at a superior level, are of a higher order, transcending the common values considered in the last chapter. This is so because they extend across the whole of life and are not a single or particular value. They are something in the order of an ultimate worth. For example we previously reviewed the values of health, safety and mental ability, each a single value unit. But an ideal value such as confidence, contentment and fulfillment extends across the sum of living. They are not outside of personal living as something not attainable but on the contrary are very much a part of the whole life of an individual. These values of the ideal will now be reviewed.

A MEANING TO LIFE

It may be that the most forceful but still the most vague term in language is the word 'meaning,' when used in such phrases as "a meaning to life," or "meaningful living." It has no simple definition for it refers to such broad areas as a satisfaction with life, a completeness in behavior and a gratification in living. Such life conditions are difficult to define even though they are a common experience, are ideal values that give meaning to life, that bestow a meaningful existence.

Before we turn to the values that engender such a meaning to life, which is the central theme of this chapter, we shall briefly note certain elements that tend to detract from a richness to life. They detract not because they are unworthy but because they are beyond the capacity of the individual to fully cope with.

- The great discoveries of science which are intelligible only to the scientist and only vaguely so to the layman.
- The great mass of products that flow from the maw of technology,

half drowning and fully confusing to the individual.

- The rapid change in life style resulting from scientific and technological advances, in work type and habits, in family living, in leisure activity.
- The great emphasis in the schools and the media upon "social man" and neglect of the individual person, the de-personalization of the human.
- A sense of unstability in the person that results from the above.

This multiple newness and change is not fully accepted nor assimilated by the individual. Perhaps the old way of living — easy, placid, slow-paced — has existed for so long that it is inbred in man and much time will be needed to adjust to the new way. In the meantime the loss of surety, of firm faith and hope, has also caused a loss of meaning to life. Not despair, although there are many prophets of doom, but rather a lessening of assurance. To restore the loss will be a long range project that must be lived out over an extended period, for richness in living cannot be injected with a hypodermic needle.

The values that lend meaning to life will be reviewed under two headings, the guidelines that enrich and the ends in enrichment.

GUIDELINES THAT ENRICH LIFE

When guidelines are the topic it is necessary to use normative language because guideways are norms, are rules. In codes such as laws and strict moral regulations the term is "you must," or you will pay a penalty. In guidelines this is modified to "you should" and "you ought." This is so because guidelines are only suggestive and the only penalty is a failure and the loss of a desirable goal or end, the loss of a benefit in living.

The four major guidelines are as follows:

A self-sufficiency. One acquires a real self-sufficiency through the pathway of the twelve goals of life shown in Part II. These are goals of worth that upon reaching a reasonable level of attainment in each, imbue the person with a feeling and knowledge that he or she is capable to meet the challenges of life and overcome the difficulties. Epicurus said that self-sufficiency is the greatest of all riches. It is an accumulated resource of abilities and skills to perform the tasks of life.

A golden mean. The alchemists of yesteryear sought for a Philosopher's Stone that would change the baser metals such as iron into gold. In the field of human behavior man has ever sought a philosopher's stone that would turn humans from baser ways and guide them in a golden way of life. We see it in such instructional titles as the Golden Rule, the Guide to Life, the Way to Happiness, the Governing Principle. It is a search for some universal rule that would apply to all human living. The nearest approach to such a guiding light seems to be that which is known as the Middle Way and the Doctrine of the Mean. This middle way is a mid-point between two extremes and means a life course that is one of moderation, of temperance, of prudence.

This teaching of a mean as the best course in human living has been part of the ethics of the two hemispheres, both East and West, since ancient times. Here are two examples from each:

1. In Chinese ethics, dating from the time of Confucius, the Doctrine of the Middle Way has been a core instruction. It was developed in depth by Tzu Shu, the grandson of Confucius, and emphasizes the absence of immoderate ways and extremes in anger, sorrow, joy and pleasure. The Confucius school taught moral order and the golden mean of conduct.
2. In India, in the teachings of Buddhist ethics, the mean is found by suppression of desires and the limiting of human motives and actions. It is sometimes called the System of the Middle Way.
3. In the West the Greeks were the early teachers of a middle way. Various terms were used: Doctrine of the right, principle of the mean, Aristotle used 'doctrine of the mean' and taught that each moral virtue was an intermediate between extremes. Moderation, temperance, and "nothing to excess" were all part of Greek moral teaching.
4. Christian, Jewish and Islamic moral teachings all emphasize moderation and the avoidance of extremes in living.

Aside from the great counsels of the moralist and religionist each individual must find his or her own golden mean in life as a guideway. All values have their positive/negative sides such as health/illness, physical skill/inability, safety protection/danger, social well-being/ill-being. There is a mid-way point between these extremes that one must reach, not in the exact center but well up on the positive side, which is to say on the value side. For example, the middle station between life and death is health, a condition that separates the two extremes of living and dying. Now one cannot say "that man has health" which is nonsense, for he would not be a man alive without some health in the body, if only a thread, for otherwise he would be a corpse. The fact to be known is whether the man has good or bad health, some level of health. And of course the desirable level is well up on the positive side of the health continuum.

Every value embraces the extremes of excess and insufficiency and the mean of these is the desired position. A value is something like the word temperature which includes the extremes of hot and cold. For our personal comfort we do not desire "temperature" but rather a certain level of temperature, not too hot and not too cold but rather a golden mean that satisfies, that is comfortable. And in one's daily living there must be a similar mean, a high center between the Nth degrees.

A criterion. A criterion is a rule or a standard by which to make judgments or decisions, a guiding principle. It is a model rule for guidance in life, not a list of Do's and Don'ts. A list of Do's and Don'ts serves well for particular necessities but are not a guiding light, not a criterion. Only a great standard or rule will serve this purpose for, as noted above, it is the basis for decision making in human behavior. One of the widely known guides is the Golden Rule of the Bible: Do unto others as you would have them do unto you. There can be no better guide in social associations. Other examples are: The Greek admonition to know thyself, Augustus Ceasar's counsel to hasten slowly and the Boy Scout motto of Be Prepared. But each individual must devise one's own criterion, either a rule, a code of rules or perhaps the ways of a great person, as a steersman for his or her life.

There is a second part to the personal criterion for one must not only steer the ship of life but also point it in the right direction. We have reviewed these direction points in the twelve goals of life in Part II. But the ship can only be held on course when one is inbued or permeated with a central belief, with a constant faith. This might be in a supreme being, a philosophy of life or a chosen field of work that has the merit of helping mankind. Whether or not one agrees with the devoted religionist, the patriotic enthusiast or the dedicated artist, these persons have a criterion that points their way of life. An example of extremes is St. Paul who, as a strict Pharasee persecuted the Christians. One day on his way to Damascus he was suddenly struck with a conviction that this was wrong and made a great decision to change his course in life and help the Christian cause. This change from persecution to promotion resulted in Paul's becoming the great leader of Christianity. His criterion changed from one of hindrance of a cause to one of helping human beings.

A confidence in life. Here we are speaking of a trust, a faith and a sense of surety in the order of things. It is a belief that one holds that the institutions of man such as science, technology, govenment, education and religion are good, are proper. Although some parts are undesirable, even wicked and evil, on the whole they are worthy and beneficial to the life of man, to one's personal living, and we have only to weed out the unwanted parts.

Confidence includes an acceptance of change as the natural order of things. Tomorrow will bring new wisdom, new goods from technology, new discoveries in science and new ways to living, but these will all occur within the framework of the institutions that have endured for thousands of years. Change occurs more rapidly than yesteryear and is difficult for persons to assimilate and adjust to but it need not shake one's assurance in all of life for change does not loosen the foundations, it is merely added at the top.

Confidence in the self comes through self-sufficiency while confidence in life and society resides in belief and trust in the institutions. When the individual holds these certainties in his or her person, they serve, along with a golden mean and criterion, as ideals for the enjoyment of living, they enrich one's life.

ENRICHED LIVING

There are many ways to define an enrichment of life but the key word is worthwhile. This carries the meaning that there is worth in the daily living, that life has a meaning and significance, that contentment and gratification are not idle words in the continuing existence.

Enrichment does not mean a single value such as justice or friendship which are only contributing values to enrichment, but it is rather a summary value, the culmination and fulfillment of many. This is made clear in such statements as: "It was a period of life that was full of meaning to me," and, "it was a life worthwhile, good, and with much happiness." When the events of life have this importance for a person, then the content of life has been enriched and the whole of living has been worthwhile.

The components of worth in life are as extensive as life itself but three groupings will help exemplify the content.

A sense of completeness in living. This would include such awareness as:

- A certainty of rightness in behavior, a freedom from doubt.
- A sense of accomplishment, in goals and projects undertaken.
- A satisfaction, with methods and ways and results.
- A knowing, of correctness in actions.
- A surety, in the courses of life.

The German poet Johann Goethe compiled a list of the conditions that bring contented living and named the following:

- Health enough to make work a pleasure;
- Wealth enough for the needs of life;
- Strength enough to overcome the difficulties of life;
- Patience enough to toil in good works;
- Grace enough to confess your sins and forsake them;
- Love enough to be helpful and useful to others;
- Charity enough to see some good in other persons;
- Faith enough to see the work of God;
- Hope enough to remove the fears concerning the future.

A whole-life assurance. This is the felt assurance that life is worthwhile, is meaningful and that there is a core stability to the whole, even though there is constant change on the surface. It includes the belief that there is an order in all of life whether regulated by laws of nature or a Supreme

Being. And it includes a sense of certainty that one can cope with the forces of nature and of society to an adequate degree.

A known value in time flow.

- A gratitude for the past and its blessings.
- Appreciation for the present in the experiences of each day.
- A constructive hope for the future in well-being of self and society.

THE ESSENCE IN LIVING

Let us re-state the beginning, that the essence of life and living for the individual is to know and seek a meaning to that life and living. The most pitiful man is one who declares "my life has been a worthless existence, a long string of senseless actions," for this describes both a life of waste and squandered living. This should not be and need not be for any person. Whatever the station in life – high or low, rich or poor, in health or in illness – there is still a meaning in that existence. That meaning is centered in a contentment with the station or else the seeking of another station that will bring a contented living. It is in this seeking the right and a feeling of gratitude that bestows meaning and enrichment to life.

Epilogue II

THE HUMAN SPIRIT

In any discussion of human behavior there is always a sense of incompleteness, a feeling that much or something has been left out. It seems impossible to fit man into an exact frame, with a set of rules and a chart of conduct for his behavior. Something will spill over and cannot be tucked back into the frame which encloses the human being. Matter that is put in at one side of the frame will cause an equal amount to flow out the other side. And the frame cannot be enlarged because a human is just that and no more.

There is a theory in philosophy that is called holism. This is a proposition which asserts that a thing can be greater than its constituent parts. It is like saying that 2 x 2 = 4, plus a little bit more. Or perhaps it is like the cell, the smallest living thing that is a whole organism. Looking through the microscope one can see that there is only one cell on the slide and no more. It is a whole and complete one. But presto! What is happening here? The cell is splitting into two parts, it is becoming two cells, so apparently that which was thought to be one, was seen to be only one, was really greater than one all the while.

It is even so with a human being. All that a man or woman really need in life is some wholesome food, clothing, shelter and a moderate amount of intelligence. With these and a few accouterments mankind should sit down and be satisfied. But no! He must have bigger, better, faster, newer, more of, everything. He must fly across the water instead of sail, must float to the bottom of the ocean where he cannot live, must fly to the moon where he cannot exist because there is no air to breathe. It is the spirit of man at work.

There is a certain British mountain climber who is forever scaling vertical cliffs and risking his life. One day he stood before a great mountain in India, preparing to live for weeks in bitter weather and extreme danger. When asked why he would want to climb such a mountain and undergo such a terrible experience he replied, "Because it is there." And that is the way of man: He must know and he must conquer nature and life because it is there. It is the spirit of man in action.

This spirit of the human being cannot be described in exact terms because it has no form or substance. In days of yore when life was lived at a slower pace and a less complicated manner, spirits did have a real presence. They were known to live in the woods, on mountains and in the sea, and were always at work for one's benefit or downfall. And they had to be propitiated. The medicine man of the American Indian tribes had direct access to the lesser spirits and prayed to the Great Spirit. These spirits were animated things and they were real to the people of the time.

Modern, sophisticated man must define the human spirit in different terms. The German philosopher, Friedrich Hegel, spread must enlightenment when he wrote that the essence of matter is gravity and in like fashion the essence of spirit is freedom. We know the reality of spirit in activity for the action is the spirit. The more freedom one has to act means more opportunity to display one's spirit. But there must be activity or the spirit will atrophy, will wither and waste away because the activity in process is the spirit. Hence the terms "high spirited" or "low spirited" person.

The best evidence of spirit is the effort to achieve, to attain. It is in the struggle to do, to win, to succeed, that spirit is shown. It is not the seeking of the goals to satisfy wants and needs as we have reviewed throughout this book but rather the driving force with which one goes about the seeking, the spirit of the effort. It is the push from within more than the pull from without. Here is a race and all of the runners are exhausted, some fall by the wayside while others force on to the finish line; the boat is capsizing and a few slip over the side into the sea to save the remaining ones; this man is confined to a wheel chair yet rises to great heights as a national and world leader; the many-talented Dr. Albert Schweitzer devotes his life to the destitute in Africa; the country bumpkin Abraham Lincoln rises to govern a nation and strike the shame of slavery its death blow. What are the rules by which these persons conducted their lives? It was a spirit that drove them onward, not rules of behavior.

The human spirit dwells in every person although it does not propel with the same force in all. In some it lies dormant forever, in others it surfaces on occasion and for many it sparks a zest for life, for living, that supercedes all else. These may be ordinary and average persons but they perform the tasks of the high and the mighty, bringing to mankind a modicum of good or perhaps a benefit of enormous proportion. In some cases they are even a savior of man. It is the human spirit in action.